ESCAPING HELL

The Story of a Polish Underground Officer in Auschwitz and Buchenwald

4 6 1 8

Kon Piekarski

Editor: Lachlan McLennan
Design: Karen Dahlstrom
Printing and Binding: Gagné Printing Ltd., Louiseville, Quebec, Canada

The writing of this manuscript and the publication of this book were made possible by support from several sources. The publisher wishes to acknowledge the generous assistance and ongoing support of **The Canada Council, The Book Publishing Industry Development Programme** of the **Department of Communications,** and **The Ontario Arts Council.**

Care has been taken to trace the ownership of copyright material used in the text (including the illustrations). The author and publisher welcome any information enabling them to rectify any reference or credit in subsequent editions.

All illustrations are courtesy of either the Auschwitz Museum or the Buchenwald Museum with the exception of the drawings on pages 25, 38, 45, 47, 49, and 133 which were done by an inmate but whose provenance is unknown

J. Kirk Howard, Publisher

Canadian Cataloguing in Publication Data

Piekarski, Konstanty R., 1915-
    Escaping hell: the story of a Polish underground officer in Auschwitz and Buchenwald

ISBN 1-55002-071-4

1. Piekarski, Konstanty R., 1915- . 2. World War, 1939-1945 — Prisoners and prisons, Polish. 3. World War, 1939-1945 — Prisoners and prisons, German. 4. World War, 1939-1945 — Underground movements — Poland — Biography. 5. World War, 1939-1945 — Personal narratives, Polish. 6. Auschwitz (Poland: Concentration camp). 7. Buchenwald (Germany: Concentration camp). I. Title.

D805.P7P54 1990   940.54'7243'092   C90-095152-4

Dundurn Press Limited
2181 Queen Street East, Suite 301
Toronto, Canada
M4E 1E5

Dundurn Distribution
73 Lime Walk
Headington, Oxford
England OX37AD

Table of Contents

▼

Foreword

This is a true story based on my five-year incarceration in German concentration camps during WW II. This is not an historical account, for we, as prisoners, had no knowledge of our captors' plans, nor is it a re-telling of the Holocaust. I have chosen instead to narrate the events in the form of an adventure, believing that this best captures the heroism and despair that were so much a part of our daily life.

Perhaps the noblest example of heroism I observed occurred in September of 1940, when a captain in the Polish Intelligence, Witold Pilecki, allowed himself to be captured by the Gestapo and sent to Auschwitz in order to establish there a resistance unit among Polish army officers. It was an almost impossible task considering the extraordinary cruelty of the German kapos and the vigilant security of the Gestapo. But Pilecki was no ordinary man. His courage and determination gave myself and others the will to overcome tremendous obstacles — the constant threat of torture, execution or starvation — despite our limited means.

The other characters in this story represent a variety of nationalities and personalities; their values, religious outlooks and political leanings are also indicative of the diversity of opinion found within the perverted world many of us learned to accept as normal. Most of the characters retain their real names; the post-war fate of those I have been able to track down forms the content of the epilogue. I have allowed myself the freedom to present other characters as a composite of two or more people and I have chosen events and activities which illustrate the day to day conditions under which we lived. I believe the resulting story is an accurate depiction of those times. Despite the multiformity of background and belief, I observed one characteristic shared by all humanity — our instinctive motivation to survive against the equally pervasive instinct for violence.

Unlike several writers about life in concentration camps, I do not believe that the violence we witnessed or experienced was unique to our German captors. Extreme cruelty was displayed by Polish, Ukrainian or even by the most non-violent group among us, Jewish prisoners. Indeed, it is almost needless to describe violence as a significant phenomenon within our post-war culture. More significant, I think, is to recognize this phenomenon as instinctively based and to combat it with our equally potent ability to reason and understand. Only then might we prevent the recurrence of events out of which my story is but a brief moment.

I am grateful to Richard Lawrence for his assistance in editing the original manuscript.

K. Piekarski
March, 1989

Part I
AUSCHWITZ

Main gate to Auschwitz Concentration Camp

CHAPTER

RECEPTION AT AUSCHWITZ
(September 1940)

Ⅰt was almost a relief to be notified that my interrogations with the Gestapo were finished and I was to be shipped the next day, September 3rd, to the labour camp, Auschwitz.

I was lucky — one of the few men who survived those trips from Pawiak prison in Warsaw to the Gestapo Headquarters. Men had been coming back blinded or with broken legs, pulled nails and smashed testicles. We were accused of belonging to the Polish Resistance Organization (ZWZ)* and we had little hope of getting out of our predicament alive. We knew nothing about Auschwitz, but labour camp sounded like a sanitorium after our encounters with the Warsaw Gestapo.

The cell door opened and my friend Mietek Lebisz and I were called out. We had both been professional officers in a cavalry brigade, the cream of society in pre-war Poland — a fact which only intensified for us the shock of prison life. Though we did indeed belong to the "underground," we had continually countered the charge during our frequent interrogations. Armed, however, with a list of names that included our own, taken during an attempted arrest of a fellow officer, the Gestapo naturally remained deaf to our denials.

---

* In 1940 there were many resistance organizations in Poland. One of them was"Zwaizek Walki Zbrojnej" or ZWZ (Organization for Armed Resistance) formed by the Polish officers who escaped being interned in German Prisoner of War Camps. ZWZ was a nucleus of the future "Armia Krajowa"(Home Army) as opposed to the Polish Army under British Command and another Polish Army formed in the Soviet Union from Polish prisoners of war captured by the Soviet Army during the 1939 Polish campaign.

How much things had changed since the days preceding our arrest, when I had made a livelihood of operating a small jewelry store in a Warsaw suburb. Now I was marching down steps and along corridors into the gloom of the prison yard. I glanced at my watch. It was one o'clock in the morning. The night was cloudy and humid, and the searchlights, directed towards the yard, pierced through a heavy steam rising from wet concrete. It must have rained not long ago. The prison yard contained a foul smell, but compared to our overcrowded cell, it seemed as if we had emerged into heaven.

After about 200 prisoners had assembled, we were loaded onto trucks under the armed escort of the SS men* The voice of the commander rang loudly from the top of one of the trucks: "Do not even think of escaping! If you dare to move from your place on the truck, you will be shot dead!" The convoy moved noisily into the dark streets of Warsaw.

"Mietek," I whispered, "what are our chances of escaping?"

"Not great, Kon. Apart from those bastards on the trucks, there are motorcycles on both sides of our column."

The trucks rolled on through the sleeping city. All windows in the passing houses were dark, their occupants asleep and unsuspecting of what was going on in the streets below — perhaps not even caring. Probably my wife was also sleeping soundly in our apartment. I wondered what she thought about my transport to Auschwitz. How much did she care?

Suddenly the trucks stopped. My whole body was immediately alert.

"Watch out, Mietek!" I whispered.

At an intersection another column of trucks was crossing. Because of the darkness we could not see who it was. Perhaps a military convoy. Looking down from our truck we noticed that the motorcycles were gone. Mietek grabbed my arm and pulled me towards him.

"Maybe we should knock out our two guards and the whole truckload of men could run. Some of us could make it."

---

* SS was an abbreviation for the German name "Schutzstaffel" (Protection Squad) formed before the war. They were bound by a personal oath of complete loyalty to Hitler himself. Later they served as an elite Nazi security corps.

Unfortunately, we were sitting at the front of the truck and the guards were at the other end. Two rows of ten men each sat between them and us; the guards also maintained a small space between themselves and the nearest prisoner.

We started to push our row towards the guard on our side. Understanding our manoeuvre instantly, the men in the opposite row also started to push. As a result, the last man in the row moved ever closer to the guard, almost touching the barrel of his rifle. In our excitement, however, we were no longer watching the street. Although the motorcycles had gone, the pavement was full of armed SS men walking along side our column of trucks.

"What's going on there?" one of them shouted, pointing his rifle menacingly at us. "Why are you crowding the guard? You have enough room in front. Move or I shoot!"

We moved back to await another opportunity. In the meantime, the long column of trucks we had stopped for, had passed by. Moments later our own column started up, turned and followed them.

No further chance to escape was granted us, and we finally arrived somewhere outside the city where a long freight train stood waiting in the glare of the searchlights. We watched an unusual, almost orderly activity taking place. The occupants of other trucks were jumping down, forming into groups of about forty, and then climbing into empty boxcars. There was no shouting, no brutality, no threats; it seemed as though all these men were simply filing onto a holiday train.

Immediately we knew who these people were.

"Those fellows were caught on the streets," said Mietek. "It looks good for us. They must be going to Germany as forced labour and no doubt that's where we're going too."

"I'm not so sure," I replied, "but at least we're not being shipped somewhere for execution."

Indeed, when our turn came, we were counted and added to the men we had been watching so keenly. Joining one group, we climbed together into a boxcar, carefully noting that SS men were posted on each end of the roof; they would also be riding in the passenger cars at the beginning and end of the train. When everybody was loaded, the train hissed, jerked, then proceeded to move us to our new destiny.

At first we could not see anything. People were moving

around in the dark trying to find a place in our crowded quarters to sit down. Mietek and I found ourselves in a corner. When our eyes adjusted to the faint light coming between the boards of the boxcar, we were able to assess our situation. This only made me worried and upset, but Mietek sat calmly with his legs crossed and smoking a cigarette as if he were in the officers' mess.

I leaned over to him and said, "Mietek, we have to try to get out of here! I don't want to be a prisoner until the end of the war."

Giving me a tolerant look, he replied, "Do you think we'll lose the war without you? When we arrive I'll tell them I'm an officer and that I was mistreated. I am sure the German officers will understand this and will transfer us to some officers' camp."

Mietek had been thoroughly indoctrinated to believe in the high social standing of officers and the chivalric treatment they considered their due. As a result, he was reluctant to attempt an escape, especially if it involved soiling one's hands and garments. I was not so sure of our status and persisted in trying to convince him to think of ways to escape.

"We're not going to an officers' camp," I said bluntly. "The best we can expect is hard labour. You know, digging ditches, that sort of thing."

"They will never make me do it," he proclaimed. "But perhaps you are right. Maybe we should try to escape."

The only possible way out was through the wooden floor of the boxcar. Desperately we tried to pry away some of the boards. With no tools but Mietek's pen knife, the work was extremely difficult.

"This is a hell of a job," he grunted and continued attacking the floorboards.

In about three hours we managed to remove one board. The second would be easier. During this time the train kept slowing down, at moments even stopping long enough that we could hear the voices of the SS guards as they walked alongside. Obviously our best chance would be to slip down to the tracks as the train started to move and let it pass over us.

Once again we felt the train apply its brakes, only this time it shunted between tracks. This was the opportunity we were waiting for. As we pried up the second board with all the energy that we could muster, the train came to a full stop.

We could hear the SS guards jumping off, shouting something and running along both sides of the cars. Through the cracks in the boards we saw strong searchlights directed towards one side of the train, the other side still in darkness. No buildings or train station of any sort was visible, though we thought we could make out a high embankment. It appeared we had stopped somewhere in the country — an excellent place for our getaway. Shouting voices and the incessant barking of dogs pierced through the night at some distance from the train.

"Get ready, Mietek. Once the train starts moving again, we'll drop down to the tracks and let them go on without us."

"Listen!" he said, raising his hand to silence me. Then soberly, "This train's not likely going anywhere. I think we have arrived at some German paradise. Can't you hear them shouting?"

We strained our ears to detect what was taking place outside. Sure enough, the shouting was moving to the end of the train and the barking dogs got louder. Then we heard the rolling sound of opening doors in some distant boxcars and voices yelling "Out! Out! Out!" There was also the sound of men screaming either in terror or terrible pain.

For some reason, our transport train was being unloaded in the middle of a field.

"This doesn't sound like an officers' camp, Mietek. Why are we unloading? They're shooting at somebody!"

Gunfire cracked repeatedly over the clamour of shouts, screams and barking.

"Maybe some idiot tried to escape," said Mietek.

The shifting sounds of the rifle shots and barking did give the impression that someone was being chased. We concluded that something terrible was happening and anticipated a violent reception when our own door opened. I pulled Mietek back to our corner, thinking this would be the safest place for us; it might give us those split seconds needed to make the right decision.

"If we can find out what's happening," I said, "we might avoid being shot right away."

Finally the door of our boxcar shot open. We could see nothing in the sudden glare of the floodlights. Voices shouting "Out!" and "Fast!" were coming from somewhere below, but how far below it was impossible to tell.

Nobody moved. Blinded by the intense lights, we stood paralysed, not knowing what to do. It did not last long. From our corner we saw several men, enormous silhouettes against the light, climbing into the car carrying things resembling baseball bats. Dressed like sailors, it was immediately clear they were not SS men. In no time they were swinging their clubs, hitting left and right at anybody seeking protection at the back of the car. To avoid being hit, those furthest from the door began to push forward, while those in front either fell or jumped from the car. Two men, whom we later recognized as "kapos," stood on either side of the wide doorway using their clubs to bat the prisoners out.* One after another they plunged into the night, swallowed up by the darkness except for their voices that trailed further and further away.

It was time to act.

We had to avoid the clubs of the kapos, especially those of the obviously dangerous ones beside the door. In the commotion of unloading, someone stepped on our loose floorboard, sending it flying in our direction. This was a weapon I could use. Reacting instinctively, I shoved the board between the ribs of the nearest kapo, sending him tumbling out of the car.

"Jump now!" I shouted to Mietek.

The embankment was not as steep as we had anticipated, but it was quite long. Upon landing we sprang to our feet, only to find ourselves face to face with the kapo I had just helped down with the loose board. We ran on both sides of him. On this occasion, it happened that luck was with us. For some reason, he believed the one who had hit him was still in the car and climbed back through the open door.

But the danger was not over. Surveying the scene, we noticed a corridor formed by more kapos and SS guards with dogs. Through this gauntlet we had to run, avoiding both the clubs of the kapos and the teeth of the dogs. Not so fortunate were those who moved more slowly or were already injured. Many older men had either broken their legs in the fall from the train or had had their heads split open by the kapos' clubs. At the end of the corridor the previously unloaded prisoners were forming into a column, five men abreast.

This time it was Mietek who grabbed me, pulling me towards

---

* "Kapo" originates from an Italian word for a head or a boss. Kapos in Auschwitz were recruited from notorious German criminals and were given the power of life and death over camp inmates.

the column with the words "Let's fall in . . . this must be what they want us to do."

Again guided solely by instinct, we ran to join the middle of the next row of five. Men were immediately added to our left and right. Those to the sides of us, as it turned out, were directly exposed to the kapos and SS men, buffering us from their wrath. We were also lucky not to be at the beginning or end of the columns. Men in the first five rows were taught by the swinging clubs which way and how fast to go. The last four rows were compelled to carry injured or dead colleagues and still keep up with the column.

"I think they expect us to march as though we were on parade," said Mietek. "Tell the fellows beside you to stay in line and I'll try to do the same. Maybe that will keep those kapos off our backs."

In this manner our column finally reached the entrance of the camp displaying its enigmatic sign, embraced in curved iron above the gates, *Arbeit Macht Frei* (Freedom through Work). Later on we were told what it meant. The only freedom to those who entered was through the chimney of the crematorium.

2

CHAPTER

TERROR AND CONDITIONING

We had had little time to think about what was happening to us. What kind of a camp was this? Who were these cruel kapos? Where did the Germans find these men who behaved worse than animals? Was all this savagery just a form of intimidation to enforce their authority on new arrivals?

In time we discovered that we had stepped into a world with new rules for human — if it can be called human — behaviour. In the beginning, there was nothing that could be called "good" or "bad" in the camp. It was more like a game of hunter and hunted, one side out to destroy while the other sought to survive. The kapos, we learned, were the most hardened of prisoners carefully selected from German prisons. They appeared to work hand-in-hand with the SS guards. In these surroundings, the more quickly a prisoner learned and adapted to the rules, the better were his chances of surviving one more day.

We marched through the gate and stopped between two rows of red brick buildings. Most of the SS men turned back, presumably to escort in another group of prisoners. At the end of the building in front of us we could see men in white and dirty blue striped uniforms running out to arrange themselves in columns, five abreast. Our metamorphosis, like those before us, was about to begin.

When our turn came, we entered a room and stood facing ten men, also prisoners, also Polish. They had already been here perhaps two or three months. We were instructed to undress and as we did, they wrote down, very thoroughly, a list of our belongings which were then packed into large paper bags. This gave us a false sense of security. Surely, we reasoned, if the Germans wanted to kill us, they would not make such a fuss about our personal property.

Yet, strangely, all future events in the camp were as well organized: the mass executions of Jewish people, the killing of Russian prisoners of war and the systematic extermination of Polish prisoners were each conducted in an orderly manner. Files were kept on every prisoner; records were maintained with respect to every occurrence in the camp; all bodies were counted precisely, whether alive or dead.

From our belongings we were allowed to keep only our shoes and a belt. Once stripped, we were marched to another row of prisoners called the barbers, who shaved our heads and body hair, then sprayed us generously with disinfectant. The barber who shaved me looked with great interest at my shoes.

"Someone will take those away from you," he said. "Why don't you sell them to me for three pieces of margarine."

They were good skiing boots, waterproof, with a double leather lining. I decided to make a counter-offer to my friendly barber.

"I've smuggled in two packs of cigarettes inside my shoes. If you help me save these shoes, I'll give you both packs."

We hastily struck a bargain and the barber took my shoes into another room. Meanwhile our group was told to move on to make way for the next lot of prisoners. Just when I thought I'd said goodbye to my footwear, the barber re-appeared carrying something that turned out to be my shoes, smeared with paint and tar.

"Here you are," he said, proudly. "No shoemaker would do a better job."

"These are ruined!" I complained. "Now neither of us has a decent pair of shoes!"

The barber looked at me as if I were out of my mind and remarked dryly: "Auschwitz is not a sanatorium. You'll learn a lot in a hurry here, particularly that shoes looking like that won't be stolen from you. They'll wipe clean later. Now, where are my cigarettes?"

We were led next to a shower room where we deposited shoes and belts on the floor before climbing beneath the shower heads with one little piece of soap. Right away I realized how helpful my barber had been. As we showered the kapos kicked around our shoes and belts, selecting the best for themselves. Nobody touched my shoes.

It was in the shower room that I witnessed for the first time an incident that thoroughly shocked me. A sudden commotion erupted and two kapos chased some naked men across the floor. A Jew had been found in our group.

"Look," I whispered to Mietek. "What are they doing to this poor guy? They actually want to kill him, for no reason other than that he's Jewish."

Mietek turned to watch what was happening and his officer's pride again dominated his common sense. He walked slowly towards the kapos — tall, handsome and naked, but with the authority of an officer — and exclaimed in Polish: "Why are you trying to harm this man? This is ridiculous, let him go immediately!"

For a moment the kapos were stunned. Fortunately for Mietek they did not understand a word of what he had said. He must have looked very comical to them, standing there naked with soap on his serious face, because they burst out laughing.

"You must be one of those crazy Polish lunatics!" one of them shouted in German. "You'd better get out of here in a hurry or we'll play circus with you too!"

With these words he raised his club and struck Mietek over the shoulder. As Mietek turned, the kapo kicked him so hard that he fell and slid, on the soapy floor, back towards our group under the showers. The kapos then turned back to their prey who had been trying to hide among the others. Dragging him out in front of an SS man, they started their vicious circus again.

Two SS men came over to watch and the kapos entertained their guests by torturing the man. It took me a long time to comprehend this role playing. The kapos apparently felt no animosity towards their victim; he was merely a prop to act out their scene. The SS men viewed the spectacle like two Roman dignitaries engrossed in a gladiatorial exhibition. Since the "gladiators" themselves were prisoners, their lives depended on the fancy of their audience. It was thus not unusual for the kapos to try to incorporate some crude kind of storyline into the killing. Almost always the prisoner would be hit so hard that he would tumble to the ground.

"Get up! Get up!" the kapos shouted. "You shouldn't be lying down in the presence of the SS!"

They then proceeded to kick the man, generally in the kidneys or testicles. When he struggled back to his feet, he was beaten

My own red triangle

further as punishment for his misbehaviour. There were variations on the theme — for example, breaking a prisoner's legs, then ordering him to run. Since he obviously could not do so, he had to be administered a "just" punishment. The SS men meanwhile stood by and smiled with approval, adding an occasional encouraging remark to a kapo or an insult to the tortured man. The kapos, in turn, performed to the best of their abilities, showing how strong they were and how well they knew where and how to hit a man to cause the most pain.

After the poor man fell unconscious or dead, we were herded into the next room where we received our striped uniforms. Those without shoes had to wear Dutch wooden shoes. We were also given items of identification which, from then on, substituted for our names: a piece of white cloth with a number printed horizontally on it and a piece of red cloth in the form of a triangle. These we had to sew on the left side of our jackets and pants. Above the number went the red triangle bearing the letter "P," identifying us as Polish political prisoners. We learned the meaning of other colours as time passed: kapos wore green triangles with no letter and a one- or two-digit number, indicating that they were German criminal prisoners; there were also purple triangles for Jehovah's Witnesses (conscientious objectors), pink for homosexuals, and black for people caught trying to emigrate from Germany.

Jews wore a double triangle made of red and yellow cloth formed into the star of David, as well as a black dot. These people were assigned to Block 13, a place reserved for dangerous prisoners who had to be specially punished. Inmates of Block 13 were strictly forbidden from mixing with the other prisoners.

Mietek and I were assigned to Block 3, one of many buildings formerly used as stables and military barracks. Dressed in our striped attire, we were marched reasonably peacefully to this next destination. Here we learned quickly about a new authority: a "blockelder" named Hans Bruno and his assistants. They were kapos assigned to be in charge of "blocks" (buildings) as blockelders, or else in charge of a room as roomelders. Bruno was a large, muscular man with broad shoulders, a wide face and small, light grey eyes. His face and voice were completely devoid of expression, and he moved like a robot. Only his green triangle indicated to us that he was a dangerous criminal. He and his assistants took command of our column in front of the block, divided us into four groups and led us into one of four rooms that was to become our new home.

It was by now four o'clock in the morning, though time for us had already lost much of its earlier significance. Our "bedroom" was about five by ten metres, its only luxury being the thin layer of straw strewn across the floor. Twenty-five of us were assigned to this room. We had to remove our shoes and crowd inside. Shoulder to shoulder we stood, not even imagining that there could be space to lie down. Bruno and his assistants soon came with help. Propped imposingly in the doorway, he announced in German, not caring whether any of us understood:

"You are now in the concentration camp Auschwitz. The only way out of here is through a crematorium's chimney. I am the blockelder and these are your roomelders. Anybody who doesn't obey orders will be killed."

Only a few of us made some sense out of his speech. His next command, however, had a universal impact.

"Lie down!"

Many could do no more than shuffle around; some attempted to crouch while others made an effort to sit. We simply had barely enough room to move.

Bruno and his helpers acted swiftly to rectify the situation. Jumping into the room, they trampled over the men already on the floor and struck out with their clubs at anyone who still stood. In twenty seconds everyone was lying huddled on the cold floor. The next command came like the sudden report of a rifle.

"Get up!"

This time we all jumped as fast as possible, even if it meant stepping on someone else's head or stomach. Then a third command rang out.

Kon Piekarski

"Lie down!"

Everyone was down instantly. The blockelder switched off the light and said: "Have a good night." Each of us lay there very quietly. Immediately, the light went on again.

"I said goodnight," said Bruno, "and I expect the same good manners from you." Then he repeated "Goodnight," adding "Tomorrow I will teach you how to be polite."

The lights again went out and Bruno departed. In the darkness we tried to adjust our bodies to the small amount of floor space without uttering a sound. Lying on my right side, I was disturbed by asthmatic breathing and groaning from someone behind me, but after whispering to him to be quiet I went almost instantly to sleep.

I do not know if my companions fell as quickly to sleep as I, but I think I knew instinctively that I would need strength for the following day and should get as much rest as possible. I felt no self-pity, no need to speculate about what tomorrow would bring. There was no fear, no excitement that could have kept me awake. My brain simply stopped functioning, saving the necessary energy for what was to come. The ability to conserve energy was, for me, the major reason why I was to survive five years of hunger, cold and exhaustion — both physical and mental.

We were awakened early to the charming voice of Hans Bruno.

"Get up and all out! Up and all out!"

I sat up, wide awake. To my surprise, some of my fellow prisoners were still asleep. I shook the guy in front of me and he jumped as if something had bitten him; so amusing was his reaction, I even found it in me to laugh. Ready to go out, I picked up my shoes which had served me as a pillow and noticed that my other neighbour remained curled up on the floor. I shook him hard but he was cold and stiff. For a moment I experienced a strange feeling — I had slept with a corpse. When I had poked him to be quiet a few hours earlier, he was probably dying.

Suddenly one of Bruno's assistants appeared in the doorway. I took my shoes and ran into the yard, instantly forgetting the dead colleague.

The location of the Auschwitz concentration camp had been well chosen. Situated in the middle of a small swamp, the camp occupied what was formerly a Polish military barracks, including horse stables, on the banks of the River Sola. On the opposite side of the river, about four kilometres away, was a small town bearing the same name as the camp (Oświęcim, in German, Auschwitz). In later years the main camp expanded into the surrounding farms between the rivers Sola and Vistula, an area which also gave birth to the infamous camp Birkenau, named after the farm which it occupied. By 1942, Birkenau was a hundred times larger than the original camp Auschwitz, with facilities to exterminate daily Jewish transports of 3,000 to 6,000 men, women and children.

The strategic location of the camp was, of course, far from my mind that particular morning. In the cold dampness of dawn, the heavy fog and partial darkness were somehow very welcome. I felt more secure, as if I could hide in this fog — perhaps even escape. Putting on my shoes, I found myself next to Mietek.

I recalled Mietek's episode with the kapo and his narrow escape from death. His assumptions about a Polish officer's status in the hands of the Germans were, of course, preposterous and dangerous. And yet, I could not help reflecting on how much he looked the part of a true officer. He was tall and very handsome — a young and dashing second lieutenant; the rest of us never had a chance with the girls when Mietek was around. Aware of his attractiveness, he carried himself with self-assurance and an air of superiority that made him even more desirable to the young women.

Now he was sitting beside me putting on his light, elegant shoes, more suitable for a business suit than the striped pyjamas we were wearing. As I was suggesting to him that we explore the surroundings, a host of uniformed prisoners emerged through the fog. Their pyjamas, however, were dirty and their faces gray and thin, indicating that they were part of the first transport from Warsaw that had arrived in Auschwitz two months earlier.

Anxiously, we started to ask all sorts of questions: How is it in the camp? What are they going to do with us? Do people die here, and why? Are we going to work? What should we do?

The older prisoners seemed reluctant to give us precise answers. They only said it was very tough and that we had to have eyes in the backs of our heads. We could relate to this advice already, but its full significance took a few days to dawn on us. They also informed us that the first two or three days would be particularly hard, consisting primarily of a military drill. Neither Mietek nor I thought gravely of this — we knew all about military drills from our training in the academy. What we did not know was that this drill would be one with a difference we could not anticipate.

The main reason the prisoners had come to us was to barter. Everything was offered on the camp's black market, from clothing to food. Bread was the measure by which the value of all items was estimated; it was to the prisoners as gold is to the international monetary system.

At that moment I was interested only in water and set out to find some to drink and to wash myself. I did not have to look long, for daybreak revealed a water pump in the middle of the yard — the only pump in our camp of 5,000. As I approached the pump I was warned by a prisoner that the water came from the swamp and would make me very sick. I noticed, however, several men with their shirts off washing themselves without soap. Finding a few pieces of soap, saved from the shower, in my pocket, I quickly scrubbed my face and hands in the icy water.

To remain clean under these conditions later proved essential for survival. Lack of hygiene resulted in the spread of skin disease, a kind that covered one in itchy pimples which, when scratched, bled and later resulted in badly infected wounds. A dirty or diseased prisoner was, to an SS man or a kapo, like a red rag to a bull. Punished for their neglect, these men became the first to be exterminated.

It was much later, however, that we realized we were in an extermination camp and not a concentration or working camp. The entire routine in Auschwitz was designed to intimidate prisoners and keep them in constant terror, thus facilitating the control our superiors had over us. I think it was also designed as a training ground for SS men destined to rule conquered nations. Intimidation was included in every detail of a prisoner's life.

The least expected place for terror was the camp's latrine, located behind our block and surrounded by a low fence. I noticed that from time to time a kapo would rush into this retreat, beating people left and right until in no time the place was empty. The kapos' action puzzled me for I could not see why one should be attacked in a latrine. Later I understood it as part of the German character: everything must be done in an orderly manner, in the latrines or elsewhere. Only a certain number of people could be allowed in the latrines at a certain time, and for a limited period.

Standing in line was not allowed and all attempts to snatch a few extra moments of comparative peace in those surroundings must be prevented. The most dangerous time to be caught there was when a kapo from Block 13, the so-called "penal" block, led to the toilets his pathetic squad who were strictly forbidden any contact with others. It was then advisable to be indifferent to everything but getting away like a streak of lightning. These kapos did not beat — they slaughtered.

But this was our first morning in the camp and we did not yet understand from where the danger might come. Suddenly, as if a silent alarm had been raised, everybody interrupted what they were doing and rushed towards their barracks, much like a flock of birds startled by a hidden predator. I took it as a danger signal and also ran.

In this instance, however, my instinct was wrong. It was breakfast time. From out of the camp kitchen came prisoners carrying 50-litre kettles of hot coffee, two men to a kettle. Within our block, bread and pots of margarine had already been divided into even portions by the blockelder's assistants. Each loaf of bread was carefully measured before it was divided into five equal portions.

Everybody watched the assistants like hawks. This first morning we still had not experienced the real pain of hunger, so the ceremony appeared unnecessary and even unimportant. Not long after, however, it became the most important event of the day and the division of bread was regarded by all of us as something sacred.

In time, we also discovered why the blockelder and his assistants looked so healthy. After the first night four men were lying dead in our barracks. The number of portions, however, had been assigned the night before, and the four extra portions had gone to the management. It occurred to me that perhaps the violence of the previous night had had another purpose besides discipline. I later learned that this was a regular practice of the kapos and blockelders, through which they arranged more food for themselves.

After breakfast I found Mietek walking around with a cigarette in his mouth, and asked him where he got it, since we did not have any money to buy it in the camp store.

"A fellow gave me the whole pack for the miserable piece of bread we were delivered this morning," he said, contentedly.

I also smoked, but I knew one had to pay a high price for this luxury, in prison or in a camp. A piece of bread did not seem a high price for a pack of cigarettes, but at the time we were not aware that the bread would be our major source of nourishment. As a matter of principle, I decided to quit smoking for as long as I was in the camp. Mietek was to pay dearly for his weakness.

Our discussion about the business aspects of bartering was soon cut short by the announcement of roll call. Each block had its place in the central yard. Block 3 assembled a short distance from the entrance gate,

Roll call

where Bruno and his assistants arranged us in two rows, laying the dead or half-dead at the end of the rows. Arithmetic was evidently not one of their strongest assets, for they counted and recounted our group several times before they were satisfied that we were all present.

After a while the gate opened and several SS men entered the camp. They went to the other end of the yard first, from where we heard the commands of a blockelder.

"Attention! Hats off!"

The whole block responded in military manner, first standing to attention, then raising their hands to their caps and removing them with a loud slap against the thigh. Those who had not yet been issued caps, such as ourselves, were still expected to make the same motion. SS men recounted all prisoners, dead and alive, and, in the military manner, reported their findings to a higher ranking SS man called a Raportfuehrer. This man then commanded the entire camp to stand to attention and in turn made his report to the camp commandant. The next command was "To work!" The old prisoners ran in all directions, forming squads which were taken over by kapos, and marched to their daily chores.

The Raportfuehrer at that time, and for the next year, was a young corporal named Palitsch. Clean-shaven, with a wide forehead and long, thin mouth, he had the look of an arrogant schoolboy about him. Because he and his wife lived just outside the camp, prisoners could often see this happy couple playing with their two small children and hear them call each other by affectionate names. Ironically, inmates at Auschwitz would remember him best as the most cruel of executioners.

Only a few of the SS men liked to beat or torture prisoners themselves. Most of them preferred just to watch the spectacles put on for their benefit by the kapos. But Palitsch was different. He decided to make a reputation for himself as a man who could far outdo the brutality of any kapo. On occasion, local Gestapo units supplying prisoners to Auschwitz would send as well a list of men to be executed. Initially, executions were carried out by a firing squad commanded by Palitsch. Later the young Raportfuehrer assumed this duty alone.

Prisoners to be executed were led to Block 13. There they were undressed, their hands were tied with wire behind their backs, and then, one by one, they were led into the courtyard within the block where Palitsch would shoot them with a .22 rifle in the back of the head. Sometimes men, women and children brought from outside received this treatment from Palitsch without even being admitted to the camp. I was told by other prisoners who had witnessed these executions that when he was delivered a woman with a baby in her arms,

Raportfuehrer Palitsch
(The Camp Executioner)

Palitsch would not bother to shoot the child. Instead, he would smash its head against the end wall of the courtyard, taking pleasure in watching the mother's despair, then shoot her in the normal manner.

I observed this man for three years. Outside the camp, he was a loving husband and father who behaved as though he were completely normal. In fact, it seemed that the more he loved his family, the more he wanted to decimate his family's enemies. He probably believed himself to be a very patriotic German.

A good deal of the work assigned to prisoners was at times carried on outside the camp. The working "commandos," as they were called, marched through the gates singing jubilant German songs that sounded like "Holla-Reya, Holla-Rha." It confused me that these men were so cheerful, until I discovered that these songs were taught by the kapos who forced squads to sing them going to and coming back from work. Almost every working squad carried back with it several dead bodies — prisoners killed by the kapos while on the job — and assisted the many injured who could hardly walk. Viewing the spectacle on a daily basis, the gay melodies sounded both bizarre and obscene.

Our block did not go to work that first day. Bruno needed some helpers whom he intended to select from among our ranks. He began by asking those of us who had been in prison before the war to step out. Nobody did. Obviously he did not inspire much trust. Then he explained that conditions in the camp were like those in prison; in short, he needed experienced helpers. Most of the men in our transport had been rounded up at random from the streets of Warsaw, so it was unlikely that all deserved the designation of political prisoner. In any case, six people stepped forward to be counted.

Bruno then asked who spoke German. This time about 16 men stepped out. He asked them several questions, such as: What was their education? What did they do before the war? He appointed the man with the least education as block translator, and used him to interview the first six who had previously been in prison. Their offences ranged from theft and assault to murder. He selected one murderer and three thieves. They were to be our immediate authorities responsible for keeping order in the rooms, bringing and distributing food, enforcing bedtime and wake-up calls, restricting use of the latrine, and generally ensuring that we behaved according to Bruno's whims and desires. They were also told to learn German by the following week or have Bruno "teach" them.

The last position to be filled was that of the block registrar. It was his task to keep an accurate count of our group — who was dead and who sick — primarily to determine how much food our block should receive from the kitchen. Bruno expected the writer to cheat in his count so that more portions would be allocated than we had mouths to feed. This was called "organizing." The term was common among all prisoners and in time everyone tried to organize what they could — food, clothing, cigarettes, or any other necessities.

We learned subsequently that Bruno had selected what became a privileged class of prisoners, intended to replace his assistants who, as kapos from working squads, were too busy to help him keep order in the block. Indeed, the new management did not prove much better than the former. This was, for many of us, our first introduction to the elaborate system of privileges one can find in any prison setting at any time. The greater the responsibility, the bigger the pay-off.

While the selection of our supervisors was being made, several kapos approached our block. Bruno collected his six new appointees and announced that the kapos were now going to teach us the camp's basic drill. The first instructions were to stand at attention and pretend to remove and replace our imaginary caps. (We did not receive our caps until early December, almost four months later.) We then learned to march in step, a relatively simple exercise had it not been for the German "military punishments" that were instantly administered when our group failed to respond in unison. These included running in step around the yard, duck walking, walking with the knees bent and the hands suspended above the head, somersaulting, rolling sideways across the ground, or simply turning around with the eyes closed. When these punishments — which took much more time than the actual drill — were not executed to the satisfaction of the kapos, the real punishment with clubs was generously administered.

The punishing exercises were, in fact, another test for survival. Rolling around too quickly would provoke dizziness, which was what the kapos were waiting for to inspire their crippling clubbing. One could not be too slow either, however, for a kapo at the end of the column was always ready to punish those who failed to keep up with the rest. The first victims were generally older men or the ones who had made their living working at desks and consequently were in poor physical condition. At the end of two hours, as many as a dozen of them remained lying on the ground unable to move. It made no difference whether they died then and there; those still alive could no longer walk, and nobody was allowed to help them. Indeed, no one wanted to help them.

Our metamorphosis was well underway, conditioned as we were to abandon our sensitivity to another's suffering. We all knew that the men stretched out before us were condemned to die or were dead already. This was an instinctive rationalization, the same as exists in a grazing herd when a predator kills one among them. The rest know very well they cannot help; furthermore, they are only too aware that the predator's preoccupation with the dead or injured buys their own lives a little more time.

The bell sounded for lunch. We collected our dead and injured companions and marched back to our block where we were allowed to disperse.

In the meantime, our newly elected "roomelders" had been very busy. They brought from the kitchen a large, round pot containing 50 to 75 litres of a black coffee substitute, its only redeemable feature being that it was hot. Each of us, by then, was the proud possessor of a tin bowl in which we received one litre of coffee to go with the remaining bread left over from breakfast.

The lunch break gave us unbelievable joy. It was as though we were allowed to catch our breath after a long and exhausting run. The kapos returned to their barracks and left us alone. Although we ourselves were not allowed to enter the barracks, the weather was good; the fog had dispersed over the marsh and the sun was shining through the hot and humid air.

Sitting on some stones next to Mietek, I examined his badly bruised shoulder. Being a tall man, he had to perform the entire drill in the first five of the column and in closer proximity to the aim of the capos' clubs.

"Those bloody kapos," he complained bitterly, "know nothing about military drill. If they'd only let me take charge, I could have the whole block marching like it was on parade—and without hitting anyone!"

This remark took me so much by surprise that I could not restrain my sarcasm.

"Where do you think you are? In the military academy drilling cadets? Look at yourself — you look more like a bum or a convict than an officer. We must forget what we were and do the best with what is left of us."

Apparently our discussion was overheard and understood by another prisoner sitting nearby who came to join us.

"Excuse me," he asked, "but are you both officers in the Polish army?"

I considered this a very indiscreet question. During my interrogations by the Gestapo, I had never admitted to being in any way connected with the military, fearing possible repercussions. Mietek, however, had not been as cautious, informing them he was an officer while denying that he belonged to any underground organization. (Such admissions were later to be regretted: in the fall of 1942, all men known to the Gestapo as former officers were executed by firing squad.)

Suspecting such a direct question, I became silent. But Mietek, in his customary fashion when the military was mentioned, stated his rank quite openly and asked why the prisoner wanted to know.

The man smiled shyly and introduced himself: "My name is Thomas Serafiński. I was a captain in the cavalry of the Wilno Brigade."

He did not look like a cavalry captain, perhaps because of his non-athletic build and youthful, freckled face. He also spoke very softly, without authority — a man who preferred to listen rather than express opinions. His soft eastern accent, however, immediately endeared me to him and no doubt accounted for him later becoming my closest friend after Mietek.

At that moment my sole concern was to find out more about him.

"You're from the same part of Poland as I am," I said. "Maybe we have some common friends. My name is Piekarski, does that mean anything to you? I've heard that my parents were captured by Russians and sent to Siberia."

"If your father was a physicist," answered Thomas, "he was my professor in my first year of university at Wilno. Science was not my best subject but he was an excellent teacher, so even I could understand it. But because I wasn't in Wilno when the war broke out, I don't know what happened to him or even to some of my own relatives."

Although disappointed that he had no news of my parents, I was delighted to hear that he knew and respected my father. But things were still not clear to me.

"I suppose I can tell you that I also was in the cavalry of the Wilno Brigade, which makes me wonder why we didn't meet. Surely you'd remember a second lieutenant from the 9th Horse Artillery Division who used to beat all the cavalry officers in horse jumping?"

"I'm sorry to disappoint you," said Thomas with a smile. "But for the last five years I've been in Warsaw and must have missed witnessing the triumphs of horse artillery over the cavalry."

I saw that my boasting did not go unnoticed and quickly responded: "I didn't mean to brag — and I'm sorry we missed each other before the war and during the past year in Warsaw. I feel I owe you some explanation of why I gave up my riding career. You see, I always wanted to be an engineer. However, after matriculating from high school, my parents could not afford to send me to the school for the artillery reserve cadets in Wlodzimierz. As you know, many young men were deciding to finish their one year military service before further studies. But, after one year the situation at home did not change and I decided to become a professional officer and applied for admission to the Military Academy in Torun. I graduated in 1936 as a 2nd Lieutenant of Artillery. Having very good marks in mathematics and technical subjects along with excellent riding ability, I was assigned to the 2nd Horse Artillery Division in Dubno."

Only half of our lunch time had passed when Bruno emerged from the barracks and shouted for ten volunteers. It struck me, however, that he said nothing about why he needed them. Already I had established one important rule that could be applied to camp life: do not volunteer for anything. My assumptions were borne out some time later when Bruno asked for men who could play the piano. The request was so unexpected I almost raised my hand, but immediately decided against it. Three men happily stepped forward in anticipation of displaying their talents, without questioning whether the camp even had a piano. Bruno then playfully announced that three was just the right number to clean the latrine; since he had no tools for the job, he required men with the proper manual dexterity.

This time, however, there were no volunteers. This did not

surprise Bruno. He merely selected ten volunteers himself. Thomas and I were among them. We followed Bruno into the barracks and noticed that our roomelders were already hard at work stuffing wood shavings into the mattresses. A new luxury was being added to our accommodation!

Thomas was appointed my working partner. Together we developed a system: work only when someone is looking. Thomas picked up our previous conversation and asked me how I had ended up in Warsaw and now in Auschwitz. It sounded like an interrogation, which later on I found out that it was, nevertheless I was glad to talk to someone from my home town. "After two years in Dubno, in spite of riding opportunities, I came to the conclusion that I was not cut out to be a professional officer. Shortly after being transfered to the Wilno Cavalry Brigade, I discovered that there was a competitive examination for the whole Polish Army for the possibility of studying engineering. I was studying at every free moment and as you can guess I won the Military Scholarship and was admitted to the Warsaw Technical University."

"That must have been a very hard examination," said Thomas, "but that was two years ago. What did you do to deserve your glorious assignment to Auschwitz?"

"The rest of the story is probably similar to yours. After finishing one year of University, the war broke out and I was assigned to the 22nd Light Artillery Division. I was wounded in this war fighting Germans, but then the Soviet Army invaded Poland, and while in the hospital I became a Soviet prisoner of war. I escaped from the hospital, came back to Warsaw and married the girl I was engaged to before the war. Being a professional officer, it was only natural for me to join the Polish Underground Army. Our commanding officer, a captain in the cavalry like yourself, was an idiot. He kept a list of our names, and kept our addresses and pseudonyms right beside our names. This is why Mietek and I are here!"

Thomas smiled his shy enigmatic smile, said that not all cavalry captains were idiots, and suggested that we should talk about other, more pleasant things.

We found other common friends whom we had known before the war and as a group decided not to finish too early, hoping to stay in the barracks when the rest of the block returned for the afternoon drill.

Luckily, it worked out that way. Stuffing mattresses was much easier than straining one's wits to stay alive during drill or the inevitable accompanying exercises that the kapos called "sport."

That afternoon I was introduced to the camp's special transportation method. Five men, including myself, had been sent to the store rooms to receive blankets. Bruno and the blockwriter went with us. We were directed behind the kitchen where we found several wagons of the kind pulled by two horses each. Little did we suspect that the five of us would become the horses: two men in front at the thill, one behind, and one on each side of the wagon. This system, as I later discovered, was common in all German concentration camps. Our vehicle, referred to as a "rollwagon," had to be pulled at the run when empty and as fast as possible when full. In this manner we transported about 400 blankets between the kitchen and our block. It was difficult work, but as we ran past the men rolling on the ground, the slower ones encouraged by the blows of the kapos' clubs, we were glad to be pulling our rollwagon.

Stuffing mattresses, piling them with blankets at the end of the room and sweeping the floors took us all afternoon. Not until shortly before evening roll call did we have to join the others for sport. It was then that we saw the working squads return. Singing German songs, they came marching through the main gate where they were counted by the SS men, to be sure their numbers were the same as when the squads marched out that morning. Behind every squad were men riding in wheelbarrows pushed by their colleagues; some were dead and others badly injured. It looked as though going to work was not much better than staying in the camp to do sport.

After the roll call we received our first major meal — a half litre of soup. A concoction of hot water, barley and potatoes, the soup did not have much taste but seemed sufficiently nutritious. Later we found out that receiving this soup was a mistake; it was generally distributed only on Sundays. On weekdays the common fare was yellow water with some turnips floating in it.

Finishing supper, Mietek and I discovered we had some time to ourselves before being called to bed, so we decided to explore the rest of the camp.

In 1940, the concentration camp at Auschwitz consisted of 20 barracks, nine on one side of the camp and 11 on the other. In the middle, facing the kitchen, was the roll call square. Later on, a

Gallows in front of the kitchen

second storey was added to all buildings and eight new barracks were built around the central square. The kitchen was also expanded in order to feed more prisoners and long gallows, made from steel rails, were placed in front of the building in full view of the square.

At public executions 20 people could be hanged there at a time, their bodies left to dangle from the ropes until the following day. The placement of gallows in front of the kitchen constituted another kind of intimidation. Prisoners who went to the kitchen to receive their only real pleasure, the highly treasured food, had to dodge the hanging bodies of their friends.

The same perverted sense of humour inspired the camp commandant, Höss, to order the formation of an orchestra in 1941 to accompany the singing prisoners going to work and later returning, when they would be dragging the bodies of their dead comrades. Once, to verify the humane treatment of prisoners, the camp was visited by the Red Cross; at such times, the orchestra played a deceptive role in helping to persuade the visitors that Auschwitz possessed a contented, even cheerful atmosphere.

Mietek and I walked across the roll call square, approaching the other side of the camp and penal Block 13. We had noticed a conspicuous void in the vicinity of this block. Everybody seemed to walk around it, as if it were infested with some terrible disease. No one was allowed to come out of it and nobody wanted to go in. As we got closer to the block, a rollwagon arrived at full gallop pulled by the inmates wearing black dots. The blockelder of Block 13 stood on the wagon with a long whip, thrashing his "horses" and enjoying the fast ride. Prisoners either in the square or between buildings ran to both sides to avoid not only the rollwagon but the swinging whip of the blockelder. I imagined this man as a Roman emperor driving his carriage through crowds of slaves. No doubt he shared the illusion.

When the rollwagon finally came to a stop in front of the penal block, the doors opened almost immediately. From the depths of the block and amidst shouting and swearing emerged prisoners carrying by arms and legs the naked bodies of their colleagues. When they got near the wagon, they would swing the bodies from side to side and throw them onto a pile of corpses already forming on the wagon floor. It was not a pleasant job. The bodies were dirty and covered with human excrement, but the men carrying them did not display any visible emotions.

The whole scene was macabre, even for those of us who had seen enough death. When the corpses went flying through the air, waving their arms and legs, they looked like horrible ghosts on their way to some sinister ritual. Also shocking was the number of bodies removed from the block; the wagon, which had side walls, was filled to the top. It was so heavy the men could not even budge it, giving the blockelder a good excuse to whip his slaves in the most vicious manner. The effort was not co-ordinated, however, so when one whipped man was straining to move the load, the others were recuperating from the previous beatings. Finally the blockelder tired of his whipping and called for four men from the block. With their help, the rollwagon started to move slowly towards the crematorium.

We asked one of the older prisoners what had happened within the penal block that had killed so many people. Apparently a large number of Jews had been discovered in our transport, all of whom were sent to Block 13. Among them was a famous Polish strong man named Schmelling who succeeded in impressing the Germans with his tremendous physical strength. Some kapos had tried to match their strength with his, but were no competition for the big man. Consequently, Schmelling became a privileged prisoner within the penal block. As a Jew he could not leave the block, but he received as much food as he could eat. In return the SS men required demonstrations of his muscular power — in particular, to prove that he could kill a man with one blow. Other Jewish prisoners were supplied as the subjects, and the SS men eagerly bet on either Schmelling or his victims.

In 1940, the average life span of a Jew sent to the penal block was four days. By comparison, extermination methods used on the Polish prisoners were mild. In spite of this, however, a count made a year later of prisoners left from our transport revealed that out of over 2,000 men, only 120 of us remained alive. Many of the Jews who accompanied us from Warsaw faced an early execution, as did others who came after.

Schmelling was an exception. He lived almost a year.

Another exception was a rabbi who arrived at the camp with a good knowledge of the German language. Unlike other Jews, he was sent to our Polish block and went to work every day to the German office where he translated the Talmud into German. I recall that he was in much better shape than the rest of us, but do not know whether he survived Auschwitz.

Mietek and I were returning to our barracks when we noticed another crowd of people in front of Block 16, the camp's hospital. Although later expanded to occupy a total of three blocks (numbered 20, 21, and 28), the hospital facilities at Auschwitz were never adequate. Indeed, many of the camp building programs attempted to keep pace with the constant increase in prisoners. The penal block would also undergo expansion to include the neighbouring Block 12, both blocks changing their numbers to 10 and 11 respectively. The infamous wall where Palitsch performed his executions was then connected with the penal block itself; today's visitors to the camp can readily identify the wall by the decorations of fresh flowers left by the families of those who lost their lives in the fight to free Poland.

This particular crowd lined up outside the hospital was trying to get medical attention — something many prisoners could only hope for. Because Polish doctors initially were not allowed to work in the hospital, the task of treating patients fell to "Doctor" Bock, a German criminal who was also in charge of the facilities. To look the part, Bock was always dressed in an immaculately clean white coat, sporting a stethoscope around his neck. He was allowed to wear long hair that framed a face both serious and full of authority. Prisoners randomly appointed by Bock to serve as orderlies said he performed all kinds of surgery with disastrous results, but human life in Auschwitz did not have any value anyway.

Bock's orderlies were now "seeing" patients in front of the building. Looking over the crowd, I estimated its size at over a thousand men, all near death. The hospital, however, had only enough room to admit about ten people per day. Those ready to die were the first admitted, helped by their companions through the main door and into a room where Bock conducted his medical practice. Even among those few Bock found some healthy enough to give an aspirin, a kick in the pants and instructions to get out.

The main criterion for admission was the patient's temperature. Visible physical injuries were treated with iodine and sometimes wrapped in paper bandages. Prisoners dying because they were weak and hungry did not have a high temperature; in fact, their temperatures were often far below normal, permitting Bock to pronounce them healthy and return them to the regular camp chores and drills.

It was among this crowd before the hospital that I first saw people actually dying from hunger. They were known in the camp as "Musselmen" (a corruption of the German word for Moslem, Musselmännen), so called because their weakness caused them to sway from side to side, or from front to back, giving the impression they were bowing in prayer.[*]

German documents found after the war estimated that prisoners subjected to the hard physical exertion of camp life and receiving 1,500 calories of food per day survived an average of about three months. Perhaps initially this number of calories was given to each prisoner. But because all the privileged prisoners (such as kapos, blockelders and others) ate as much as they wanted, the amount of food remaining for ordinary inmates was well below that expected.

The Musselman condition started after a man lost about one-third of his normal weight. Physical symptoms, apart from the weight loss, included swelling of the feet and often the entire leg, stiffening of the joints which further hampered movement, and diarrhoea. Their faces wore a greyish-blue colour and indicated

---

[*] The symptoms and condition of these men are well described by Dr. W. Fejkiel who was a Musselman himself. He later worked in the camp hospital where he had the opportunity to study and diagnose the condition. See *Wspomnienia więźniów obozu oświęcimskiego* (The Publication of the Museum in Auschwitz).

Musselmen

quite clearly that they no longer cared about anything or anybody.

Their only interest was food, about which they could talk for hours. Those who had been cooks or connoisseurs of food would describe to others, in great detail, how gourmet dishes were prepared and how they tasted. Such speakers always drew an appreciative crowd who would ask for further details to imagine better the taste or appearance of the food. Otherwise, Musselmen were antisocial, irritable and non-communicative. They generally gathered around the kitchen where they could at least smell the food, or they searched through the garbage which in the camp rarely yielded many edible delicacies.

They were not very choosy. Musselmen would eat raw potato peels and rotten pieces of turnip; they would lick dried fat from the garbage cans or spilled soup from the ground. Only in eating were their movements fast. They were always first to finish their soup, after which they would stand around to watch those still eating, following with eager eyes each spoonful. The purpose of this vigil was the sheer pleasure of imagining the ingestion of food, as well as the hope of receiving small handouts or even permission to lick an empty bowl for the service of washing a dish.

Musselmen still in the early stages of this stupor tried their luck by mixing with working squads who received extra soup from their kapos for performing special tasks. I never could find out what these tasks involved or how one managed to become one of their kind. I did notice, however, that few Musselmen were successful in obtaining their goal. The kapos, who could spot them immediately by their appearance, rewarded their efforts with nothing more than a hard smack on the head with the ladle.

Quite often Musselmen would hang around the kitchen when some late delivery of food was to be made. Though Musselmen generally were unable to act as an organized group, blockelders and kapos knew of their possible danger and consequently escorted the food carriers past the starving men and into the kitchen.

One day bread arrived late and had to be delivered to the blocks after evening roll call, when all Musselmen were on the loose. A crowd of perhaps 50 watched as the bread was carried in wooden crates towards the blocks. All eyes were on the bread. They were as though hypnotized, unable to see the kapos escorting the baskets or the SS man, armed with a rifle, who accompanied wagonloads of bread into the kitchen.

I could understand what was going through their minds. No reasoning, no consideration of the consequences if the bread were snatched occurred to them. In fact, they had no thought even of taking it. Only one image passed before them: to take a big bite out of an entire loaf and have the heavenly taste of bread in their mouths, and then to swallow it, and swallow it, and swallow some more. Nothing else in the world mattered. No price was too high even for a single bite.

In a flash, as if at some sharp command, they flung themselves on one of the baskets, rushing at the loaves with their mouths open in an attempt to eat them then and there, like a pack of wolves tearing apart a fallen deer. Naturally the crate bearing the bread fell to the ground, breaking into pieces. In seconds a seething mass of human bodies tumbled on top of each other, biting one another, punching and kicking to get at the loaves. The kapos rushed in with their clubs, striking at the struggling mass with all their strength. Their clubbing was as bad for the bread as for the men, but could make no impression upon the ravenous throng.

The SS man emptied his gun into the middle of the crowd. But by then the Musselmen had achieved their dream. They were taking big bites out of the loaves, unaware of their cracked skulls, broken bones and bleeding bodies. Kapos and blockelders came running from the neighbouring buildings and began slashing down their victims like a machine threshing grain. Dead bodies lay scattered about; others, half-dead, swayed to and fro with movements of scarcely conscious despair, attempting to salvage some bread crumbs from the dirt which they instantly stuffed into their mouths. The rest stood by watching with sharp interest in case, in the clamour, a chance should present itself to obtain a scrap of bread for themselves.

The state of the Musselman was the final stage to which most men in Auschwitz were driven before death. All previous patterns of behaviour were peeled off like the skin of an onion, until only the instinct of self-preservation remained. Never did they hesitate to steal food from a hungry companion, even if this meant instant death. Fathers were caught stealing bread from dying sons, and sons from fathers. Some Musselmen admitted to the hospital had to have their hands and feet tied at night to prevent them from taking food from dying comrades. Finally, the thought must have entered their minds that even survival was meaningless; they were going to die anyway, so why should anyone stop them from doing the only thing that mattered and would ever matter.

The almost irreversible pathway to the crematorium was often the result of constant diarrhoea and the never-healing wounds caused by scratches, boils or injuries received in the camp. Untreated, diarrhoea led to dysentery and infection which, in the conditions at Auschwitz, was nearly always fatal. For these reasons, as well as for their proclivity to steal food, Musselmen were not well tolerated by other prisoners. Not only did they present a health risk, but their clothes were constantly soiled with excrement since they were unable to control their bowels. They were therefore shoved together in a corner close to the door, where at night they would not have to step over the other sleeping men.

Considering the hopeless conditions, it is interesting that there were relatively few suicides in Auschwitz. Those who did commit suicide were generally in reasonably good physical condition.

Indeed, when I reflect on my own existence in the camp, I often wonder why I did not end up in the crematorium. We did not receive underwear and coats until late November, and our striped pyjama suits offered little protection against rain, cold, or frosty, foggy mornings. Perhaps as much by luck as by design, I somehow managed to escape getting the flu, a cold, or even a sore throat; and though I received no more food than my fellows, I never reached the Musselman stage. One practice I followed religiously was to eat my food very slowly, having decided to derive from every bit all possible nutritional value. To bolster my resolution, I made a sober assessment of the situation: there was only so much food and a limit to what one could do about the conditions in which we lived. I therefore had to do everything in my power to survive.

Before my arrest I had been very interested in yoga, through which I learned about breathing exercises, conservation of energy and meditation. When there is nothing else to fall back on, one grabs at anything that might fend off death. A large number of studies today show that the mind can influence the physical condition of the body. I did not know about such things at the time, but I must have done a great deal right because in three years, fewer than one per cent of the 2,000 or so people sent to Auschwitz in July of 1940 survived. Fewer than 20. Those who survived had, of course, a lot of luck. But even luck could not help when almost the entire camp was dying of hunger.

I had been in the camp barely a day when I first discovered I was hungry. It was a hunger quite different from that which I was to experience later on — what one might call a healthy hunger. I wanted to eat something, but I could also do without it.

It was dusk, and Mietek and I were walking silently between two rows of brick buildings. We still had one hour to wait before we could enter our block to crawl into bed. The autumn evening was so beautiful and we were so deep in our thoughts, we did not notice that, moments later, we were standing in front of our barracks.

Witold Pilecki (Thomas Serafiński)
Organizer of Polish Underground Army in Auschwitz

WARPED LIFE
IN A WARPED WORLD

Thomas was waiting for me. He took me to one side and said he had something very important to discuss with me. It was all very mysterious. We went behind the block where he began to talk in a serious tone.

"What I have to say to you, Kon, is in great confidence. You must swear on your officer's honour that you won't mention it to anyone without my consent."

"Thomas," I said, as gravely, "if it is such an important secret you have my word."

"Good," he continued. "My name is not Thomas Serafinski. It's actually Witold Pilecki."

"If that's your secret," I said, "then perhaps I should tell you I'm really 24, one year older than the Germans think I am. I've given my new birthday a date I won't forget — the 3rd of May, Polish Constitution Day. What's more, I'm an engineering student who's supposedly never been in the army."

"Don't interrupt," said Thomas, hesitantly. "I've more to say that is of greater importance."

I eyed him carefully, still unsure if I could trust this man.

Thomas continued: "I could not have been in the Wilno cavalry brigade for the last five years because in that time I've worked in Warsaw for Polish Intelligence. It is they who organized the underground army after the Polish campaign. In September, I volunteered to come to Auschwitz to organize a resistance unit here."

I was now definitely confused about the soft spoken fellow who stood before me.

"Thomas," I exclaimed, "you must be nuts! Who in his right mind would do such a thing? How did you do it? Don't tell me you asked the Gestapo if they'd be so kind as to send you to Auschwitz for a couple of years?"

"Please don't joke," said Thomas, now observing me more closely than I had him. "Polish Intelligence thinks that Auschwitz is going to be expanded into a very large extermination camp to house Polish freedom fighters. Here is an important place for our unit to function. Because I knew the Gestapo was rounding up people on the streets to send to this camp, I just happened to take a walk at the right time."

"If what you say is true," I replied, "you're either the greatest hero or the biggest fool."

It was even harder to believe Thomas's story because he looked so unheroic with his nondescript face wearing an almost naïve smile. If anything, he seemed every bit the fool. But I liked him nonetheless, recognizing in him both honesty and a certain vulnerability. What I could not see was the confidence and strong will of a commanding officer, and for this reason expressed my reservations to his anticipated offer.

"You know, of course, that I have not volunteered to come here. I'm here because of the stupidity and overgrown ambitions of our high ranking officers, all competing to organize the underground units in Warsaw. Every one of them kept a list of the officers he had recruited. They were too stupid to memorize the names. When the Gestapo tried to arrest the bigwig whose list contained my own name, they found a ready roll call with which to go hunting. This is why Mietek, myself and others are now here for you to organize."

"You're absolutely right," said Thomas, evidently oblivious to my complaint. "I recognize here many senior officers, but I'm not planning to recruit them for our organization. Older people may not be able to cope with the stress in the camp. For that matter, some young people may not be suitable either. I propose to build a purely military unit with full responsibility resting on the shoulders of young officers like yourself."

I still had my doubts, despite his assured manner.

"Why should such an organization exist," I asked him, "and how much can we accomplish in these conditions? Are the risks not greater than the possible benefits?"

"Those are good questions," said Thomas. "I will try to answer them for you. To minimize risk, our unit will operate on a system whereby only five men know each other. Only a contact man from the five and one other man will know me. The purpose of this is self-defence—against kapos and in an emergency, against the SS should a possible uprising of the whole camp occur. The first and most immediate purpose is to help the weaker among us survive the camp."

I reflected briefly on the sense of his proposal and found it surprisingly plausible "You can count me in. I may be as nutty as you are, but let's give it a try."

"In that case, you will be pleased to know that your friend Stan Kazuba is in your five-man unit," he

Suicide

concluded and by sudden impulse, hugged me.

Later events showed how important it was to have such an organization functioning in Auschwitz. At that moment, however, the scheme provided an effective psychological boost, allowing me to think a joint effort might actually be successful. This hope was much needed, particularly as the Germans had intimidated us into believing that none of us would leave the camp alive — a rational belief shared by others who had been inmates for more than a year.

My hope was transformed into confidence in one's ability to survive when, in 1942 and 1943, I helped to organize escapes from Auschwitz.

According to our colleagues who had been in the camp for three months or more, our drills and sport would last between four and six weeks. The thought of even a few more days of this barbaric treatment left some men in a state of complete despair. They were the ones who walked into the barbed wire surrounding the camp.

Any prisoner who approached within three metres of the

fence was shot. It made little difference whether the man made it to the fence or not, for to touch it meant immediate electrocution. But the SS man in the guard tower knew he would receive a day off in town if he shot a prisoner attempting to escape, so very seldom did anyone reach the wire. Men who were shot did not always die immediately; the SS men generally had poor aim. In the event that they wounded their target, an SS man from the main guard room would come to administer the *coup de grace* by shooting the prisoner in the head with a hand gun.

I asked Stan, who had been in the camp for two months, how he managed to survive so long.

"I guess I am stronger than the others," he replied. "Our transport occupied two barracks when we arrived. Now we're in one and have more space than before. A man has to be very alert to avoid the kapos' clubs and at the same time conserve his energy."

This was valuable advice, especially coming from someone as reliable as Stan whom I had worked with in the underground in Warsaw. He was an infantry captain and a very pragmatic, no-nonsense man — of medium height, strongly built, and possessing a firm sense of Christian ethics. Stan never had difficulty making up his mind about what to do in any given situation. I always felt very good in his company; he did not talk much, but his behaviour was steady and reassuring.

The following days in Auschwitz proved to be more of the same — drill and sport. Each day our number was reduced by five or six. On the evening of the third day we got news that tomorrow there would be no sport; we would go to work instead. Older prisoners who had been working outside the camp brought back rumours that building materials were arriving for the expansion of Auschwitz. There was need for more labourers. Indeed, the next day about a hundred men were assigned to a working party in the so-called "industrial park." It was arranged that they would be supplied from our block, so sometime before six o'clock that morning, following roll call, we were added to the existing column of workers for an indefinite period.

I considered myself very lucky to be included in this group and no longer exposed to the senseless sport, the only purpose of which was to kill. My joy, however, proved somewhat premature.

The kapo in charge of our squad was a man called Siegrud, the first intelligent-looking kapo I had seen in Auschwitz. But his

On the way to work

green triangle gave me reason to be cautious; as it turned out, he also was an infamous killer with a background of murder and bank robbery. Glaring out from his otherwise handsome face were the eyes of a predator. Although he had only one arm, he could beat his victims more effectively with that single appendage than most kapos could with two.

Siegrud was disliked by his fellow kapos because he was always showing off his intellectual superiority. His strength and cunning were further supplemented by a special martial art technique he had adapted to the conditions in the camp. I once watched him dispose of a man by beating him to death with his feet alone. A favourite with the SS men, Siegrud always occupied a position of power, which on this particular day meant complete authority over a working group of 300 to 400 prisoners. His two helpers, Alois and Alfred, simple brutes lacking in both sophistication and intelligence, shared in our fear. Siegrud did not have to say anything or even make a threatening gesture; his presence itself meant danger.

I was assigned to a group of about 40 men whose task was to unload sewer pipes from railway cars. Alfred, who was made responsible for our group, reported in turn to a foreman given charge of the immediate operation. The job involved selecting two men to climb to the top of a pile of pipes in an open car. The pipes were then handed down to others who carried them to storage areas a few hundred metres away. Work had to proceed at top speed — the usual demand in the camp. Because the best foremen, which usually meant the most brutal, were rewarded by being appointed kapos, they made liberal use of their clubs to control the traffic to and from the cars.

The physical condition of the workers varied widely: some were young, some old, some healthy and some almost in the Musselman state. Those who were old and weak collected all the beatings, giving the stronger the occasional chance to rest. To take this opportunity meant being constantly alert not only to the kapos and foremen, but to the SS guards who, because we were working outside the barbed wire of the camp, patrolled our group from all sides. As one of the younger and stronger workers, I found invaluable the older prisoners' advice about needing eyes in the back of one's head. It supplied me with the necessary moment or two to catch my breath.

However, these moments were few. Part of the unloaders' task was to keep the carriers busy, so the foreman paid special attention to their pace. Unloading the pipes was a tricky business in that it required both strength and a good sense of balance. When an accident occurred — for example, if a pipe were to fall to the ground and break — it was considered sabotage and the man responsible was killed on the spot.

The worst accident happened when Siegrud was watching. One of the unloaders lost his footing on top of the pile and began to slide down. To stop his fall, he grabbed at a pipe which in turn started an avalanche. Pipe after pipe crashed down from the car, some landing on the backs of carriers, while the unloaders rode desperately on the peak of the avalanche.

Alfred and the foreman immediately rushed for protection from the rolling pipes. It was then that I saw, for the first time, Siegrud in action. With the agility of a cat, he took several leaps to reach the top of the tumbling mass where he grabbed the first unloader and smashed his fist across his face. The man did not move again. Then he jumped like a monkey to the top of the car where the second unloader was scrambling to get up from the

Work

pipes. Two blows from Siegrud's feet, one to the man's kidneys and the other to his head, sent the fellow flying to the ground. He then leapt to the ground himself, briefly surveyed the damage, and said to Alfred in a quiet and composed voice: "Clear those pipes at once."

Alfred jumped as if something had bitten him and almost hysterically began tugging on a pipe lying nearby.

"Not you, stupid!" Siegrud shouted. "Make those men do it!"

In no time the unbroken pipes were carried away and the broken ones were piled up beside the car. Siegrud picked one man from our group and sent him to the next car to be the unloader. Looking around again, he pointed to me. I was ready to climb onto the car when he stopped me and asked: "What is your profession?"

This was a most unusual and unexpected question. I was momentarily startled, thinking perhaps he knew that I had been a cavalry officer. Collecting my wits, I told him I was a university student.

"What did you study?"

"Mechanical engineering," I answered.

My reply must have come as a surprise to him, for he immediately continued chatting with me as if we were old friends.

"I am a mechanical engineer myself — graduated from the Polytechnic Institute of Berlin. What year were you in when the war started?"

"I had just finished one year," I said.

"Then," he continued, "you must have passed courses in physics, chemistry, some mathematics — let me see — engineering design, descriptive geometry. Is that right? Did you have a similar curriculum?"

"Yes, exactly," I said. "The curriculum at Warsaw Polytechnic is based on the Berlin Polytechnic, I think."

For about ten minutes we compared notes about the two institutes and the courses we had taken. Nobody worked. Alfred looked at us with his mouth agape while my colleagues stood by completely stunned.

Finally Siegrud decided to finish our pleasant conversation and said to me: "Now you climb to the top of the pipes on this car and if any more accidents occur, Alfred is going to kill you."

It sounded like a good joke to him and he walked away smiling. Fortunately, this was my first and last encounter with Siegrud, though I could observe him for the next three months supervising work in the industrial area. I could not help but wonder at his intelligence, which perhaps in itself was not worthy of my regard; in fact, it merely served, under these conditions, to make his treatment of others that much more inhuman. The love of violence in his brain was the same as that found in the simplest of men. He had the intellect, however, to apply this same primitive behaviour in more cunning and sophisticated ways.

Upon returning to the camp I saw Mietek, who had just finished a day of drill and sport. He informed me that things had improved somewhat since several kapos had joined work squads, leaving fewer to supervise the exercises. During the next few days, more and more men were required to join labour crews and eventually drill was officially ended. Most of the work force dug foundations for new buildings, built roads, drained swamps, excavated ditches for sewer and water pipes, or simply shovelled for sand and gravel. It was very difficult to get out of this trade; squads with better working conditions were already filled with older prisoners who would not be displaced by newcomers.

In the meantime, the weather grew steadily worse. Frequent rains turned the ground, mostly clay, into a slippery muck. Some days were bitterly cold and our wet pyjamas clung to our damp skin. This was when the first clothing appeared on the black market. It consisted, at that time, of cement bags with holes cut for the head and arms; a lining of a few layers of waxed paper offered reasonable protection against wind and rain. The transactions were generally carried out in the latrines, for anyone caught wearing or distributing these fashionable garments invited rough treatment from the kapos. I managed to "organize" a vest for a portion of my soup, and I must say it was an unbelievable improvement.

I was very fortunate to have good boots, particularly as none of us had socks. Within a few days, however, I succeeded in organizing a couple of rags which I wrapped around my feet to protect them from injury.

Mietek was not so lucky. His elegant shoes were in pieces in no time and he received Dutch wooden shoes as replacements. It was very difficult to walk in these shoes and almost impossible to run in them. Unless one's feet were covered by a couple of layers of rags, bad sores could easily develop that eventually became septic and remained open. For this reason, such things as shoes sometimes decided the life or death of a prisoner.

I was to work with Mietek for the next couple of months in the industrial park, still under Siegrud's command. I had met up with Siegrud several times after our initial meeting, but he either did not recognize me or did not care to let on he had. Partaking of intelligent conversation with someone may have been simply a one-time fancy for him.

One day we were working in the group where Alois was in charge. Alois was just a common thief by profession. He did not have any education or any trade, and his only redeeming characteristic, from our point of view, was his laziness. Too indolent to beat up his men continuously, he only did it two or three times a day — just enough to maintain his good name. These beatings, however, were concentrated on one or two people and generally resulted in the death or near death of his victims.

Our job was to dig a long and deep ditch, God knows for what purpose. Freezing rain had made the ground difficult to dig and harder still to throw out of the ditch because it would stick to our shovels. In rare moments when Alois, a foreman or an SS man was not watching, we managed to catch a little rest and warm each other up by standing back to back, always keeping a sharp look-out for danger.

Alois had a small shack built in which he organized a wood stove. The sweet smell of smoke coming from the chimney indicated he had a cozy place there. From time to time he would run out the door swearing loudly to show the SS men his eagerness, then disappear again into his makeshift shelter to hide from the rain and cold.

This time, after emerging to discharge his tirade of elaborate swearing, he announced: "I need two professional carpenters to set up a woodworking shop!"

I immediately recognized this as a promise of better work, perhaps even under a roof. Several hands shot up, including mine. Alois looked over the candidates and selected me and another man. We followed him into another shack where he again announced: "This is going to be the woodworking shop. You will find here all the lumber and tools you need to make a workbench."

My companion remained silent, but I thought I should at least sound professional by asking him some questions.

"Where would you like us to put this bench? And have you some idea of how large it should be?"

Alois looked at me with the recognition of an expert.

"Just make a good bench. I don't know much about these things, but I sure will know if it's not good and then you'll wish you were never born."

Then he left us in the shack saying he would check back later to see how we were getting along. When he was out of sight, I turned to my carpenter friend with obvious anxiety.

"I hope you're a carpenter because I'm certainly not. But maybe I can help you if you'll tell me what to do."

While I was talking I detected sheer terror in his eyes.

"You're not serious!" he exclaimed. "I thought you were the carpenter and I could help you!"

He paused briefly to regain some of his composure.

"I'm sorry, but — my name's Marcinek. I'm a mathematics teacher. Perhaps you've seen some of my books in high school?"

I recognized the name immediately and said: "Yes, I know your books. They're very good. In fact, I relied on them to prepare for the competitive entrance examination to the Warsaw Polytechnic and won the scholarship."

A faint smile quivered on his lips.

"Now let's see about a workbench," I said, attempting to get down to business. "Do you know what it should look like?"

"No," said Marcinek. "I've never seen one before."

I looked out at the rain which was now mixed with snow, trying to picture in my mind how a workbench was constructed. It was comforting to be sheltered, if only temporarily, from the cold and wet. But we had to produce a bench. If Alois discovered our ignorance, we would meet a miserable end in the muddy trench outside. I was determined to fool him.

We began by making the top, cutting boards to the same length which we laid on the ground and nailed two pieces across. We looked proudly at our work and decided to hold a conference on how to attach the legs to this contraption. Neither of us had a clue where to start. My professor of mathematics used a stick to make complicated drawings on the ground, showing me the distribution of forces. But even after this lesson we were not convinced the bench would be stable without nailing it to the wall.

Now it was lunch break and Alois returned to inspect our work. The first thing he noticed were the nails from the crossboards sticking out through the top piece.

"What is this? A bed for some Indian Fakir? I will roll you on those nails until you're so punctured the stink leaks out of you!"

I had to think quickly what to say to save ourselves. Alois was not joking, he could do anything.

"Those nails are obviously too long," I said with as much assurance as I could muster. "That's why they're sticking out. We used them temporarily until you could get us some shorter ones."

He seemed uncertain whether this was a true carpenter's argument, but agreed anyway to bring us shorter nails. We were still faced with the problem of attaching the legs to make the surface of the bench rigid, for Alois would not even hear of nailing it to the wall. We decided to nail the legs at each corner using long nails from the top piece and to lean the structure against the wall, hoping Alois would not notice how wobbly it was. By the time we had finished this job, Alois was back with shorter nails.

He stopped in front of the bench, looked satisfied, complimented our work and slapped the shorter nails on the bench for our finishing touches. He was about to leave when the bench started very slowly to lean forward. As he slammed the door shut, the structure collapsed to the ground. We almost stopped breathing! But Alois did not hear the crash and walked away.

It was now near the end of our working day and we decided not to press our luck any further. We gingerly lifted the top piece and put it back on its legs. There was no time to replace the long, protruding nails so we just hammered them in, which made the bench even more wobbly. We then balanced the whole thing against the wall and quickly made our escape. Grabbing some extra spades which we found behind the shack, we ran into a ditch supervised by a different kapo and immediately began digging.

About ten minutes later we saw Alois returning to the shack. Seconds passed, then we heard a crash and saw Alois bounding out of the shack, swearing furiously and swinging one of the legs from the bench above his head. He rushed alongside his ditch trying to identify his carpenters, but of course, we were not there.

After this encounter with Alois I naturally tried to stay as far from him as possible. There was a continuous competition of wits among all prisoners to get attached to a working squad where better conditions would enhance one's chances of survival. An important factor that autumn of 1940 was finding shelter from the cold and the rain. A few men worked permanently in stables and in cow and pig sheds; they were among the privileged because of their ability to organize some animal food for themselves to ward off hunger. The top class were the scant few who worked in the SS kitchen outside the camp and in the prisoners' kitchen.

With the expansion of Auschwitz, a new opportunity arose for improved conditions because the SS needed tradesmen. Men who could work as bricklayers, stone masons, carpenters, electricians, glaziers, painters or in other trades were protected from the extermination practices of the kapos. The expansion also resulted in the resettling of Polish farmers within a ten-kilometre radius of the camp, and all buildings in the annexed area were to be levelled to reduce the number of places an escaping prisoner might hide. By accident, I was assigned for several weeks to this demolition squad.

This job had its benefits, for on the farms we could sometimes find old clothing to use as rags or underwear. Barns also yielded small amounts of spilled grain which could be chewed to provide a few more of the calories we so badly needed. Since our diet did not include fresh fruit or vegetables, cases of scurvy were widespread in the camp. But in the gardens and fields we sometimes found an odd carrot or turnip which gave us supplemental nutrition.

The work itself was not easy because we had no machinery. Everything had to be done with picks, sledge hammers and crowbars. Also, safety was not one of the kapos' concerns, nor was our system itself very safe, so accidents were not uncommon. We tried to remain as long as possible under the roof, demolishing first the inner walls and shovelling out the debris until only the supporting structure and roof remained. We then had no choice but to hack at the exterior walls in the rain and snow. The job turned out to be a mixed blessing: our kapo, who while supervising sheltered himself inside the house, was in no hurry to complete the demolition; the SS man forced to patrol the operation from outside, however, did all within his power to rush us to work faster.

Upon returning to the camp I found Mietek in very poor condition. He decided to join the lines of men requiring medical attention and stayed in the camp instead of going to work. Unfortunately for him, the first man to examine him was Leo, the campelder. Not only was Leo in charge of all blockelders and the top authority within the camp, he also had good reasons for wearing a green triangle. His powerful position was the result of his tremendous physical strength and astounding ability to display a variety of ways to kill people.

He pronounced Mietek healthy so instead of getting the care he obviously needed, my friend had to join a group of prisoners doing sport for infringements of camp regulations. These exercises left him covered with bruises and barely able to stand. We decided that after the evening meal we would try to get him into the outpatients group, hoping that by this route he might find a place in the hospital.

Following the evening meal, however, Mietek felt much better. He was still very much in need of medical attention, but the cigarettes he obtained in return for soup and bread seemed to give him momentary comfort. It became evident to me that my companion was among those who turned into Musselmen psychologically before developing any physical symptoms. Our discussions revealed his indifference to practically everything but the occasional smoke that he said killed his hunger. Neither food nor the will to live mattered much to him any more.

Arriving at Block 16, we found the situation even worse than before. The crowd had grown larger. Men were pushing and clawing their way to the door, trampling over the fallen bodies of those weaker than themselves. We stood there in a state of hopelessness when some male nurses came out to announce the hospital was full, that there would be no more admissions, and that the outpatients reception had closed. In stark contrast to those seeking help, the nurses were dressed in clean striped uniforms and looked healthy and well fed. Among them we recognized Fred Stoessel, a junior colleague of ours at the military academy before the war.

We started to shout his name: "Fred! Fred! Here! Come here!"

He finally spotted us and pushed his way through the crowd. As he came toward us, I marvelled at how he had retained his youth and handsome features while others, like Mietek, had slowly withered away.

"Germans got you too, I see," he said, standing next to us. "It's strange that our first meeting after school is in Auschwitz. Can I be of help to you?"

"I'm okay," I replied, "but Mietek has been done in by sport. Can you get him aid for his injuries?"

While the crowd in front of the hospital dispersed, Fred took us through the back door to the washrooms. Here all admitted patients, many of whom were already half-dead and unable to stand, were required to shower themselves. In order to save water, five or six patients were showered at the same time. They simply lay on the cement floor while frigid water was poured on them by one of the Kieliszek brothers, a somewhat retarded pair without much ability to contemplate human suffering.

Bill Kieliszek had developed his own method for diagnosing the condition of a patient. He would direct a very strong stream of cold water on the patient's body; if the patient moved, it was assumed he might survive. Those who remained still were pulled to one side and generally pronounced dead within an hour or two. Bill was proud to be regarded as someone who could make an accurate diagnosis. The SS doctor who inspected the hospital called him "Doctor" Kieliszek though the man was a cobbler by profession. Bill could not see the irony in this title.

Another duty of the Kieliszek brothers and a job they were more suited to was keeping track of the numbers of dying men. When a patient was stripped of his clothing, one of the brothers would write in ink a number on his chest. Patients diagnosed to die were kept together, each bearing a randomly inscribed number given him by a Kieliszek. In the fall of 1940, two or three bodies were often cremated together. At that time the camp authorities still shipped the ashes of the deceased — who always died of "natural causes" — to the family for a price. The random numbering on the bodies did not matter because the ashes were mixed later anyway.

After we had ample time to observe the admitting procedures, Fred returned with some peroxide and iodine. He washed Mietek's bruises, applied iodine generously and then, in the midst of the dead and dying, engaged us in a discussion about the camp, the reasons for our arrest and old times.

We discovered that Fred had a very low three-digit number. He had arrived at Auschwitz with the first 700 prisoners from Tarnow.

"We were the first Polish prisoners here," he told us. "You might say we were the founders of this camp. To have a proper reception for us, the Germans shipped here 30 kapos from the concentration camp in Sachsenhausen. Leo, who's responsible for Mietek's problems, received Number 1. We got numbers from 31 to 720. There was no work at that time. For one month we were doing sport which reduced our numbers by half.

"Hans Bock was given the responsibility of organizing the hospital. Although he's a criminal, for a long time he was a chief doctor and thanks to my knowledge of German, I became his assistant. Actually, Hans isn't a bad guy when the SS men are not watching."

Although Mietek had never been formally recruited by Thomas into our special unit, he had overheard enough of our talks and in his usual carefree manner asked Fred if he knew of our organization. The younger man was more cautious and barely nodded in assent.

"I know we're not supposed to talk about it to anybody, isn't that right?" he asked, looking quickly at me. "In any case, we now have a Polish doctor in the hospital whose name is Dering. He's a friend of Thomas, from Warsaw."

It was now almost curfew and briefly exchanging a word of thanks, I urged that we hurry back to our barracks.

"Come again tomorrow night," said Fred as we parted. "I might be able to talk some kapos into putting you in a better working group."

Next day we were back in the hospital washroom where Kieliszek greeted us like old friends and went to fetch Fred.

"I have good news," Fred announced. "Mietek is to work in the kitchen peeling potatoes and should report there directly after morning roll call."

Fred also gave me the name and number of a man he called Jan who worked in a surveying group. In case they were looking for another worker, Jan was to give my number to the kapo in charge. Now, I thought, this is work I am much better qualified to do than carpentry. I later found Jan, who turned out to be Fred's junior in the military academy, and he promised to talk to his kapo at the first opportunity.

The following day I went back to my demolition work while Mietek joined the potato peelers. He was very pleased with the job which involved sitting all day scraping potatoes and throwing them into a barrel of water. I also learned that Thomas had been placed with the carpenters, a job arranged with the kapo through Dr. Dering.

Thomas would rarely volunteer to say to whom he talked or who else had joined the organization. The fewer names we knew, he argued, the safer it was for us. By 1943 I knew most of the names anyway, for by that time I was making contact with a membership that had expanded well beyond our original five. After I confronted him several times, however, Thomas eventually admitted that he knew about Fred and Dr. Dering. He also told me to pursue my possibilities with the surveyors since this group worked outside the

camp where we could make valuable contacts with the underground.

I went to see Jan again and in a couple of days I was
summoned to join the surveyors by their kapo, Fritz, who turned
out to be an unbelievable contrast to his counterparts. Despite his
green triangle, Fritz was kind, helpful and hated violence. He
would assist at work drawing our maps and would write the titles
of our project in a beautifully ornamental Gothic script. He was a
counterfeiter by profession.

My knowledge of surveying instruments and cartography
came in very handy and in a couple of days I was working on my
own, with two helpers. The three of us were always guarded by one
SS man. However, we soon found out that not all of them were
exterminators. Some, especially the older men, were actually quite
human. We could even impress them with our surveying skills and
partake of a friendly conversation.

Sometimes we used our profession to our own advantage by
placing instruments close to farmhouses or in farmyards. Polish
farmers, knowing about the camp conditions and the hunger, often
tried to treat the SS guard and then pass pieces of bread, with bacon,
to us. Since the guard was forbidden from accepting anything from
a civilian, tempting him with food worked as a sort of blackmail; by
taking things for himself, he also had to allow us some food. Of
course, the majority of SS men would treat even the Polish civilians
like a lower race and any contact between us was regarded as either
attempts at escape or as spying. We had learned to recognize these
types. When under their guard, our surveying would always be
done far away from any buildings.

Besides the occasional bits of food which kept us in better
condition than others, our surveying work removed us, at least
temporarily, from the daily threat of being killed. Our contacts with
civilians also proved very valuable in the future. Sometimes we
were able to send letters to our families in which we wrote the truth
about Auschwitz, instead of the sentence dictated by the Germans:
"I am healthy and feel good."

Letters were also sent to the Polish underground and soon
underground men were making direct contact with us. Later,
regular reports went out describing the main events in the camp.
The underground transmitted this information to the headquarters
of the Polish army in London, England, and from there it was

broadcast to the rest of the world. In 1942 and after, this contact was also used to prepare the underground army for intercepting escaping prisoners.

SS men who sought assignment to the group to obtain extra food and cigarettes could also be persuaded, when the price was right, to allow us more in return than the bacon and bread passed to us by farmers. Sometimes these prices were high indeed, for the guards knew that, if caught taking bribes, they would end up in the concentration camp themselves. But greed is a powerful force and we always had several SS men conveniently working for our cause.

One day, returning from work, I again found Mietek in a very sorry state. Apparently Leo had decided that peeling potatoes was light work for weak people who had left the hospital as convalescents. Not that the room between the camp kitchen and the outside garbage box offered a perfect place for recovery: sitting on benches or on logs around a water-filled barrel, the peelers were constantly adjusting to alternating drafts of hot steam and cold air. From time to time, Leo would raid the group and inevitably find men who, in his opinion, should be capable of doing harder work. Those selected were punished for feigning sickness by being attached to a group doing sport for other offences.

Such was the treatment accorded to Mietek who, as a result, collected more bruises and a very nasty cut on the head. He turned almost instantly into a Musselman both physically and mentally. We decided to seek help again and finding Kieliszek at his customary chores, asked him to fetch Fred.

"You should not give up, Mietek," our colleague said upon seeing my companion. "When you look like a Musselman, you're fair game to be beaten up by anybody. Try to straighten yourself and walk with your head up."

"I know you are right," answered Mietek, "but I've just run out of steam. I don't think I can fight any longer."

"Don't worry," said Fred. "I'll talk to the hospital blockelder, Bock, to persuade him to admit you. Instead of going to work in the morning, join the group in front of the hospital."

The next day was very cold and rainy. I went to work with my surveying partners to find that one of those young, eager representatives of the "super race" had been appointed our SS guard. Although an empty farmhouse stood near our work area, we would be given no chance to get out of the rain. Instead, our SS man took the place for himself and set up a shooting gallery on the front porch. He had us bring a chair from the house, build a wooden support for his rifle, and in appreciation fired a couple of practice shots into the field ahead of him.

"Now you march out there," he told us, pointing along his line of sight. "For targets, I prefer you to those logs, and maybe one of you will give me a day off this lousy post."

We knew very well this was not just a threat, that SS men before him had earned their holidays shooting "escaping" prisoners. Our only hope was that the camp's top management regarded our work as urgent and important, a fact I tried to remind him of.

"If you shoot me," I said, attempting to sound matter-of-fact, "no work will be done and you'll have to take the responsibility. And if you shoot one of my helpers, you'll have to work in his place because the camp commandant expects this job to be completed today."

With these words we took our instruments and went into the field. The SS man sat in his chair taking aim at each of us in turn. He obviously enjoyed our fear. I told my helpers to ignore his antics and to avoid even looking at him.

Just before noon, while I was aiming my instrument at the rod held some distance away by my helper, a shot rang out. The bullet hit the ground just under my feet.

Turning to the SS man, I shouted: "You may have to finish the work yourself if you hit me!"

Even at the distance he was from us, I could see him reload his rifle and take careful aim at me. There was no place to hide, and running would certainly precipitate his shooting by giving him a good excuse to do so. I could only hope he was bluffing. The next few seconds were an eternity for me and my watching colleagues.

Finally the SS man raised his head, laughed loudly and shouted: "Midday break!"

I heard afterwards that this same SS man, assigned to guard a demolition team, had asked one of the prisoners to fetch him a sunflower from a neighbouring garden. When the man started to walk there he ordered him to run, then shot him in the back.

Though I had survived this ordeal, the day still turned out badly. In addition to the shooting scare, I was soaked through by the cold rain. Also, the results of the triangulation were not accurate enough; intimidated by our trigger-happy guard and preoccupied with keeping warm, I had at some point made an error in my calculations. Our kapo was concerned he would be punished for our unfinished work and reproached me for making an enemy of the SS man, whom he said would likely shoot me at the next opportunity.

CHAPTER 4

THE DEATH OF MIETEK
AND FATHER KOLBE'S SACRIFICE

After evening roll call, I was shocked to see someone resembling Mietek lying at the end of our rows among the dead. Approaching the bodies, I discovered it was indeed Mietek, half-conscious and displaying the wounds of a severe beating.

There was no time to be lost. He had to be taken to the hospital at once. I succeeded in pulling him to his feet, but his legs were so stiff he required all the support I could give him. I desperately looked around for help, but men had begun lining up for evening soup and no one wanted to risk losing his portion of the food.

I do not know how I managed to drag my friend across the roll call square to Block 16. By the time we arrived Mietek was unconscious, so I laid him on the ground in the rain and rushed into the washroom to find Fred.

But the one man who could help was unhappy to see me.

"I can't possibly admit him," Fred told me. "Do you know what this silly ass did? Bock examined him and was ready to admit him only because Mietek's my friend, but that wasn't good enough for Mietek. He had to be doubly sure so he rubbed the thermometer so hard it registered 42° Celsius. Bock knows these tricks, of course, and for attempting to fool him sent the guy to Leo for a special treatment of sport."

I had to agree with Fred; Mietek could not have done anything worse to jeopardize his chances. Bock, playing the role of medical doctor, was especially sensitive to any attempt at interfering with his official diagnoses. If a man dared to undermine his power, he had to pay for it. But understanding the situation did not change the fact that my friend needed care immediately.

"Mietek is dying," I said. "Would you at least come out with me to look at him?"

The sight of our badly beaten companion must have soothed Fred's anger somewhat.

"Let me see if Bock will be forgiving and compassionate enough to admit him now. I doubt it very much, but let me try."

A short time later both Fred and Bock emerged from the hospital. Bock examined Mietek, gave me a lecture on honesty in the camp, then ordered Fred to admit him. It was an unusually magnanimous gesture from a German criminal.

When I returned to my block all the soup was distributed; I had missed my main meal. However, I was glad that Mietek had a friend in the hospital and a good chance to get better.

Next day the weather improved significantly and my surveying team got a previously tamed SS man as our guard. We went first to the farmhouse where each of us received a piece of bread with bacon and coffee. Watching the guard as he munched on the bacon together with his prisoners, I thought of how little he looked like a member of a super race. His gun stood against the wall within easy reach of any one of us, offering an ideal means of escape; we were also a long way from the camp. It did not even occur to us, however, to use this opportunity. An escape at that time brought responsibility on the prisoner's family, who were brought to the camp and hanged in front of the kitchen. The remaining prisoners were also punished by having to stand at roll call while ten men were selected to starve to death in specially constructed concrete cells called bunkers. Without windows, they were so small one could not stand erect and so narrow one could not sit down. This punishment was later "improved" by putting ten men in a bunker at a time. What happened in that cell before its occupants died was difficult to imagine — even for us, who had become used to all sorts of brutality.

The Germans liked this type of punishment so much they apparently devised a means of watching their unfortunate victims and ensured that plenty of these chambers were constructed in the penal block. Prisoners would sometimes spend 12, 24 or 36 hours there for such minor infractions as "sluggishness" in removing one's cap in front of an SS man.

Fearing such severe repercussions, the underground army agreed in 1940 to discourage escapes. Indeed, those of us who found opportunities to flee had to make very tough decisions for the next year and a half, until the regulations were changed.

Bunker with bricks removed from one corner
to show the smallness of the interior

I went immediately to the hospital at the end of our working day to check how Mietek was doing. Fred informed me that the poor man could not pass even Kieliszek's diagnostic procedures. He had died on the cement floor of the shower room without regaining consciousness.

Deputy Commandant
Hans Aumeier

Late in 1940 the camp was surrounded by two tall encirclements of barbed wire, punctuated at intervals by guard towers perched high up for the benefit of SS men armed with machine guns. During working hours an outer as well as an inner ring of sentries guarded every working area in the camp and its surroundings. The sentries of the outer ring, though far removed from the working squads, were also positioned on high wooden towers within sight of each other.

If, at evening roll call, all prisoners were accounted for, the outer ring was withdrawn. Should someone be absent, the outer guards remained in position and we were kept standing in the square while a special detachment of kapos and SS men with dogs went out in search of the deserter.

Very often the "escapee" proved to be one of the Musselmen who had retired into some tight spot to die in peace. But whatever the reason, no prisoner could budge from his position until the man, living or dead, was found. On one occasion we stood at attention for 36 hours. Many among us were killed or severely beaten by furious blockelders who had to join us in waiting out the search without food.

There inevitably came a time when someone actually was missing. Kapos and SS men searched every inch of the outer ring but came back empty-handed. Apprehension on a new scale ran through our ranks: because the missing man was from our block, ten of our block-mates would now be chosen for slow death in a bunker of the penal block.

The wait was unnerving. We were standing in two rows about five paces apart. Up came Höss with his deputy, Aumeier, and the infamous Palitsch. Behind them marched the SS men responsible for the roll call procedures and a couple of SS guards with dogs.

The Death of Mietek and Father Kolbe's Sacrifice

Aumeier walked slowly down the ranks, often stopping and looking into the eyes of the terror-stricken prisoners. Occasionally he would point at a man with his riding whip and the victim was immediately dragged out in front of the block. Several of my colleagues were already standing there. A grave silence prevailed during this procedure. Even the usual shouting of the SS men was absent.

When they finally approached my row, I noticed a look of complete indifference and even boredom in Höss's eyes.

Rudolf Höss
Commandant of Auschwitz

My face has an unfortunate characteristic: my mouth is shaped so that it appears I am smiling even when I am in a most serious mood. I was obviously as scared as everyone else, but my face did not show it. As Höss came up to me he looked surprised, paused, lifted up his whip — his eyes showing curiosity and interest for a second or so — then he walked away. Looking back at him I somehow knew that it would not be my turn to die, though he went through almost all the motions to select me. Perhaps it was that moment of eye contact that saved me. I will never know.

Höss passed along, followed by Aumeier and Palitsch. As Palitsch walked by me, he said: "You were lucky this time." I knew that I was lucky but I regretted that Palitsch had registered my face— he was a dangerous man to know. At last ten men were selected. The commandant returned to his place in front of our block, said something about the joint responsibility for escapes, and was prepared to walk away when an incident occurred unlike anything else in the history of the camp.

From our ranks a prisoner suddenly leapt forward. He was about 50 years of age, quite thin from hunger and wore Dutch wooden shoes, but his face and light blue eyes were lit with a radiant smile. Boldly and in a loud, clear voice, he said: "I would like to speak to the commandant!"

Everyone stood astounded. A prisoner asking to speak to the commandant? At this time and in such a daring voice?

Even the kapos were dumbfounded and did not move to silence him. The SS men just looked at Höss, wondering what he would say. Höss seemed to be interested. Turning to the prisoner, he asked him in an almost polite voice: "What would you like to talk to me about?"

The prisoner pointed to a man standing among those condemned to die and who was crying like a child. Then he said, strongly and evenly, the smile still clearly visible: "I want to ask you, sir, to let me change places with this man."

"Is he your son?" asked the commandant.

"No sir, I have never seen him before. But he is young and I haven't a very long time to live anyway."

The commandant frowned, then simply nodded his agreement and walked away.

The prisoner went up to the man, tapped him on the shoulder and gently pushed him back into the ranks. Then, still smiling, he took his place among the condemned.

The man who displayed this heroic behaviour was a Roman Catholic priest named Father Kolbe. Sometime later Fred informed me that our Doctor Bock went at night to the bunker, dragged out the semi-conscious Kolbe and injected phenol into his heart, causing instant death. We interpreted this as an act of euthanasia, delivered by a German criminal to a saintly Catholic monk.

The Death of Mietek and Father Kolbe's Sacrifice

Father Maximilian Kolbe, the guardian and founder of the
Franciscans Monastery before his arrest by the Gestapo

CHAPTER

OF MORGUES AND HORSES

It was on a day in late November, when a heavy snow fell and the temperature dropped below freezing, that the camp had its greatest mortality. Musselmen froze to death and squads working in the industrial park had to drag back unusually large numbers of dead or dying colleagues. That same day these working parties unloaded countless boxes that had arrived from the concentration camp in Dachau. According to the rumours, the boxes contained under- wear, coats and caps.

This time the rumours were correct. After roll call each man received a pair of underwear and a cap, and those of us working outside were also delivered striped coats. The shipment, although late, was a real blessing, since the winter of 1940-41 was particularly cold and started unusually early. However, it also brought unwel- come guests — lice. These pests spread so fast in the dirt and filth of the camp that a new ritual had to be performed before going to bed: everybody would undress and try to catch lice in their under- wear. Deemed our "social hour," it was the only entertainment granted us. One ingenious fellow collected especially big, fat lice that he conscripted into a louse circus. There were lice pulling a rollwagon, lice with banners named after kapos and blockelders, and lice accorded personalities like those of Leo and Bruno.

Auschwitz officials carried out many unsuccessful attempts at delousing the camp. Men in block after block were obligated to surrender all their clothing to steam ovens, and mattresses were thoroughly disinfected. But as the unsanitary conditions prevailed, so too did the lice.

By now the numbers assigned to newly arriving prisoners had risen above 15,000, though the actual number alive was about half that figure. In order to accommodate the newcomers, three-storey bunks were built by the carpenters and eventually additional blocks were erected. The camp officials also decided to segregate "professional workers" from the others. I was transferred to a block where, to my delight, I found that my friend and fellow officer Stan Kazuba was a roomelder. Also moved to our new block was Thomas, then working as a carpenter. This gave us more opportunities to talk about the underground army and in time, Thomas sent out his first reports through my civilian contacts to our headquarters in Warsaw.

Unfortunately, I was unable to perform this mission because two days after changing blocks Fritz told me I must find another working group. Apparently the SS man who had used me for target practice spoke to our kapo in confidence about assigning me to a less important task. His intent was to show me how good a shot he was by shooting me in the arms and legs without killing me. I did not relish the thought of proving his marksmanship, particularly since we both knew that a prisoner was only to be shot for an attempted escape and, therefore, was to be shot dead. In any event, my work as a surveyor came to an abrupt and disappointing end. Once again I had to return to the general working force, exposed to all the dangers which, for a short time, I had been lucky to escape.

December was not exactly the best time to begin again carrying a shovel and pushing a wheelbarrow.

Perhaps the only consolation at the time was that my number, 4618, considered low in comparison to those given recent arrivals, earned me a little respect from the kapos and even the SS men. The kapos knew that I and others like myself bearing "old numbers" must have influential friends somewhere to survive so long and therefore deserved better treatment. Such special considerations, however, did not extend to working times when we stood side by side with newcomers digging ditches.

"How did you last?" the kapos would ask, adding "if you didn't get a good taste of my club before, I'll show you how tough it is now!"

I thus began desperately trying to find a working group that would give me a better chance to survive.

Also important to me was to be allowed to stay in the tradesmen's block. This in itself was a privilege since the block contained no Musselmen, was generally cleaner (we still had lice but in smaller quantities), and we were more frequently and better treated for scabies, an infectious skin disease that had spread throughout the camp, leaving men scarred as if they were the victims of some terrible plague. The treatment of scabies consisted of smearing a tar-like paste all over the body until we were all black; another kind of paste, containing sulphur, was also used. As showering was infrequent, the paste tended to irritate the skin, especially around scratches and open wounds. The medication always seemed in short supply — so once again my friendly relationship with Fred proved helpful.

Dr. Wladyslaw Dering

One day I went with Thomas to see Fred about organizing some sulphuric paste. Our friend would always assist us on these occasions. This time, however, while we were covering our bodies with the paste in the Kieliszeks' shower room, Dr. Dering walked in. He started to swear and shout at the top of his lungs, ordering us out.

At that moment Fred returned, alerted by the commotion.

"Don't you know who these men are?" he asked Dering. "I thought you'd at least recognize your friend Thomas."

Although Thomas knew Dr. Dering from Warsaw, he prepared to leave without saying a word. But Dering stopped him, his expression completely changed, now very apologetic. He even invited us to his room above the showers after we finished our treatment.

The difference in the characters of these two men was startling. Thomas was a gentle, shy, unimposing person — hardly the type one would imagine coming to Auschwitz voluntarily to organize an underground movement. Dering, on the other hand, was an extrovert — loud, domineering, egocentric, confident, full of energy and with an insatiable desire to outshine anyone in his presence. He divided people into two categories: those whom he might need in the future, and those whom he could completely ignore.

We went to visit him with Fred. The doctor was likely thinking that someday he might need the services of the underground, for he was very kind to us, even offering Thomas and me some of his meal.

"There is a half a bowl of today's soup if any of you want it. They keep giving it to me. I suppose it is the German — 'Ordnung muss sein'" (There must be order.)

He laughed at his joke and continued: "I do not eat this stuff. Cooks bring me some meat and guys here fry it for me with some potatoes. I love fried potatoes!"

This was a time when Dering could see for himself thousands of men dying from hunger. Indeed, Thomas and I did not look much better than half-dead Musselmen ourselves. We just sat there swallowing our saliva thinking about those fried potatoes. It was not very sophisticated tact Dering was displaying, but he needed to brag about his power and importance.

Still talking, he shoved the bowl to Thomas who readily accepted the offer. After finishing exactly half of the soup, Thomas passed it to me saying: "You must be hungry also." I hated Dering's attitude so much I told the greatest lie of my life: "No, I'm not hungry, thank you. You can finish it if you want."

Thomas polished off the rest of the soup while Dering continued to chatter.

"You know, I showed these German doctors how surgery should be performed. The other day I took an appendix out in three minutes flat. Those German doctors come here to learn from me.

"We had two cases of gall bladder surgery, so I let a young German fellow take one while I handled the other. You know, it took him four hours! Then I did my case. From the incision to the closing of the wound took me exactly 20 minutes!"

At this moment Thomas shyly interrupted: "Our organization is losing a very vital contact with the outside in the surveyors' group." He then described my encounter with the SS guard.

"That's no problem," said Dering. "What's the name of this SS guard? I can ask one of the SS doctors to talk to him and he will leave you in peace. Do you know I was a commanding officer in the Warsaw underground before I was arrested?"

I did not believe he could really influence that particular SS man so I immediately declined the offer, telling him that the kapo had already hired another man in my place.

"This is no problem either," said Dering. "Fred can fix you

temporarily with the potato peelers and next week I will be looking for someone for our surgical outpatients' department. If I do not find anybody better, you could have that job."

This was an offer I could not refuse.

"Thank you," I answered. "I think it would be the best solution."

That was the end of our conversation. We went back to our barracks while Dering continued talking to Fred.

Next day, after the morning roll call, I reported to the kapo of the potato peelers. He already knew I was going to work in the hospital and assuming he might eventually need me to organize some medication, promised to help me dodge Leo. That was a very important promise. One day the kapo was in the kitchen and Leo appeared on one of his raids. Among the old and sick, my face stood out like a sore thumb.

Leo came directly to me.

"What are you doing here?"

"I am peeling potatoes," I said politely.

"What kind of a stupid answer is that?" he barked.

"There was need for extra help and I volunteered to do it."

Leo grabbed me by the shoulder.

"Now you are volunteering for sport!"

At that instant the kapo of the potato peelers walked in from the kitchen.

"Let me punish that man!" he shouted. "What did he do?"

"He is too healthy to work as a potato peeler," Leo replied.

My kapo laughed and said: "You're right, he is healthy. But he's not a potato peeler, he's a cook's helper!"

"Then what is he doing here?" pressed Leo, without letting go of my shoulder.

"We needed a lot of potatoes in a hurry. I had to use anybody I could spare!"

It was merely accidental that this statement coincided with what I had said earlier. Releasing his grip, Leo slapped me on the back and said: "All right then, show these Musselmen how to work fast!"

With these words he turned and left without examining the other men in the group.

This incident merely illustrated the system of mutual favours that had sprung up in the camp. Because Leo needed, from time to time, some extra food, he would not harm anybody working in the kitchen. My kapo, in turn, needed medication from the hospital and knowing I would be working there, protected me. The SS men also organized food from their kitchen and were therefore unusually polite to kitchen personnel. Each of us relied on a plan of mutual interdependence.

The SS men in the surveyors' group also required our help to get goodies from the civilians; consequently, they too treated their prisoners well. "To organize" something was a motto of the day: the better a man was at using his contacts, the more likely he would get what he needed. To organize also meant to steal, generally from the common supply rather than from an individual. The lives of prisoners, kapos and SS men consisted of the continuous process of organizing. It was also the reason some of us who could organize lived, and those who could not died. To survive at Auschwitz, one had to adapt to the laws of camp life. Some, of course, organized not only to survive but to satisfy their greed.

While waiting for my position in the hospital to open up, I stayed with the potato peelers for three weeks. It was a job that could keep one alive. Cooks would occasionally pass extra food to the peelers and we were spared direct exposure to rain and snow, though we were in no way protected from the cold. The shed in which we worked was unheated, but because our job was indoors we had to surrender our coats. Peeling potatoes in near-freezing temperatures was not the greatest pleasure. But it offered, most of the time, no direct threat to our survival.

At last I got the job I had waited so anxiously for. I had a shower, received a new, clean uniform and underwear, and was assigned to Dr. Dering's surgical outpatients' department.

Dering began his instructions by saying: "As I recall, cavalry officers do not have to think — they have a horse for that. Now let's see what I can teach you about treating injuries."

The man's arrogance irritated me beyond measure. Obviously he was making little attempt to endear himself to me.

"Please do not assume everyone besides you is stupid," I advised.

"You misunderstand me," he said. "I was also in the cavalry and let the horse think for me, but by then I had proven myself as a medical doctor."

"Then there's no misunderstanding," I said. "The medical

men I saw in the cavalry couldn't ride. Obviously the horse had no choice but to take responsibility for the good doctor."

Dering was visibly annoyed and without further digs at the cavalry, continued his instructions. Because the camp hospital had a very limited number of medications, my training as a male nurse only took about five minutes.

"There is iodine and antiseptic powder for uninfected wounds, Ichtyol, a cream for slow healing wounds, and potassium permanganate for cleaning septic wounds. You will learn how to apply them today after roll call."

With these words Dering finished his remarks and walked away.

Directly after roll call I was inside the hospital door. Dering had introduced a new procedure to speed up the processing of patients. He first appointed two men to arrange the patients in line outside and separate out the "emergencies." Inside, two men sorted the patients needing surgical help, a change of dressing, or other medical attention. The temperature and the pulse rate of the patients was taken and only then were they permitted to see the doctor.

He performed with astonishing speed, ordering aspirin for colds, charcoal tablets for diarrhoea, or admission to the hospital in extreme cases. Each patient was granted no more than a minute or two of his time, yet he managed to see, in an hour, everybody who had been waiting outside. During these visits he made a large number of enemies. Perhaps 80 per cent of the men sent out the door were ill enough to deserve admission. But the hospital had room for only a few each day and Dering would admit only the number he could accommodate. Needless to say, his decisions were harsh; those unable to survive one more day were admitted and those who could last another two or three days were sent back to work.

Dering was eventually appointed chief surgeon of the hospital and Dr. Diem succeeded him in charge of admissions. A short, kindly man in his mid-forties, Diem offered a welcome change; he would see at the most 20 patients in two hours and examine them very thoroughly, admitting almost everyone. A more sensitive and compassionate man than Dering, he had no difficulty winning the admiration and respect of his patients. Perhaps his only flaw was that he was too methodical, for not infrequently several hundred injured and dying men were left waiting outside, many of whom did not have a chance even to reach the front door. Although Dering's practices seemed heartless and brutal, they were in those grim circumstances more rational. Of course, under normal conditions Dr. Dering should not have been a physician, but such conditions never prevailed at Auschwitz.

A common ailment at the time I began my apprenticeship was infection. Very often it would spread deep into the flesh and burst open at some other place on the skin. Dering showed me how to treat such cases. With one quick movement, he would insert long forceps into the wound until their end came out the other opening. Then he would pick a piece of gauze saturated in potassium permanganate and pull it back through the wound until he could draw the forceps free. Gauze was left in the wound until the next visit.

I received a lot of scolding for the way I performed this treatment. Instead of ramming the forceps through the wound, I attempted to find the path of the infection. This method was never fast enough for Dering, but the patients appreciated it and very soon all the men needing it done lined up in front of me whom they regarded as the "specialist." Dr. Dering was furious.

"If you continue to dilly-dally with patients like that," he warned, "you'll go back to work with Siegrud!"

Then, perhaps trying to justify himself, he added: "It is a painful procedure, but when I do it the patient doesn't even have time to scream."

I think that he believed in what he said because I later had the opportunity to see him in the operating room. He was indeed an extremely skilful and efficient surgeon. His darker side emerged as a consequence of his program for survival, based almost exclusively on a desire to gratify influential people. Dering was never too busy to treat a kapo or blockelder, even for a minor skin cut. He would also go out of his way to impress the SS doctors with his skills and his readiness to be of service. I suspected the majority of operations he performed were for the benefit of these doctors, with whom he would spend hours in the surgery discussing various techniques and strategies. Once, while performing surgery for a hernia, he removed a large portion of skin from the scrotum of a patient. To please a German surgeon, he had the skin tanned and then found someone to make a tobacco pouch out of it.

His indulgence of the camp authorities was later taken to

extremes. Perhaps his most infamous decision resulted in him cooperating with German doctors on experiments in sterilization methods. After applying various doses of X-ray radiation to men's testicles and women's ovaries — using Jewish prisoners as guinea pigs — Dering removed the irradiated organs by surgery to examine the results.

When I asked him after the war why he did it, he replied: "They were all destined to follow the 3,000 or so Jews killed in gas chambers every day. The Germans could have killed them first and then removed the organs. I was actually saving their lives."

Ironically, following the war some Jews whose lives he "saved" were among the first to testify against him for war crimes.

In the winter of 1940-41 the first Jews were allowed to visit the hospital for treatment. Apparently, the order had come from Berlin that all prisoners should have access to medical care. Little did it matter whether the men sent to us were to be killed the same day; everything had to be done according to the regulations.

One day 12 men suffering from frostbite arrived from the penal block accompanied by their blockelder. I was on duty at the time. The men were herded into a corner of the emergency room. No one was allowed to talk to them. They were treated as all others from the penal block, although their only crime was that they were Jewish. Polish prisoners in the penal block were at least proven enemies, either captured as members of the Polish underground or taken prisoner in armed combat. The Germans kept these men alive, temporarily, in case more information could be extracted from them at a later date. Jews, on the other hand, were assigned to this block simply because they were condemned to die.

An armed SS man stood guard over the 12, excusing his presence by telling us, with the utmost conviction, how dangerous these men were and why it was necessary to maintain their isolation. It was later confirmed each of the Jews had been rounded up on the streets of Warsaw.

Dr. Dering was summoned to examine them. After a while he called me and another orderly to apply the treatment. In the hospital we were used to seeing all kinds of human misery, but what we saw now thoroughly shocked us. The man assigned to me removed his wooden shoes to reveal the two feet of a skeleton, completely devoid of flesh. The bones were brown in colour, probably frozen as well. Many of the other patients were in similar condition. How these men were able to walk, let alone perform the work expected of them, was beyond my comprehension. I had no idea what kind of treatment to attempt; it seemed impossible that anything I could do would help.

Dering, as usual, had a ready solution.

"Just sprinkle the bones with disinfecting powder and apply some bandages," he said and walked away. It was even too much for him.

While putting the powder on, the smell of rotten flesh and bones was so overpowering I had to interrupt the work from time to time in order not to throw up. I decided to complete the treatment by wrapping the bones in a thick layer of bandages, to make it easier for the men to walk.

But that idea was cut short by Dr. Dering who, monitoring me at a distance, barked: "Paper bandages!"

I interrupted my work, went up to Dering and said very quietly: "When they walk out into the snow, those bandages will last less than five minutes."

"Yes," he replied. "And how long do you think they are going to survive after they leave this place? More than five minutes? One hour? Maybe two? We have only a few cotton bandages and we need them where they'll be useful."

In hindsight, the logic of his response was perhaps irrefutable. These men certainly had not long to live and such rarities as cotton bandages could no doubt have served a better purpose. But I remember that at the time I was outraged. I also knew not all the cotton bandages were going to be used for people who really needed them — that Dering had established a cache for kapos and other influential people.

As time passed, Dering gave less and less of his attention to the underground, fearing his involvement might endanger him personally or compromise his position in the hospital. On one occasion, however, he agreed to the placing of a stolen radio under a sink in the German doctor's office; while underground men were installing it, he was conveniently at the other end of the camp establishing his alibi. He was too busy to see Thomas, and I also suspected I would be fired at the first opportunity.

The mortality rate reached its peak in Auschwitz in the winter of 1940-41. Deaths attributed to "natural causes" included killings by kapos and blockelders or the incidental shooting of prisoners by

SS men. In 1942 began the mass exterminations in the gas chambers of Jewish men and women, most of whom never entered the camp as prisoners. Executions on a smaller scale, however, started in early 1941. Prisoners put in the penal block who survived too long or whose use to the Gestapo had expired — such as Polish officers or men the Warsaw Gestapo believed to belong to the underground — were led to the gravel pit behind the camp kitchen. One by one they stood before a firing squad and were shot at the command of an SS officer. After 1942 the Germans dispensed with this ritual. Small numbers, including those brought to the camp by the local Gestapo simply to be executed, were taken by Palitsch to the yard of Block 13 (later renumbered Block 11) and shot in the back of the head with a .22 calibre rifle, while larger numbers were sent to the gas chambers.

It was the job of the hospital to collect dead bodies wherever they happened to lie, undress them, write numbers on their chests and deliver them to the crematorium. The morgue, located in the basement of the hospital, was presided over by two prisoners, Albert and Alex. They had to attend all executions, collect the still-warm, bleeding bodies — often of their very good friends — and deliver them to the crematorium. Not infrequently, the corpses far outnumbered those they could handle, at which times other hospital workers were called in to help.

Fortunately, I managed to avoid this job, though by Auschwitz standards it ranked among the more favourable. I was always kept informed, however, by Albert and Alex, who were never too busy to miss giving me a first-hand description of who was executed and how.

On Christmas Eve, 1940, I was invited by Albert to come down to the morgue for a Christmas dinner. It was a curious place for such an occasion, but then it was also one of the safest places in the camp. SS men did not go there; even kapos and blockelders avoided it. In the evening, when the last outpatients left and for lack of a better place to celebrate Christmas, I decided to accept the invitation.

The basement consisted of a large room with a cement floor and drain in the middle. At one end, a collection of corpses were stacked high to provide more floor space. A sort of table, made by stacking three coffins one on top of the other, had been erected in the centre of the room. It was covered with a white bed sheet and at its centre stood a Christmas tree. Around the table were more coffins which served as benches. In a corner opposite the corpses I spotted Alex leaning over a hot plate, busily preparing our feast. He was frying potato pancakes — our main dish.

We were joined in this setting by a Catholic priest who, after we were seated, said a short prayer for the dead and the living, blessed the food, then opened an envelope and took out a Christmas wafer. Breaking the altar bread into small pieces and passing them to everyone, he wished us all survival and a reunion with our families. Then we dug into the pancakes. Albert even treated us to a drink organized from the hospital's alcohol supply. I think it was rubbing alcohol because it was generously spiced with the camp's marmalade to kill the bitter taste.

We had no good news about the war or from our families, but somehow we managed to whip up some hope that eventually the Germans would lose the war and we would get home. We even sang a few Christmas carols. The general mood, in spite of the gruesome surroundings, was reasonably happy. Our celebration was certainly more than that provided to other prisoners who had to be content with eating their regular portion of food, killing a few lice and going to sleep.

Upon deciding to go to bed ourselves, we had to pass by an even livelier party going on above in Dr. Dering's room. Walking quietly by the door, we were horrified to see Leo suddenly emerge. Fortunately he was dead drunk, as was Bock who followed closely on his heels. Shortly after came Fred Stoessel, who had started the party with us but then joined the "upper class" upstairs.

Although I regarded him as a friend, it soon became evident to me that Fred was a power-hungry man. Because he spoke perfect German, he was popular among the kapos and blockelders for whom he would do little favours. In fact, a year later he himself became a blockelder of one of the hospital blocks. For now, he made himself useful to Bock and Dering and they gladly used him to expedite some of their orders. Fred was an early member of our organization and I am sure he hated the German authorities as much as we did, but he just could not help pushing for power.

The constant exposure in the camp to human suffering and death inevitably blunted in all of us both sensitivity and compassion, but the effect on many was nothing short of dehumanisation. Fred, Dering and others fell victim to this transformation which, of course, was what the SS authorities desired. As more and more Jews were discovered among the new arrivals, the Germans were incapable of exterminating them fast enough. Eventually groups of them were sent to the hospital where an SS doctor injected phenol directly into their hearts. Fred Stoessel and Mietek Panszczak were his assistants. I later learned they took over his job and also killed large numbers of Jews from the penal block.

"Why do you do this dirty work for them?" I recall asking Fred.

"Just think," he told me, "would you rather die instantly or be clubbed to death over several days?"

"You ask the wrong question," I said, "conveniently forgetting that the Germans have set up these camps to exterminate Poles, Jews and others. Why should we Poles, who are fighting Germans even here in Auschwitz, help them in this terrible scheme?"

But he was not convinced. He had been in the camp longer than I and had already become fully convinced that all of us would die there. As for the Jews, his excuse that "they cannot live longer than a couple of weeks anyway, so why not give them an easier death?" sounded remarkably like Dering's.

Attempting to imagine the gruesome business from his point of view, I asked: "Are these men not panic stricken when they see your long needle?"

"Oh no!" he replied confidently. "They never even get a glimpse of it. I simply tell them that before being admitted to the hospital they must have a vaccination. I seat them back to back on two stools, insisting that they hold each other with linked arms in case one of them faints. Then, hiding the needle with one hand, I handle each at a time. The injection takes only a fraction of a second. There's no sound. The other guy is still holding his already dead colleague and I do the same thing to him. Then Albert and Alex take them out through the door to the morgue downstairs and the next pair is admitted."

I thought I knew this man quite well, and yet I could not be sure whether he really believed what he was doing was right. No doubt others, including Palitsch, also had ready justification for the atrocities they committed. However, I am equally sure Fred Stoessel, injecting Jews from the penal block with phenol, and Palitsch, shooting condemned prisoners in the back of their heads, derived special pleasure from their actions.

Fred's willingness to kill was also utilized by the Auschwitz underground to eliminate spies.

The SS political department as well as the camp security were always actively seeking informers to reveal any dangerous movements among the prisoners. The conditions in the camp were so terrible that, unfortunately, many weaker inmates agreed to supply the Gestapo with news of any suspicious activity in return for extra food or protection against beatings. The underground army had to deal with such people. The most common way was to frame such spies for stealing food from a kapo or blockelder and let the German criminals do the dirty work. However, the Gestapo also implanted in the camp special German spies who could speak Polish and pretended to have been arrested for activity in the Polish underground. These were the most dangerous and the most difficult to unmask.

By 1941, prisoners were employed as clerks in the SS offices to help administer the camp's complex organization. There were simply not enough Germans to fill all the positions in their highly bureaucratic system. Some of these prisoners were recruited by our organization and often supplied vital information about implanted Gestapo spies.

The system used by the Gestapo was at times very crude, enabling us to recognize immediately such spies. Once an SS man brought to Bock a new prisoner to be employed as a male nurse. Things like that did not normally happen. The special privilege demanded for the new prisoner naturally gave rise to suspicions. Fortunately there was also animosity between the SS doctors and the Gestapo. Dering promptly reported to an SS doctor that the Gestapo had implanted a man in the hospital to spy either on the prisoners or on the SS doctors. The SS doctor was furious, but because he was also afraid of the Gestapo, he insinuated to his superiors that everyone knew who this person was and that there was no point in keeping him in the hospital. Sometime later the man's number was called to report to the front gate. That was the last we saw of him.

Another incident proved much more serious. A new prisoner arrived with the transport from Krakow. His profession was listed as carpenter, so he was assigned to the carpenters' group in which Thomas was working. He claimed the Gestapo arrested him on suspicion of belonging to the underground army, that he had been suspicion of belonging to the underground army, that he had been interrogated several times, but after ten days in prison was shipped with others to Auschwitz.

It was a normal state of affairs. There were hundreds of men in similar circumstances and the fellow was accepted as trustworthy. After several days Thomas confided to me that a new man in his working group was eager to organize an underground movement in the camp. Following extensive questioning, Thomas decided to recruit him for our work and introduced him to four of his immediate contacts. A couple of days later, members of the group that had arrived by train from Krakow told us they suspected one of the men among them to be a Gestapo agent. This suspicion was quickly traced to our carpenter.

The men who shared a cell with the new prisoner informed us that each time he was taken for interrogation, the Gestapo found out exactly what was said in their cell. Moreover, two of their colleagues had been executed as a result of information leaked from the prison. We started to watch the man more closely. He was indeed pumping everybody for whatever they would tell him. We then asked one of our spies to check his file in the political department of the camp. The file was normal, except that it omitted such obvious details as a home address and proceedings from interrogations with the Gestapo. In their place we found one sentence: "Special assignment."

Now that we knew he was not just an informer but an SS man, we were faced with the problem of getting rid of him without any reprisals from our own Gestapo. He already knew too much and we had to stop him from talking to any of his compatriots about his discoveries. Arrangements had no doubt been made for him to meet with some high ranking officers and to attend other very important meetings. Our plan was to somehow get him into the hospital where Fred could take care of him. Unfortunately, he insisted on being in perfect health and did not want to go, even for a visit. Then one of our men who worked in the stables brought us some laxative used for the horses. On an evening when the carpenters were cooking for themselves special food which happened to be stolen from the SS magazines, we implanted it in the man's portion. Our spy liked the food, although he was curious how it had been removed from magazines he believed were so well guarded.

After the roll call he started to run to the latrine. I think he to the front gate. Two of our men took him under the arms, arguing it was dangerous to go there at that time because the SS sentries were under orders to shoot. It was true and he knew it.

The only place for help was the hospital. Fred arranged the admission and performed several tests to mislead the SS doctor into thinking the man suffered from meningitis. Next morning, at the routine check-up, Fred described the symptoms to the SS doctor. It turned out, however, that the doctor recognized the spy as one of his own and demanded a more thorough check-up. Expecting this, Fred proceeded to carry out a great deception.

One of the check-ups involved a test of the spinal fluid. While the SS doctor was watching, Fred took a fresh syringe from the autoclave and pretended to prepare himself for extracting the sample of fluid. At that moment, he switched to another syringe full of pus taken from the infected wound of a prisoner. He then injected the pus into the man's spinal column and invited the SS doctor to take the actual specimen. The doctor had never before performed this test and, pleased the needle was already inserted, promptly obliged by drawing out some of the contaminated fluid. After examining the specimen under a microscope, the doctor was so alarmed by the condition of his special patient that he immediately arranged to transfer him to the SS hospital outside the camp. About an hour passed before an ambulance arrived to take him away. By then the man was delirious. He died two days later.

The doctor admitted to Fred several days after the incident that the man was a member of the SS from the Krakow Gestapo.

"If I hadn't taken the spinal fluid from the fellow myself," he told him, "I'd have been sure you Poles killed him."

One day in March, 1941, Fred came to me and said: "I think that tomorrow you'll have to start looking for another job. Dr. Dering has decided to fire you and hire one of those important lawyers who arrived from Warsaw a few days ago."

This was terrible news, for it meant returning to the general work force in the industrial park only to experience again the hunger, cold, hard labour and constant danger of being killed.

"Could he not give me at least a week to find another job?" I inquired.

"Don't let him know I told you this, but you could ask him to suggest you to some kapo. He knows them all and I'm sure that on his recommendation you'll find some safe place of work."

Without wasting any time I sought out Dering, who was busily manicuring his fingernails in his room.

"May I talk to you for a few minutes?" I asked in the most composed manner I could muster. I knew that at this moment he was in a position to make a decision on which my life would depend.

He was not pleased to see me and said very abruptly: "What do you want to see me for? I've got a lot on my mind and don't have time for small talk."

It was not the best start, but I had to get confirmation of Fred's report. Discreetly omitting names, I asked if he intended to let me go.

Dering practically shouted at me as if I had done something terribly wrong.

"I need people who are fast workers and who don't dilly-dally with patients! This isn't a sanitarium — one has to work hard or else you're out!"

I understood this hostility was intended only to reinforce his decision. He had recently complimented me several times on my ability to grasp medical problems and had even been surprised that I could, after his surgery, close the wound almost as fast as he could. Knowing he would dodge the real reason for my firing, I wanted to obtain from him at least a little time to find something else.

"Would it not be possible for me to stay a few more days, so that I can ask around about the availability of another reasonable job?"

"The decision has already been made by Bock and as you're aware he is the highest authority here. Besides, I've made arrangements for your replacement."

There was no point in prolonging this conversation. I decided to waste no more time and to start immediately looking for other options.

▼ ▼ ▼

Of Morgues and Horses

The first people I visited were Stan Kazuba and Thomas. Not only were they good friends, but I had been able to help them get extra food from the hospital and any medical attention they needed. Stan tried to talk to his kapo in the carpenters' shop but without much success. We also asked his blockelder about a job in the block but he too brushed us off with the excuse that everything was running fine. My one consolation was that, because I still worked in the hospital, blockelders and kapos were at least talking to me instead of using their clubs for faster communication.

One of my former patients was a foreman with the electricians. I found him in his block and asked if his group had a vacancy.

He gave me a puzzled look, then said: "The kapo is examining everybody before allowing them in and you, as a male nurse, haven't a chance. Besides, you're the best male nurse in the hospital, so why are they letting you go?"

"I have to tell you this secret," I said, drawing close to him. "I'm not a male nurse at all. In fact, I learned everything I know in the hospital. I'm actually an electrician."

His face registered disbelief, then he grinned sympathetically.

"Listen, I'd hate to see you hurt, but if the kapo were to find out you're not an electrician that would be the end of you."

I agreed with him, but still maintained that this was my profession. My insistence eventually won out.

"If you're so sure of yourself, let's go to the kapo and let him examine you right now. At least your only risk is that he won't have a job for you."

The kapo, Hans, wore a green triangle and was a safecracker by profession. My request pleased him, primarily because it gave him the opportunity to boast about his own abilities. He stated proudly that he had studied electrical engineering at the university and would soon find out whether I was telling the truth.

The interview began with the question: "If you want to drill a hole in a safe, can you plug your drill into an ordinary wall outlet?"

"Yes," I replied confidently. "The drill won't consume more than 15 amperes, so there should be no problem."

"Oh!" he said. "That's very good, but now tell me — if you want to drill a big hole in the concrete wall around the safe, can you still use the outlet?"

"It depends on the size of the drill's motor," I told him. "There is usually a little plate that gives you that information, and from it you can determine whether a wall outlet is sufficient."

Not expecting this answer, he paused briefly to recover his composure, then exclaimed with a self-satisfied smile: "You see, there you are wrong! The kind of drills used to put holes in concrete would burn fuses every time you tried to use such an outlet."

Our conversation continued for about an hour, during which time Hans exhibited his wide knowledge about different kinds of wires, electric motors, and even the kind of insulators required on electric poles. I had only to agree with him to make him happy. After the examination he pronounced me a professional electrician and said he would admit me to his working group the moment he needed someone. When we parted, I noticed the foreman regarding me with admiration.

"You must be a very clever man," he told me. "At times, I myself didn't know what the kapo was talking about."

I refrained from answering, thinking that Hans did not know what he was talking about either. My satisfaction was short-lived, however, when it occurred to me that I was still without a job.

Stan Kazuba offered me another hope. Next morning he was to start a new job in the tannery working under a kapo with real expertise in tanning; he was a Pole from Silesia but spoke better German than Polish. Stan proposed to talk to the kapo in a few days about hiring me.

I could always return to the potato peeling group, but Leo had come to know me as a male nurse and once I was out of the hospital, he would be only too glad to treat me to some very special "sport." My possibilities were almost exhausted when I saw Lui, the rollwagons' kapo, heading for Block 16. Since I was still employed there, I offered him my help which he gladly accepted. He had received a nasty cut from a dirty nail and the wound was getting septic. At the hospital I cleaned and disinfected his cut and applied a dressing. I also gave him a piece of gauze and bandage to allow him to change the dressing. When he discovered I had been fired and was anxiously seeking work, he became very concerned and suggested that I join his rollwagon to replace a man he had recently lost.

I inquired: "How did you lose this man?"

"Well," he said, "it was very unlucky. The man was caught

Rollwagon driven by human horsepower

stealing food from the SS kitchen and Mamma killed him."

"Who is Mamma?" I asked.

"He's a kapo in the SS kitchen. Mamma is just the nickname given him by men working there. His real name is Fritz Biesgen. He's got a green triangle and can be very nasty, but because he's usually good to his men they call him Mamma, sort of out of affection."

"In that case," I said, "he sounds like the type one should avoid."

"Not at all," said Lui. "My rollwagon works around the SS kitchen all the time. We carry out garbage, deliver potatoes or other produce and sometimes even deliver bread, sausages, ham — that sort of thing. Mamma always lets us have some extra food but he doesn't like it if someone steals from him."

On hearing this, I became more interested in the job. It seemed as though one could survive there in spite of the heavy work and the exposure to all kinds of weather. In any case, I had no immediate alternative so I gratefully accepted the offer.

Next morning, after roll call, I reported to my new job as a human horse.

The group consisted of eight people and Lui. It was responsible for transporting goods to and from an area outside the main camp occupied by the SS quarters, magazines, storerooms, offices and SS kitchen. Our main task was to collect garbage and take it to the dump. At the request of the SS, we hauled almost anything.

My seven companions were not very strong, nor were they in the best physical condition. Also, Lui's promises of extra food turned out to be slightly exaggerated, but within the first couple of weeks I received a small portion of raw turnips we were delivering to the SS kitchen. Food conveyed to the SS sentries was always precisely counted and the soup was enclosed in 50-litre kettles, so we had no chance to organize anything.

Worst of all was the cold and damp March weather. The roads over which we had to pull our rollwagon were unpaved and often we found ourselves ankle-deep in mud or slush. A full load made for particularly hard pulling. The men were always hungry and after several weeks I was as hungry as they were. I knew extra soup was usually waiting for me at the hospital, donated by Fred or other men with whom I had worked, but the fact that I had been fired made me reluctant to accept their offers. Intense hunger eventually rules one's will, however, and soon my workmates and I were planning together how we might steal some extra food.

A hobby of mine before the war was to perform magic tricks for my colleagues. It occurred to me that this small talent might again be brought into service.

Normally, the food for the sentries was transported from the kitchen, with Mamma supervising the procedures. To steal from Mamma was very risky. I never forgot that I was the replacement for a man who had attempted to do just that. But my hunger constantly provoked me to consider ways of succeeding without getting caught.

One day the SS kitchen failed to receive the regular delivery of bread that usually came by truck, so our rollwagon was sent to the bakery to collect the goods. Among our team was a professional baker. I asked the kapo to appoint him and me the official counters of the loaves. Lui knew well what I had in mind and warned that the counting was done by the German baker who was also an SS man. All I needed, however, was a brief moment to divert his attention. I asked our baker to talk to this fellow about baking, as one professional to another, or to occupy him in some other way.

When we arrived at the bakery, the bread was ready to be counted on the table near the door. I started taking it, two loaves at a time, putting these into our bread baskets. Each time I took two loaves the SS baker counted them aloud. Our baker, whose name was Fred, tried to strike up a conversation with him, but to no avail. The SS baker kept counting religiously. Fred was desperate. He began demonstrating, with large gestures, how the bread should be kneaded. In his eagerness, he knocked an empty basket to the floor. This was the advantage I had been waiting for. By then I was also counting aloud with the SS man. When the basket fell I took three loaves, continuing to count, of course, in the usual two's. The SS man counted with me but Fred noticed my manoeuvre. He repeated his diversion by knocking some metallic forms down off the shelves. This, of course, resulted in another loaf to our credit. At the end of the count we were two loaves short. Lui demanded a recount but the SS baker was adamant about his calculations.

"Don't be stupid!" he told our kapo. "You'd better take two more loaves or your heads will roll."

We humbly accepted two more loaves of bread and started back to the SS kitchen. Extra food in the rollwagon would have been sure evidence that we were stealing from the SS, so the bread had to be eaten as fast as possible. The first loaf was cut into nine pieces with the largest for Lui; it was eaten almost instantly. As we were about to cut the second loaf, however, one of the SS cooks came out of the barracks and joined us on the way.

At the kitchen, Mamma called for men to unload and count the bread again. I hastily volunteered and jumped on the wagon to help with the unloading. Pretending to be hot I took off my coat and threw it on the floor of the wagon. We unloaded basket after basket while Mamma watched and no doubt checked our count. One basket, of course, contained an extra loaf. I turned this basket over to show it was empty and the loaf rolled right under my coat. Mamma could not possibly have seen it because his vision was obscured by the side of the wagon. When we finished unloading the number of loaves proved correct. Mamma smiled broadly at me, obviously satisfied, and I breathed with relief, waiting for him to return to the kitchen. But Mamma did not do so.

Instead, he jumped into the wagon with me. His face turning serious again, he looked at my coat, then at me, and then with the tip of his boot lifted the edge of my coat. I stared him right in the eye, wondering at the same time how I was going to avoid being killed. Then Mamma suddenly burst out laughing, slapped me on the back and said: "You old crook, you! How did you do it? You almost fooled me! Nobody can fool a super-crook like me! What are you going to do now?"

Without much thinking, I said: "I guess we're going to eat it."

Mamma almost choked with laughter.

"I like clever men. You've done well. Go ahead and steal from the SS, I do it too. But don't get caught or I'll have to kill you like I did the other guy."

He then hopped out of the wagon and disappeared into the kitchen. In a few minutes he returned with a half kilogram of butter under his apron.

"Eat it fast and remember, you never got this butter from me."

We had a real feast that day.

Unfortunately, we were not called again to haul bread and our hunger returned. Prisoners invented many ways to combat their cravings. Some chewed wood to a pulp and swallowed it, giving them the impression they had a full stomach. But the worst thing, perhaps, was to talk about food. While we pulled our rollwagon our baker would describe to us how one made cakes, tarts and French pastry. Each of us paid full attention to his methods. I think I could probably make a French pastry today — a testimony not only to the accuracy of his description but to the interest his words commanded.

I continued to check with friends for any opportunity of getting a better job, but with no success. It seemed as if I were stuck with Lui's crew, though I maintained hope that Stan Kazuba might arrange a transfer. There was still no possibility of my working in the tannery, but one day Stan brought me a gift that looked something like boiled meat.

Noticing my uncertainty about what to do with his present, he smiled and said: "Eat it and tell me if you like it. Then I'll tell you what it is."

My ravenous stomach told me it tasted delicious, whatever it was, and I thanked Stan heartily for it. I knew that carrying any food through the front gate was forbidden and in bringing it to me he was risking his life. I was so happy at finding my hunger momentarily abated that I almost forgot to ask Stan what it was I had eaten.

"You probably never thought steer's ear could taste so good," he remarked. "I can bring you more, every day in fact. When we tan the skins I cut out the ear, then boil it in the drying room on the coal heating oven."

I gratefully accepted the offer, warning him to be careful not to get caught.

Spring finally came, even to Auschwitz. Snow melted, the ground began to dry and in the fields the first green blades of grass poked up to face daylight. Buds gradually appeared on the few trees left around the camp and, as usual at this time of year, new hope was shared among prisoners that perhaps this year would bring an end to the war. Unfortunately, events proved quite the opposite. The German armies attacked the Soviet Union and advancing with astonishing speed, proclaimed victory after victory. We found the news hard to believe, but the broadcasts over the BBC confirmed almost all the German claims. In their jubilance, our guards treated us with even more cruelty.

One day, two blocks were separated from the rest of the camp by barbed wire and the first Russian prisoners of war were brought in.

They were a sorry looking lot. Dressed in torn and dirty uniforms, they appeared tired and hungry. Apparently they had had no food or water during their two days journey from the Russian front. They told us the situation was hopeless. The German Army was so much better equipped they had no chance at all against it. Many officers and prisoners of war had been shot on the spot, their bodies left to decay on the ground where they fell.

The first Russian prisoners of war, though not required to work in Auschwitz, were exterminated in another way. Left alone in two barracks, their food rations were cut in half on the grounds that they did not work. That meant they received fewer than 700 calories a day. Hunger and unsanitary conditions soon started to decimate their population.

Our lot, in the meantime, was not much better. I was still pulling the rollwagon, unable for at least two weeks to organize extra food. Our hunger increased as our strength lagged. One day the wagon got stuck in the mud while loaded with garbage from the SS quarters. No matter how hard we pushed and pulled, it refused to budge. We decided to make it lighter by unloading some of the garbage onto the sidewalk. This time, however, luck was not with us.

An SS man caught us in the act and furiously ordered Lui to beat us up for this misbehaviour. But Lui was not a violent man; he tried to appear angry and shouted a lot, but the confusion left us uncertain whether to pull our wagon out first or remove the garbage from the sidewalk. Then the SS man took out a pencil and paper and wrote down our numbers.

Before leaving us he announced: "Since your kapo does not know how to punish you, we'll see you get proper punishment in the camp."

It was hard to imagine anything worse, for the SS rarely made idle threats. We were now faced with undergoing one of three types of punishment administered for such an infraction. The first was flogging — the usual dose being 25 strikes on the naked bottom. This ritual was performed by Leo while all prisoners were forced to remain standing and watching. Leo, the campelder, used either a bullwhip or a wooden club, which inevitably resulted in severe bleeding and such deep haemotoma that the victim would lose almost all the flesh, whatever was still there, from both buttocks. The second possibility was to be hung on a pole by the hands which were tied together behind one's back, a treatment that generally dislocated the shoulders and elbow joints. The last punishment was to be shut away for a number of nights in a bunker of the kind in which people were condemned to die of hunger.

Needless to say, we returned from work that day without much to look forward to. I informed Stan about our situation and asked him to save my food ration for me, knowing that if our numbers were called we would not be able to visit our blocks before the punishment was administered. Any hope for a pardon was immediately dismissed at roll call when we caught sight of Palitsch holding the list with our numbers. Each was called in turn and we stepped forward. I will never forget how the rest of the prisoners looked at us. To be summoned by Palitsch meant only one thing — execution.

At the conclusion of roll call, Palitsch turned to Leo and said: "Take them to the penal block, I will be there shortly."

At least we knew there would be no flogging. Our destination was either the bunker or the pole.

Upon arriving at the penal block we noticed, apart from prisoners going about their normal activities, several people dressed in civilian clothes whom I assumed were brought from outside to be interrogated by the Gestapo.

Leo delivered us to the blockelder of the penal block and left.

We were locked together in a small room, probably used also for interrogations, and were told to wait for Palitsch because he wanted personally to hang us on the pole. Several minutes later Palitsch appeared with the assistant of the penal block, a blockelder whom I recognized as one of my patients in the hospital. They chose four men to accompany them and left us to wait for our turn.

As we sat there my friend, the baker, became covered with a cold sweat and started to tremble uncontrollably. Although the rest of us seemed resigned to our fate, we too found the waiting period incredibly unnerving. About 30 minutes later the blockelder's assistant stood before us.

"You guys are lucky," he said. "Palitsch had to go somewhere and asked me to hang you up for half an hour. Let's go!"

We did not know what had happened to the first four men and were afraid to ask.

In silence we followed our "hangman" to the attic of Block 13 where, on one side, were several stools. Above them and attached to the rafters were heavy ropes suspended from blocks. The assistant blockelder had two helpers, Jewish prisoners who at the time were also roomelders. They instructed us to climb onto the stools and tied our hands behind our backs. Then the blockelder's assistant pulled with the full weight of his body on the end of each rope in turn.

I was the first to be lifted up. My arms were pulled back with a jerk, I lost my balance and a terrible pain shot through my wrists, elbows and shoulders. I desperately tried to find the stool with my feet, but it was just centimetres beyond my reach. I did not faint but the pain was so sudden and so sharp I did not even have time to cry out. When the four of us had been hung my friend the baker and the man next to him fainted. The assistant blockelder then left the attic saying he would be back in half an hour. Grabbing a bottle of ammonia, the Jewish helpers stuck it under the noses of the two men who had fainted, advising us that it was better to remain conscious so that our muscles would take up some of the tension, thus lessening the severity of our dislocations. It did not make sense to me at all; I felt my arms were already out of joint and was now able to touch the stool with my toes.

One of the helpers noticed this and said: "You are really lucky Palitsch is not here. He removes the stools and then pulls everyone down to make absolutely sure the joints are dislocated. This was what he did to your four friends. When he pulled, you could hear the joints crack!"

"Thanks for the entertainment," I gasped, "but can't you loosen the ropes so we can rest a little more on the stools?

Both of them answered almost simultaneously.

"You must be joking! Palitsch would kill us instantly! Besides, it would not help you much. Your joints are already dislocated."

I was still concentrating on putting more weight on my toes when I noticed that all feeling had gone out of them. After about five minutes I felt no pain anywhere.

"You see," remarked a helper knowingly. "You've got used to it now. But if Palitsch were here he'd pull you down every five or ten minutes to remind you what pain's really like!"

This was a terrifying thought — to be pulled down.

We remained almost in limbo for what seemed an eternity. Finally the blockelder himself arrived and without even looking at us, pulled the ropes behind us, releasing them instantly. I tumbled to the floor on my face, hitting my forehead against some wood bracing the corner, my arms still behind me. The pain returned with a vengeance, only this time there was also relief that my ordeal was over.

Our hands were untied and we heard the blockelder's voice bark "Out, you swinedogs!"

To get up without the help of your arms is not an easy matter. On top of that, my toes were still numb. But noticing the blockelder was about to kick me in the kidneys I unwound like a spring, jumping to my feet with a gymnastic skill I did not know I had. When the gate of Block 13 closed behind us and we were alone again on the camp street, my aching and useless arms seemed small payment for the joy of being alive.

Stan was waiting for me at my block with a portion of soup and bread. Unable to hold even a spoon in my hand, Stan fed me like a baby while discussing what I could do tomorrow. To work at the rollwagon was impossible without movement in my arms, but Stan had already thought about this and within minutes we were at the hospital asking Fred if I might be accepted there for a couple of days.

Unfortunately the request had to go to Dr. Dering whose response was a definite "no." The only alternative was to work with the potato peelers. I was uncertain whether I could even peel potatoes with my hands; besides, if I got in the way of Leo a real disaster might result. I thus decided I had no choice but to return to my job at the rollwagon.

Lui was surprised to see me because no one else came and he had to assemble a new team. While he was putting one together, we saw the baker being chased out of his block by the blockelder. Apparently he had tried to stay as a room helper but had been forced to rejoin the rollwagon. Lui was a decent guy and arranged a place at the wagon where we had only to pull with ropes fitting over our shoulders. The rest of the team steered the wagon and did the loading and unloading.

It was a long time before I could use my arms normally. Fortunately there was no permanent damage. Others were not so lucky.

Towards the end of May, when our rollwagon was routinely collecting garbage from the SS kitchen, Mamma told Lui that one of his potato peelers was sick and asked if a member of our squad could replace him for a day. As we were hauling no heavy loads that morning, Lui agreed. To select his helper, Mamma inspected each of us to see how clean we were, paying particular attention to our hands. I was always much cleaner than my colleagues so I was not surprised when Mamma stopped in front of me.

"You old smuggler!" he said, instantly recognizing me. "So you want to work for me, do you?"

I did not have to think twice. Potato peeling in the SS kitchen was safe. Though one had to be young and healthy, no kapo would dare to bother a worker under Mamma's protection.

I agreed enthusiastically, hoping it might become a permanent job.

CHAPTER 6

RESISTING TERROR

Thus I somehow became a permanent member of the SS kitchen potato peelers.

The former farmhouse in which the kitchen was located stood just outside the periphery of the outer circle of sentries, so special guards were assigned to patrol us during our working hours. It was a privileged duty for these guards; generally they sat chatting with the SS cooks and of course stuffed themselves with the choice food.

Potato peelers worked in what was once the sun-porch. We had a beautiful view of green meadows and a corner of a forest that extended all the way to the river. Seated at the edge of a world we had left behind, it was difficult to concentrate on peeling potatoes. Our attention was drawn to the spring flowers blooming in the meadow and the dark trees of the forest — a gate to liberty. This proximity to freedom made me realize that I was not the person I had once been. Transformed into some kind of concentration camp being, I was almost incapable of imagining that, in this other world within our sight, people were well fed and lived peaceful lives. At some uncharted time I had passed through a looking glass separating our world from theirs and was now unsure which was real and which fantasy. My speculations were interrupted, however, by Mamma shouting and swearing at us to peel more potatoes.

It was, considering conditions in Auschwitz, an excellent job. Almost daily we would get extra food from our colleagues who worked in the kitchen as cooks. These included two legitimate cooks, one butcher, and two university students from Warsaw. The German cooks, each a member of the SS, generally overlooked this special treatment because they wanted to have their work force operating efficiently. The head cook, a non-commissioned SS officer, was so pathetically stupid he might have been considered funny were it not for the power of life and death he held over his crew of prisoners.

Thwarting hunger was for almost all prisoners their sole concern. Thomas, Stan and I had discussed this problem when we set out to form the first underground units, recognizing that a man could be relied on only when not ruled by his appetite. Now that hunger no longer dominated my life, I started to pay more attention to underground activities and participated more frequently in its conferences.

We had anticipated a time when the Germans might decide to kill all prisoners at once. It was inconceivable that they would ever let us out alive after witnessing the atrocities. Thus, as early as 1941, we decided upon constructing a proper military organization divided into a series of brigades, each with a separate commanding officer. One organization would operate during the day when working groups were out of the camp and a different one at night when everyone was inside the barbed wire.

The organization's plans for taking control of the camp had to be continuously revised as members died and new ones joined. Also, with the expansion of the camp, unexpected obstacles were constantly thrust in our path. Perhaps the most significant change was the replacement of the single barbed wire fence surrounding the camp with double barbed wire supported on concrete posts curving inward. A high voltage electric current now ran through the wires while under each row of fences were buried concrete plates several meters deep. SS guards posted in high towers armed with searchlights and machine guns further discouraged any possible resistance.

We decided that success was only possible if we received sufficiently advanced information to make a pre-emptive strike during the day when the SS guards were more vulnerable and when prisoners were working inside the SS quarters and around the armoury and ammunition storage. Plans for taking over the camp in daylight were relatively simple. Our commando force would break into the armoury after silently disposing of the three SS guards who marched outside the buildings. We would replace these guards with our own men dressed in SS uniforms. A rollwagon would then distribute arms to key points outside the camp while the commanding officers outfitted their men in the armouries. We estimated that within a couple of hours we could have an armed force twice the size of the SS unit manning Auschwitz.

The most dangerous obstacles were the two rows of towers, one surrounding the main camp and the second, much larger, encompassing the prisoners' working area. This included all the store houses, SS quarters, stables, the SS armoury and even the fields, vegetable gardens and sand pits. We appointed sharpshooters, generally professional commissioned or non-commissioned officers, to set up posts on the towers once they had disposed of the SS guards. This accomplished, the few SS men directly supervising working groups would represent no serious problem.

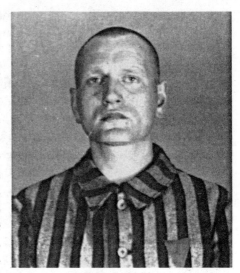

Henry Bartosiewicz

Once the plan had been worked out we faced enormous temptation to put it immediately into effect. However, as part of the Polish underground army with headquarters in Warsaw, such action had to be co-ordinated with partisan units outside. Our ecstasy about the plan and our certainty that it was workable inspired us to send a special report to headquarters notifying them we were ready to begin operations at any time.

I believe, even now, that we were in an excellent position in 1941 and 1942 to destroy the SS garrison and take over the camp within a matter of hours. The incentive was strong enough. To end the miserable existence of our animal-like life — each of us waiting our turn to be exterminated — and to pay back all the humiliations we suffered suddenly became a very real possibility.

But there was one serious problem. Out of about 7,000 men, only about ten percent were strong enough to fight and bear arms. The rest were sick or Musselmen-like creatures who, once we took command of the camp, would instantly become our responsibility. I remember very clearly the heated arguments over the second phase of our uprising. The older prisoners, myself included, were of the opinion it was worth it. Even if 1,000 men reached the partisans, it was better than resigning ourselves to extermination. Thomas, as a commanding officer, as well as Stan Kazuba, Henry Bartosiewicz and many others shared my views. Those opposed centred on prisoners in the hospital. They maintained that to drag along the sick and infirm would slow down the fighting unit to the extent that all would perish, and to leave them behind would not be fair. In any event, it was not our decision to make — we had to wait for the command from headquarters.

We kept our plan in effect for two years, but the command to go ahead never came. We were baffled. How could the underground abandon us to our fate when we asked for so little help? One possible answer was the Germans' new method of discouraging escapes. Instead of selecting ten men to die in a bunker, a practice ended in the middle of 1941, the Gestapo was now arresting the entire family of the escapee, transporting them to Auschwitz and publicly hanging them in front of the prisoners' kitchen.

To compensate for the underground's apparent reticence about our plan, we became active in arranging escapes by notifying ahead of time the families involved to change their addresses. Almost all the escaping men carried out one message: "We are being exterminated here by the most cruel methods! We can stage a successful uprising! We need direction to the nearest partisan unit and the sabotaging of roads to slow down other SS units who will try to cut us off!"

And still the command to go ahead never came.

In the meantime a power play surfaced within our organization. In 1941 some senior officers, arrested for underground activity, arrived at Auschwitz. Thomas decided against recruiting them, feeling that they lacked the stamina to endure both the camp conditions and the Gestapo's interrogations. These officers, however, were not about to obey orders of a former captain. I myself was a commanding officer of one of the camp brigades, but previous to my arrest was only a second lieutenant. They overrode our authority and in partnership with their former subordinates escalated the organization's clandestine work. It soon became obvious that the situation could no longer be ignored.

We found a compromise. For security reasons, senior officers whose rank was known to the Germans were excluded from the organization. Those in Auschwitz under false identities were admitted, however, and Colonel Rawicz was made a commanding officer.

This sudden, unhealthy expansion of the organization created new uncertainties. How would new members stand up to the interrogating tortures of the Gestapo? In the bunkers of Block 11, the local Gestapo (also referred to as the political department) used many techniques to make people talk. One of the best known was the "swing." The prisoner was hung by the feet, his hands tied together so that his genitals protruded. While swinging towards the interrogator he was struck on his testicles with a riding whip, repeatedly told to "think of something interesting" to say. Other tortures employed the usual instruments for breaking fingers or pouring boiling water into the nose of the victim. It was difficult to predict who would be the last to break down; usually older people could endure much less. Whenever someone was taken to Block 11 for interrogation, the men who had worked with him prepared themselves to go next.

The year 1941 was full of military successes for the German army. With every victory, the Germans became increasingly confident that a gigantic slave-state could actually be created. According to Hitler, all Jews were to be killed — what was called "the final solution" to the Jewish problem; other nations, including the Polish, converted into a labour force and deprived of higher education, were to work only under German supervision. It was very difficult for German nationals not to be spellbound by the promise of a "glorious future" in which they, as the super race, would govern other inferior races.

Hitler created the greatest deception in the history of mankind, convincing his countrymen that Jews, more than any other peoples, threatened the purity of the Germanic race. In Auschwitz all Jews who had any kind of physical deformity were killed and their skeletons sent to the Berlin museum as proof of their race's many imperfections. All other nations, too, were imperfect, but the danger of contamination was not as great and the urgency to exterminate them less pressing. Even our kapos, who were themselves prisoners and condemned criminals, believed themselves superior simply because their mother tongue was German.

This philosophy was reinforced by the economic success of Germany before the war and its proven military prowess during the early part of the war. The breakdown began in 1944 when the elite German army, expecting easy victory over the Russians, was forced to flee from a people whom they considered culturally inferior and akin to animals. In 1941, however, the doctrine of the German super race was at its peak and all government offices, including the camp administration, were operated according to the Fuehrer's plan.

Work began near Auschwitz on a "Buna" factory to manufacture synthetic rubber. It was to be the largest factory in Germany. Thousands of prisoners were allocated to the task and construction proceeded at literally neck-breaking speed. There was a two-fold purpose to this: to build the factory quickly and to exterminate as many of the "inferior" Poles as possible. The mortality rate at Buna Werke exceeded that of the main camp which was already so high the crematorium, working day and night, could not burn the bodies fast enough. Later in 1941, the Germans came to the conclusion that killing Jews without getting any work out of them was inefficient. From then on more thorough selections were made from Jewish transports; the fittest went to the Buna Werke and the rest were killed.

Gradually Auschwitz lost its exclusively Polish character. Small groups of prisoners from Czechoslovakia and Austria began arriving. The grand plan for Auschwitz became more evident after the visit of Adolph Eichmann, the man in charge of "the final solution." A little later, an inspection by Himmler himself precipitated more changes which we witnessed in the years following. The first change was the founding of a new camp close to Auschwitz, called Birkenau. Intended to accommodate 200,000 prisoners, this camp included several new crematoriums which later proved insufficient to handle the vast number of corpses.

Another event of great historical importance also took place in the middle of 1941: several hundred of the hospital's sickest men, as well as the remaining Russian prisoners of war, numbering about 600, were transferred to the basement of Block 11. That night the window shutters were closed and crystals generating the new poison gas Cyclon B were thrown in, marking the first extermination of large numbers of prisoners by gas in Auschwitz. The amount of gas required was badly estimated and men did not die instantly. The groans and rattling of windows were heard all through the night. Male nurses, brought in the next morning to take out the corpses, found the sight was so horrific even their hardened nerves could not take it.*

---

* A detailed description is given in W. Keiler's *Anus Mundi* (Krakow: Literary Publications, 1976).

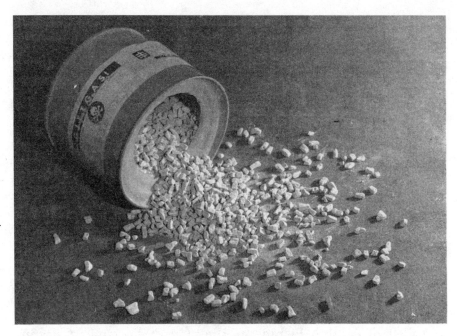

Cyclon B poison gas pellets use in gas chambers
to exterminate prisoners

In 1941 the German government began a formal program of indoctrination to help regulate the behaviour of the entire country. Soon, sufficient numbers of individuals were killing anyone who was Jewish and Hitler's personal policy ripened into an official one initiating mass extermination. The whole population of Germany was now conditioned to believe in the superiority of its race, tolerating the worst kind of modern slavery. By the end of the war not one small town or village in Germany would have failed to witness the SS escorting through its streets columns of concentration camp slaves, visibly starving and suffering from severe physical mistreatment. Every man, woman and child who saw the shadowy columns march by, nearer death than life, accepted it as a normal occurrence.

In the concentration camp violence was a way of life. It was not so much an expression of hatred as the need to satisfy the desire for power, greed for better things in life and the creation of optimum conditions for self-preservation. When such basic trends of human nature were reinforced by effective propaganda and government policy, even the great nation that produced such giants as Kant,

Schopenhauer, Goethe, Schiller, Beethoven, Wagner and Bach was reduced to the same level as the criminal elements running the camps.

The successes of the German army on the Russian front became more apparent when a large part of Auschwitz, consisting of nine blocks altogether, was evacuated and separated from the rest of the camp by barbed wire. To make room for the Russians, prisoners had to be transferred to three newly created satellite camps, the largest of which was located next to the building site of Buna Werke. The remaining prisoners had to double up in their three-tiered bunk beds. When all was ready, a transport of 12,000 Russian prisoners of war arrived and was assigned to the evacuated part of the camp.

This time the Germans dropped any pretence at treating them as prisoners of war. Each and every man was required to work at the Birkenau construction site and the usual cruel treatment was applied to them as it had been to us. The Gestapo searched continually for political leaders among the prisoners; such men were either shot immediately or sent to the penal block for a slow and painful death.

The first Russian prisoners of war did not hesitate to denounce their political leaders. The Politruks were the hated members of Stalin's régime, representing the imposed system of terror and occupying privileged positions simply because of their blind obedience to the Communist party. More recent prisoners were reluctant to comply with the Nazis, finding no clemency either from the enemy or their own government. Stalin had declared that all men taken prisoner by the Germans were, upon their return home, to be courtmarshalled for treason and put to death.

I am not sure which had the greater effect on the Russian army: German cruelty towards the Russian people and prisoners of war, or Stalin's declaration. In any event, after 1942 the Russians regained their fighting spirit and became as eager to exterminate the Germans as the Germans had been to exterminate them.

My job as a potato peeler in the SS kitchen was uneventful until early 1942.

In the meantime Auschwitz kept growing bigger and bigger, requiring more and more guards. In a small way, this showed in the kitchen. Mamma was shorthanded and came to the potato peelers to get help. I again was the lucky one to be selected. After proper scrubbing and washing, I donned the long, white cook's apron and was admitted to the kitchen.

One should understand the significance of this great moment: a hungry, half-starved prisoner suddenly enters a place where is kept an abundance of food. He imagines food will be everywhere and is prepared to be completely surrounded by all sorts of meats, fruits and vegetables. It was with great disappointment that I discovered only wet concrete floors, huge kettles, each over a metre in diameter with a separate electric heater, and men on step ladders holding something like canoe paddles in their hands, stirring or mixing the kettles' contents.

One fellow mashing potatoes called me to relieve him for a few minutes. I could hardly extract the masher from the white mass, so I leaned on it with all my weight in an attempt to squash more potatoes. Engulfed in steam, I did not think much of the job, though I took the opportunity to stuff fistfuls of potatoes into my mouth when no one was watching. At the end of the day Mamma gave me a large bowl of barley soup with pieces of meat in it. Eating it was an excruciating experience. For two years I had been deprived of such luxury; now the opportunity had come and I was full of potatoes. Though my stomach almost burst, I steadily and surely polished off the whole bowl, not knowing when or from where my next meal would come.

On another occasion I was called to help make meatballs. Four of us stood around a table supporting a large mound of minced meat. We rolled little balls from it and piled them up on one side of the table. The other three men, permanently employed kitchen cooks, were by comparison well fed and would not even think of eating raw meat. But for me it was an opportunity I could not pass by, even in the presence of SS cooks supervising the general activity in the kitchen. I applied a simple trick I had learned some time ago, "palming" ping pong balls. Meatballs were the perfect substitute.

In this trick one pretends to transfer a ball from one hand to the other, though it actually remains hidden in the palm. Then, by distracting the viewer's attention to the hand in which the ball is supposed to be, one has time to dispose of the ball from the palm of the other.

I palmed a meatball and with my empty hand pretended to put it on the pile. In the meantime, I lifted the other hand to my face and swallowed the meatball without even chewing it. I did this for about an hour and nobody noticed.

Near the end of the day one of the prisoner cooks nudged me and said: "You should sample one or two of these meatballs, they're not too bad raw."

I smiled and said: "Thank you, but I have been eating them continuously for the last hour."

"But that's not possible," he said. "I saw you put every meatball you made on the pile."

I gave him a quick demonstration.

"Do it again," he said, "and let's see if Mamma can catch you. If you don't mind, I know he'd get a great kick out of it."

The SS guards had left the room, so I agreed. The cook went to fetch Mamma while I practiced my technique. A short time later Mamma stood beside me moulding the meatballs with us.

I had eaten two more meatballs when he said: "So, let's see you steal meatballs without me catching you."

I then told him I had consumed two while he was watching me. This was a professional insult to Mamma who enjoyed boasting he was the best thief in all of Germany.

"Do it again and we shall see," he huffed.

I put the first meatball properly on the pile but palmed the second and while Mamma was watching my empty hand, popped it into my mouth. Then I slowly opened the empty hand. Mamma immediately grabbed the other hand to find only my greasy, outstretched palm. As an encore, I opened my mouth wide, showing Mamma where the meatball had disappeared.

Mamma was delighted. He slapped me on the back so hard the meatball went flying out of my mouth. Everybody roared with laughter and Mamma especially could not contain himself.

The noise attracted the SS men who came back into the room to see what was going on. Mamma was still laughing so hard, all he could do was point to me while gasping for breath. I knew the SS men would not likely appreciate a demonstration of how to steal from their food supplies, so I simply told them that Mamma had seen some of my magic tricks.

"Okay, let's see you perform," they demanded.

I asked for a coin and made the coin disappear, then took it out of the chief SS cook's ear. I also showed them how two solid matchsticks can penetrate through each other. I did not show how a meatball could disappear into my mouth.

From that time on, whenever some extra help was needed in the SS kitchen, Mamma always called on me.

Sometime in February, Thomas came to me, secretive and mysterious as ever. He wanted to talk to me alone, without Stan Kazuba or Henry Bartosiewicz, another of our organization's founding members.

As we left Henry called after us, "When you two get all the steaks from the secret steakhouse, don't forget about your friends!"

We went outside so as not to be overheard and walked between the barracks. It was a bright and frosty night. Not a soul was in sight. Our clothes were not the best for walking in the snow at about -20°C. Thomas was silent, probably thinking how to tell me whatever it was he wanted. I was getting impatient.

"Thomas!" I said at last. "If you want an inconspicuous meeting with me, this is not the best place. Who would be stupid enough to walk in this cold for pleasure? Let's go inside!"

Thomas was deep in his thoughts and seemed startled by my remarks. He looked quickly around. "You're right, we cannot walk here. Let's pretend I am sick and you are taking me to the hospital."

We turned the other way, Thomas leaning on me like an invalid, and set out towards the hospital.

"When we reach the hospital," he whispered, "we can turn around and it will look like we've just come from there. There are too many people in the barracks and someone may hear us."

"Thomas, you're stalling," I said. "What is it you want from me?"

"All right," said Thomas after a pause. "I have to ask you to make a big sacrifice for the organization. I want you to quit your job at the SS kitchen and join me for a week or two in the cartography offices."

I did not fully trust Thomas' judgement. Sometimes he would go to ridiculous lengths to preserve the secrecy of our group and at other times would rashly recruit new members knowing very little about them. I had never forgotten that he had once recruited a German spy.

"Why is it so important for me to work for the cartographers?" I asked, barely disguising my impatience. "I have a very good job and if I lose it now, I could be back in the industrial park, Buna Werke, or building Birkenau with the Russians."

Thomas spoke slowly. "You're the only one I can trust and you also can draw maps. I'm not as good a draughtsman, but both of us would have to pass for professional cartographers for at least a week. In the building where we work is stored electronic equipment for radio communication.

"I think we should have our own broadcasting station in Auschwitz and instant communication with outside underground units. In case of an emergency or the need for a sudden uprising, or even to help those about to escape, such a device would be invaluable. I know a man in the cartography offices and he'll prepare all the parts we'd need to assemble it in camp. Our job will simply involve getting it here."

I did not answer right away, still thinking of how it could be accomplished — how large was the building, where did we have to go to get the parts, and how reliable was Thomas's contact?

As I opened my mouth to discuss these concerns, Thomas continued: "I knew you'd agree, so I talked to Dr. Dering and asked him to appeal to Mamma to let you go for a week. He told Mamma he needed Bristol board and draughting instruments at the hospital to make important signs for the operating room, and that you and I were the two guys who could steal it from the cartographers. Mamma agreed. In fact, Mamma gave you an excellent reference — he told Dering you're an expert, almost better than Mamma himself.

"And all this time I thought you were a professional officer and mathematical genius, not a nimble-fingered thief!"

"Never mind the jokes," I said. "It appears I have no choice. You've already arranged everything.

"At least let me talk to the contact who's supplying the parts. I'd like to know how he's going to arrange for our safety. And how are we going to bring the radio into camp? Are the parts small or large? Could we carry them in our pockets?"

"Kon," said Thomas seriously, "not only do I not want you to meet this man, I don't even want you to know his name. You're aware of how the Gestapo works — the less you know, the better. We'll find out the size of the parts when we see them. It all depends what assemblies our man can steal without arousing suspicion."

There was nothing more to discuss. We hurried towards our barracks and as we were turning into the entrance, ran squarely into Mamma.

"Ah, there you are, you rascal! And that must be another robber," he said pointing to Thomas. "You're making unfair competition for honest thieves around here!

"So tell me, how are you going to steal large sheets of Bristol board? It's not like taking meatballs, you know. Perhaps you should consider having the rollwagon bring it into camp. You might pick up some paper and instruments for Lui, too. What an artist that guy is! He used to make beautiful 100 mark notes! And don't worry about your job. You can come back to the kitchen any time. Besides, I'd like to do this little favour for Dr. Dering. So when do you want to start?"

"Tomorrow morning, if it's all right with you," said Thomas, since I did not even know for what day the arrangements had been made.

"No!" said Mamma. "I cannot spare this crook for a weekend. We have too much work preparing for Sunday dinner."

"It's no problem," replied Thomas. "I can start tomorrow and work there Friday and Saturday, and he can come on Monday morning."

"Well, good luck to you! Remember, when you need truly professional advice — come to Mamma!"

We both thanked him for his understanding and went into our barracks.

Next Monday morning I reported to the kapo of the cartographers and walked the one kilometre or so to the building outside the camp. Thomas and I were considered a welcome addition to the original group of six because of the urgent need for maps of Buna Werke and building plans for Birkenau. Thomas was not a draughtsman and relied on my skills to get by. He spent most of his time doing lettering with stencils and visiting the washroom where he would meet with our man from the electronic stores. On Wednesday, Thomas returned from the washroom very excited and announced to me that the whole unit, including the batteries, was fully assembled.

"How large is this unit?" I inquired.

"That may be a problem. It's rather big — the size of a large suitcase —but I've accepted it and it's sitting on top of the water tank in the washroom."

He said this in one breath, obviously without any thought as to how we were going to get it into the camp. We looked at each other, worrying about what to do with it now that we had it.

"Let me look at it," I offered. "Perhaps I can think of something."

I trotted off to the washroom. There on the top of the old-fashioned water tank, in plain view, was a huge wooden box. The conspicuousness of our radio was especially dangerous since the washroom was frequently used by SS guards watching over some working groups outside. The radio had obviously been placed there in a hurry because it was resting on the toilet handle, causing the water to run continuously.

It had to be hidden immediately. Looking frantically around I noticed a large cupboard with double doors standing in the corridor leading to the washroom. I tried one door but it was locked; when I pulled harder the bolt came out of the slot and the door flew open. The cupboard was full of cartography supplies: rolls of paper, bottles of India ink, pencils and boxes containing articles I did not have time to examine. Quickly removing the supplies from the highest shelf, I placed them on the top of the cupboard, pushing them as close to the wall as possible. I then shut the door and returned to the washroom for our radio. Fortunately it was a portable unit with a handle and leather strap. I peeked through the door to make sure no one was in the corridor, picked up the box and began walking towards the cupboard. Suddenly the door at the other end of the corridor opened wide and two men in striped prison uniforms walked towards me. Because I was new to the building and the corridor was dark, I attempted to assume authority, hoping neither man would recognize me.

"Where do you think you're going?" I shouted at them in German. They paused and started to mumble something, no doubt thinking I must be a German kapo. That bolstered my courage and I shouted angrily: "Out you go, you swine dogs."

They turned tail and ran. Hastily I opened the cupboard, put the box on the top shelf, camouflaged it with some loose maps and, closing both doors at the same time, managed to shove the bolt back into its slot.

But that was not the end of my test of nerves. Walking back to the cartographers' room I met up with the kapo.

"What took you so long? I thought you'd flushed yourself down the toilet! Since you're here, come and help me get more supplies."

With these words he went to the cupboard, took out a key and opened the doors.

"Who made such a mess in here?" he grumbled. "It must have been that stupid Fred. You can't depend on anyone unless you do it yourself!"

Muttering away to himself, he removed several rolls of drawing paper and piled them in my arms. He then turned to the cupboard and snatched a few pencils.

"That's all for now," he said, briskly closing and locking the cupboard doors. "I want your job completed by Friday or we'll all get hell from the SS."

"There's simply too much work and not enough time to do it," I said. "Perhaps we should make arrangements to come back here evenings — not that we'd enjoy it much — but otherwise we can't hope to finish by Friday."

"You're all lazy bastards," he snarled, eyeing me slyly, "but just maybe you're right. I want you to work day and night until the end of the week."

When I accompanied the kapo into the draughting room carrying supplies, I glanced furtively at Thomas' anxious face and knew what must have been going through his mind. I deposited my load on the table near the kapo's workplace and returned to my drawing board next to Thomas.

I had barely sat down when the kapo approached me and asked: "What was all that shouting about in the corridor?"

"Oh, it was nothing," I answered nonchalantly. "A couple of dirty Musselmen wanted to hide in our washroom and I just chased them back to work."

The kapo was satisfied and everyone returned to their work again.

"What did you really do there?" whispered Thomas.

"I've hidden the box in the supply cupboard and will tell you all about it when we're back in camp," I answered, also very quietly.

Later that day we reviewed our strategy, discussing and arguing about how to get the radio into the camp. We came to the conclusion that we could not do it alone. Neither of us knew enough about electronics. To take it apart at the cartography office was dangerous and furthermore, we were not sure we could put it together again.

The only solution was to bring the whole thing in by any

Maximilian Grabner, head of
Auschwitz Gestapo and expert on
physical torture

rollwagon that would not likely be inspected by the guards.

Almost simultaneously we decided that it should be done by Albert and Alex who took corpses out through the main gate to the crematorium almost every night. The guards did not like to inspect corpses, especially if they knew the men had died of some contagious disease. Thomas left immediately for the hospital to make the arrangements.

He returned just before curfew.

"All is ready," he announced. "The transmitter will be picked up and delivered into the camp. We simply have to take it to the central garbage collection, about 200 yards from our building."

"But Thomas, we can't do it during the day unless we involve the garbage rollwagon, which isn't really a good idea. We might have a better chance at night if they make our group work the late shift."

Giving me a worried look, Thomas confessed he had no ready solutions. We decided to sleep on it and hope that some chance would arise for us to deliver the radio to its final destination.

The next morning and afternoon passed by uneventfully, providing no opportunity for action; our only hope was that perhaps somehow, during the night, things would change. Late in the day an SS guard strode in and announced we could not leave the room until our job was finished. At 6:00 p.m. a kitchen rollwagon brought us our evening soup. We ate and returned to our work. Everything seemed hopeless. Barely able to concentrate on my lines and figures, all I could think of was the radio transmitter, sitting in the cupboard like a time bomb. Sooner or later someone was bound to find it and when he did, Thomas and I would become intimately acquainted with Grabner and Boger of the Auschwitz Gestapo and their torture room in Block 11.

Thomas leaned close and whispered: "I will test the SS guard to see how thorough he is."

"Good idea," I said softly, "but don't be too hasty. We still have one day left and it may be safer to wait until then."

Thomas nodded, then asked the guard if he could go to the washroom.

"Go," came the reply, "but don't try anything stupid or I'll fill you full of holes."

The guard opened the door to the corridor and stood at the doorway. From there he could observe everything but the inside of the washroom.

Thomas came back shortly.

"I think we have to do it tonight. If the Gestapo knows it's there, we'll all be sent to the bunker.

"The washroom has a window that opens to the rear of the building and the dump is only about 200 metres away, in complete darkness. Somehow one of us has to get there."

"Thomas, you're nuts. How can you take that huge radio from the cupboard in full view of the SS guard?"

"I'll pretend that I have diarrhoea and will go to the toilet every 15 to 20 minutes. During one of these trips you will start performing your magic tricks for everybody. Get the guard sufficiently involved to keep him away from the door.

"When you think there's enough time for me to get the radio out, say loudly: 'Now, watch very carefully!' That's my signal.

"I grab it, take it to the washroom, place it outside the open window, then return here. All you have to do is jump from the window, run like hell to the garbage, dump the radio there and run back."

The plan sounded simple enough, but there was no time to think of how much could go wrong. When one is young, danger is a challenge: better to act first and think about it later.

I smiled. "Let's do it!"

Thomas began to groan, pretending that he had a stomach-ache, and I tried to get my neighbour on the other side interested in a disappearing coin. However, someone else went into the washroom and the kapo spotted my performance.

"No funny business there!" he shouted. "Get back to work!"

It was Thomas's turn to go to the washroom, but the kapo was watching me and I could do nothing. Thomas had been gone for perhaps only three minutes when the SS guard got suspicious and went to see what he was doing. Fortunately he found Thomas in the proper position, shouted at him to hurry up, and returned to the doorway. Thomas returned shortly after; we could not make our move. A few minutes later the rollwagon from the kitchen arrived bringing us coffee, which normally accompanies dinner. This time, for some reason, it was late.

When the large kettle was brought in by two prisoners and another SS guard, Thomas remarked: "One of those men is with the underground. They will be taking the empty kettles back to the camp. I will talk to him immediately."

He went for more coffee and I watched him explain the problem to one of the prisoners. Moments later he was at my side sipping from his cup.

"It will be much easier this way," he said with contained excitement. "The rollwagon with the empty kettles is just around the corner from the window. We'll do the same thing as before, but you must put the transmitter into the kettle instead of carrying it to the garbage."

Since we were now on a coffee break I started to show my tricks quite openly, quickly getting everybody's attention. Thomas, favouring his stomach, left for the washroom and I had a captive audience. The new SS guard then pulled a deck of cards out of his pocket, challenging me to show what I could do with them.

While the eyes of both SS guards were on my hands, I picked some cards from the deck and said dramatically: "Now, watch very carefully!" I then transformed one card into another.

I performed the trick over and over again but they still could not tell how it was done. They demanded that I explain it to them. Taking my time, I made my explanation so complicated they were none the wiser. To reassure them, I insisted it took a lot of practice before one could be proficient. By this time Thomas was back and I asked to go to the washroom. To my dismay one of the guards announced I had to wait, saying he wanted to go first.

I looked at Thomas, trying to read in his face whether the SS guard would find the radio. But Thomas's face was always the same, expressing only an innocent look of happy boredom.

The SS guard came back. Obviously he had not found any-thing because he merely ordered his men to pick up the empty kettle and head back to the camp.

That was the end of Plan B. We were back to our drawing boards, both aware that we now had to follow through with the original plan.

I leaned over to Thomas. "Do whatever you can to keep the SS guard from the washroom, I'm going out for fresh air. Wish me luck — let's hope I don't run into an SS man there!"

When I asked to go to the washroom the SS guard was surprisingly friendly.

"Okay, but hurry up because I'm taking you guys back to camp. It's enough work for tonight."

He then ordered the kapo to "start packing."

In an instant I was in the washroom.

I opened the window; there on the ledge stood the transmitter covered with a rug. I jumped out of the window, picked up the transmitter and looked around, listening for any suspicious noise. The night was quiet and so dark I could barely see where the garbage dump was. But there was no time to lose. I began a fast sprint in the most likely direction.

Suddenly I tripped and fell right into the middle of the garbage heap. Empty cans clanked noisily against each other, some rolling along the ground like renegade hubcaps, making a clamour so prolonged I thought it would never stop. I jumped up almost as quickly as I had fallen, colliding with yet more trash cans. I was still holding onto the transmitter. Thomas and I had both been warned that the tubes in the radio were very sensitive and the slightest impact might destroy them. Hoping for the best, I quickly set the transmitter down on the garbage pile in which I was standing, covered it up with the rug and raced back.

Someone came out of the next barracks and shouted in German: "Who goes there? Stop or I'll shoot!"

I glanced over my shoulder. A flashlight scanned the garbage. More SS men came out to see what the commotion was about.

With an Olympian leap, I cleared the window only to meet the frightened face of Thomas peering through the half-opened washroom door and shouting at the top of his lungs: "Get out of there! Don't you see that I'm going to do it in my pants? How can you just sit there and let me suffer?"

I understood instantly what this charade was for and shouted back: "You've camped here already for half the night! You'll get your turn soon enough!"

I switched off the lights in the washroom and ran to the window to check whether the SS men had discovered the transmitter. I was just in time to see them walking back, laughing and saying something about a cat.

I let Thomas in, gave him the thumbs up sign and returned to the draughting room.

Everybody was ready to leave, complaining about how cruel I had been to make Thomas wait, and what would have happened if he had not been able to hold himself any longer.

Later on, Thomas told me how desperate this improvisation was. At the sound of the noise outside, he rushed to the toilet and began shouting before the SS guard had time to become suspicious.

When we were back at camp, Thomas went to the hospital "to get something for diarrhoea" and notified Alfred to collect the transmitter on his rollwagon. It was delivered the same night and installed by Fred Stoessel in the basement of the hospital block.

Unfortunately our radio was only in operation for about six months. The Germans eventually picked up our signals and began a frantic search for the source, taking in several men for questioning. They did not have, at that time, the equipment to locate the direction from which the signal was transmitted, but they redoubled their efforts to uncover the activity of the underground. To the Gestapo, this signal was proof-positive of an organization in the camp and that it must be destroyed. Afraid our security was inadequate, the decision was made, in the summer of 1942, to dismantle the transmitter.

CHAPTER

SMUGGLING AS AN ART FORM

On my last day with the cartographers, I went to see Mamma to make sure I still had a job with the potato peelers.

Like a sheep to the lion's den, I approached Mamma's barracks. The chances of encountering a murderous kapo there were very good. If he felt like showing his strength or giving vent to his frustrations, or even for no reason at all, he would readily strike the first prisoner in his path. If the unfortunate victim were to show any tendency to defend himself, it would be equivalent to a swift death sentence: other kapos would join the fray, execute him on the spot and enjoy every moment of it. During working hours the kapo's authority was unfailingly reinforced by the SS guards who were always ready to shoot a man for insubordination.

Thus, my trip to the kapos block was not for pleasure. No ordinary prisoner in his right mind would dare to go there, but I was counting on my clean uniform and confident appearance to convince the kapos that I occupied some important position in the camp and should be left alone.

I found Mamma in a back room playing poker with Leo and some other kapos. On the table lay a generous pile of German marks. Stakes were high, faces tense and tempers short. I had come in at the wrong time.

Leo took one look at me and barked: "Get out of here!"

I was out like a shot.

The next day, after morning roll call, I ran to where the SS kitchen group stood, looking for Mamma. He was late for some reason, but the cooks told me Mamma had found a replacement and that there was little hope he would take an extra man. I felt lost and uncertain, not knowing where to go. Some groups were already marching out of the camp; if I stayed in, I would have to report to

Leo who was still the campelder. While I was pondering over what decision to make, Mamma was leading his group out of the camp.

"What are you doing here?" he inquired in a surprised voice.

"Don't you remember? I was to report here after I finished my job with the cartographers. Dr. Dering got what he wanted and now I'm back."

I pretended not to know I had been replaced. Mamma looked genuinely perplexed.

"The potato peelers' group is complete. I can't take more men than I'm allowed, so I don't know what to do for you. But I suppose you can come with us just for today."

That was encouraging. On Sunday, the following day, most men did not go to work, which would give me time to find another job. When we got to the kitchen sun-porch, all the potato peelers took their places; there was not even room for me to sit down. For an hour I stood while Mamma busied himself in the kitchen, uncertain as to what to do with myself.

Finally Mamma walked in and announced that the chef had no need for another potato peeler. He then paused, waiting for my response. I said nothing.

"He also mentioned that we could use one more man in the kitchen if I can find a really good cook."

Mamma stepped closer. "Are you a good cook? Tell me the truth! I want to know what your real profession is!"

I certainly did not want him to know I was a regular officer on a scholarship to the university, nor did I want to lie to him. I was tempted to tell him a partial truth — that I was a university student in mechanical engineering — but decided instead to make up a story that might appeal to him.

"No, I am not a very good cook," I confessed, "but I was once employed as a cook's helper in a travelling circus. Actually, I do not have any profession; I had to quit school because we did not have money for my education. I have worked at many jobs and always managed to be good at them."

Mamma seemed pleased. "I believe you. You're a very smart guy. I heard you're a good draughtsman, too. It's a pity you couldn't finish your schooling, you'd have made an excellent professional. Let's go into the kitchen to see just how good a cook you can be."

In the kitchen I received a new uniform and clean underwear.

Another prisoner then led me to the crematorium for a special shower and disinfecting procedure. When we returned, Mamma endowed me with a long white apron and a white cook's hat, the official emblems of my new post.

The day passed uneventfully until shortly before six. The SS suppers had been prepared and Mamma and his prisoner cooks were sitting behind the kettles, tucking into their own dinners. I was about to join them when Mamma stopped me.

"You've not had your cook's examination yet. This goulash would taste much better with just a little something more. What do you think it needs?"

I tasted it and feeling deeply embarrassed about my cooking knowledge, looked up at Mamma and shrugged.

"Well, let me help you," he offered. "What would you think if we cut pieces of salami into that goulash? Would that improve it?"

I agreed with Mamma, as was expected.

Mamma continued: "The SS kitchen received a big shipment of salamis today. They're all kept in the room where the SS cooks are working. Go and get us one."

After a pause he added: "By the way, if they catch you they may kill you, and if they don't do a good job of it, I'll have to finish you off myself."

This was not the nicest cooking examination I could imagine.

I tried to worm my way out of it. "Shouldn't you let me work here for a couple of days before trying this stunt? I'm new here and everybody's watching me."

"Hurry up," said Mamma. "The goulash is getting cold."

I walked briskly to the doorway of an adjoining room and peered in. On a side table was a small mountain of salamis. Three SS cooks who were having dinner turned and stared at me.

"What do you want?" one demanded.

Thinking fast, I replied, "It's my job as a new cook to wash dishes, and I thought I might collect some. Is that all right?"

It was all I could think of to say, though I knew it was a pretty flimsy excuse for getting into the room. I stood there, my heart pounding, feeling my confidence drain away.

"A good idea! So Mamma Fritz is finally thinking about his bosses' comfort. You can clean up the room too while you're at it."

I could not believe my good fortune.

I collected their dishes, took them to the sink and washed

them. At the other end of the room I noticed a cupboard full of cups and plates and walked over, placing my wet dishes on the table beside it. As I dried them, I puzzled about how to sneak a salami. Though the cooks were moving around the room, one always kept an eye on me. This was probably no more than simple curiosity about the new man in the kitchen, but for my purposes it constituted a considerable nuisance. I felt I had to direct their attention away from me.

I finished the cleaning and washing-up and started to walk out of the room past the table full of salamis. The cooks watched my every move.

I stopped by the table as if suddenly remembering something, turned around and said: "I'm sorry, but I didn't ask you where the clean dishes should go. I probably piled them in the wrong place."

I pointed to the cupboard and everybody immediately looked there. Quickly, I snatched a salami with the other hand and slipped it under my apron.

"No," said the chef, "that's where we keep them."

I smiled with relief and returned to our part of the kitchen. Mamma, sitting behind one of the kettles, was finishing his dinner.

Proudly, I handed him the salami. "I'm sorry it took me so long, but I'm new here and they were watching me all the time."

Mamma grinned broadly.

"You've done well," he exclaimed. "I was really upset about having to kill such a nice guy. Now you are a member of Mamma's family."

He patted the seat beside him and I took it gratefully.

"Now let me explain why I asked you to do this. You see, in my family we're all prepared to take risks for each other. I wanted to see whether you would do it for me. But I will never again expose you to unnecessary risk. And you can be sure no kapo in Auschwitz will dare to touch you. They know what I can do to them."

This lengthy explanation seemed quite logical and thus made little impression on me. The fact that I had just risked my life to satisfy the whim of some criminal did not even occur to me. Stealing was a real achievement — I had exposed myself to danger and enjoyed it.

Life in the kitchen under Mamma's protective wing proved indeed a heaven in hell.

My position in the SS kitchen provided natural opportunities for exploitation. The kitchen had better cold meats for the officers' mess and greedy SS men in the lower ranks often exchanged favours for goodies.

Prisoners returning to the main camp from work were frequently searched for food received from outside, for letters, or for any other matter the camp administration considered dangerous. SS kitchen personnel were, of course, prime suspects and searched more often than any other working group. However, the system was so corrupt, Mamma could usually pass cold meats to the guards at the camp's main gate to find out when a search was planned. These methods of exchange were not foolproof; sometimes officers would order, on a spur of the moment, an inspection of returning work groups. But with regular camp life so full of dangers, we felt the risk was worth it. I carried ham sausages, salami and back bacon into the camp on a regular basis. Others were more cautious, or perhaps did not have so many friends in need of such delicacies.

One day, as I marched back to camp with the rest of the SS kitchen personnel, two salamis nestled under my belt, several SS men ran out of the guardhouse and ordered the entire group to stop at the gate — a surprise inspection. Divided into rows, the potato peelers were searched first by two of the guards. One was particularly thorough, checking pockets, running his hands along the body front and back, then feeling each arm and leg. The two thick salamis burned against my stomach. No matter how much I pulled it in, I could not make them disappear.

Suddenly there was a commotion and shouting up front. An SS man had found a very small piece of sausage hidden in the sleeve of a potato peeler. Triumphantly, he showed it to everybody; then, joined by other men from the guardhouse, he began to beat the prisoner. The poor potato peeler was kicked, slugged with rifle butts and hit with clubs until he collapsed, almost unconscious. He was then dragged between the two rows of electric fences surrounding the camp, placed upon his feet and left standing there. But that was not enough.

An SS man picked up a heavy club, approached the swaying figure and said: "I should kill you for what you did, but I'll give you another chance. If you run fast enough between these fences that I can't catch you, I'll let you live. If not, I'll kill you with my club. Now go!"

He pretended to chase the man who stumbled along as fast as he could, dragging his left foot while one arm, probably broken, swung limply at his side.

The SS men, laughing outrageously, watched him labour on. "Look at the dummkopf run!" they shouted.

The unfortunate prisoner had forgotten that, being between the fences, he was a shooting target for the guards in the towers. Indeed, no sooner had he approached one tower than three shots rang out. The SS guard had to fire that many times, at about 50 metres, to kill him.

The guards returned to their body search of our group. What would happen to me when they found my two huge salamis, I wondered, praying for a miracle. Inside the camp gate was a small gathering of prisoners observing the search. I saw Stan and Thomas anxiously watching me, not knowing for certain whether or not I was carrying food.

During the inspection, I noticed that the SS men had slightly different techniques. The one in my row was checking the torso very thoroughly, almost neglecting arms and legs. The other guard paid more attention to arms and legs, likely encouraged by finding the bit of sausage in the man's sleeve. On approaching our guard, each of us was required to spread his legs, raise his arms and submit to the search. I watched the man who was to frisk me, then decided, when my time came, to shift the salamis to my hips in the hope that he would concentrate on my front and back as he had with the other prisoners. Deep in thought about how to outwit this fellow, I failed to notice that the other guard had finished his row.

A shout jerked me back to reality: "You there! Come to me!"

It was the sausage man. With no time to think, I reacted instinctively. I walked straight to him, spread my legs and raised my arms, and leaned with my salamis against his stomach. If he stepped back to check my front I was finished, so I made sure there was no room for his hands to touch my belly.

The guard ran his hands over my sides and my back, checked each arm and leg, and let me go.

When I walked through the gate, Stan and Thomas greeted me with relief.

"We were afraid you might be carrying some food tonight," they said. "Thank God you weren't."

A little later, as we got further from the gate, I pulled out the two salamis. My two friends just stood there, staring at the meat.

"I don't know how I got through," I said simply. "It was a real miracle. If they'd found these huge sausages, I'd be minced meat myself by now."

Thomas smiled his enigmatic smile. "Perhaps Mamma was right — you may be a better thief than officer."

This close brush with death did nothing to stop me from my practice of smuggling sausages into the camp. In a young man's mind, the hunger for adventure is often more powerful than simple logic. Thomas and Stan tried to discourage me, insisting there was no need for me to take such a risk. But I knew that this was not true — my friends were always hungry and a bribe often came in handy when dealing with those in authority. Besides, somewhere deep down I enjoyed the thrill of deceiving the enemy.

Future information about the likelihood of an inspection at the gate proved highly reliable. In time, I was able to bring quite a load of meat into the camp.

There was, however, another near miss. It was late in summer and I was again carrying two beautiful, thick sausages under my belt. Once more we were stopped at the gate and two SS men conducted a body search. This time they ordered us to take off our jackets and submit them for inspection, then each man was searched in the usual manner.

Removing my jacket would immediately expose my sausages. Quickly, I put one sausage into each sleeve of my jacket and held it at the end of the sleeves, by two fingers, pretending it was feather light. I waved the jacket back and forth in front of the SS man, twisting and turning it, then grabbed both sleeves in one hand, spread my legs and raised my arms. The body search revealed nothing more.

Through my work in the SS kitchen and my ability to bring good food back to the camp, I became one of the influential, privileged class in Auschwitz. Thanks to Mamma, no kapo would touch me and the difficult kitchen work, along with the extra food, made me very strong. I always wore a nice-fitting, clean uniform and had a good pair of shoes. Also, my number, 4618, signified that I was one of the old prisoners and had survived, suggesting that I had good connections with the camp authorities. Since a mere two per cent of the first transports were still alive, even the SS treated us better.

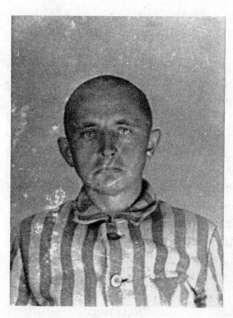

Stan Dubois
Polish Socialist Party leader

Dr. Dering's attitude towards me changed. He treated me like an old friend, apparently forgetting that he once fired me from a very good job and exposed me to conditions in which survival was far more problematic.

At 26, I was too young to have any firm political views. Three years of the military academy and a year at university had not given me much time to form opinions about political parties. Dering was a right-wing conservative, highly intolerant of all minorities such as Russians, Ukrainians or Jews. It was probably his attitude that pushed me towards socialism.

In Auschwitz at that time was a man well known before the war as a socialist. His name was Stan Dubois. He was much older than me and because I found him very wise, he became the first person to educate me politically. I had been raised as part of the privileged class and consequently knew nothing of social discrimination and injustice. My concepts were very simplistic: there was an intelligent class and an unintelligent class. The intelligent class was rich and the unintelligent class was poor. It did not occur to me then that education, not intelligence, was the exclusive domain of the rich. No doubt most of my conservative colleagues, including regular officers, never understood that difference.

Political activities became as significant in Auschwitz as our military organization. But I could see no purpose for them there, in spite of my sympathy to Dubois. Political people tended to classify others according to their pre-war political preferences, thereby judging how trustworthy they were. Nothing did more to prevent cooperation and trust between people than one's political affiliations. This was demonstrated to the extreme in Buchenwald where Communists were the blockelders and kapos. Their behaviour was not much better than that of the professional criminals in Auschwitz.

In the spring of 1942, when orders from Berlin for mass executions came into effect, Auschwitz did not yet have an elaborate system of gas chambers. We heard that the first attempt was carried out on about 1,000 Jews from Slovenia. Although they could easily have been shot, they were instead "hand murdered," beaten to death in Birkenau by a group of SS men over a period of about three days. Death was delivered person to person, in a most primitive and brutal way, serving as a training ground and test of endurance for future executioners. For those who could do it, dropping a canister of gas into a room with hundreds or thousands of men, women and children became as easy as swatting a fly.

Meanwhile, in the main camp, an epidemic of typhus broke out. With rampant malnutrition and insufficient health care, prisoners dropped faster than the kapos could kill them. Attempts to keep the typhus under control were almost impossible. As long as there were lice, typhus spread like fire; as long as the camp was unsanitary, lice multiplied. Those who worked in the SS offices, stores or kitchen were moved to a separate block. Yet the disease still struck the SS. Soon, drastic methods were adopted and block after block put through the delousing process. People sick with typhus in the hospital were brought naked to the showers and often had to wait their turn outside. Men and clothing were disinfected, the former with special soaps and the latter with hot steam, but nothing helped. In fact, the combination of heat and damp may have contributed to the proliferation of the lice, thus spreading the disease even further.

The underground decided to use the typhus outbreak to its advantage, keeping a special breeding place for infected lice in the hospital. Selected "sharpshooters" received their own little box of lice and they in turn would select pieces of straw into which a louse would fit snugly; then, like Amazonian Indians with their poison-arrow blowguns, they would shoot the lice into the necks of the most hated SS men.

The hunt was quite successful. Several SS men infected with typhus died in spite of the fact that they had received much better medical attention than prisoners. Among them was the one who had wanted to make a shooting target out of me when I worked with the surveyors. Somehow the SS guards realized that the most cruel of them were the very ones who were dying. The trick of shooting infected lice was never discovered, but the SS men began to talk about some "curse" connected with the Auschwitz concentration camp. Whether all of them believed it or not, there was nonetheless a general improvement in the treatment of prisoners by the SS guards. Besides the curse, the SS men became afraid to touch prisoners for fear of infection.

One favourite target for lice-shooting was Palitsch, though in spite of perfect scores, he never got sick. However, he must have taken the infected lice home because shortly after he had received several hits, his wife developed typhus and died.

Indirectly, this affected Palitsch himself. About a year later when more Jewish prisoners inhabited Birkenau, Palitsch started to visit a Jewish girl in one of the barracks there. Sexual relations between German and Jew were strictly forbidden. Palitsch's activities were discovered, but instead of being sentenced to imprisonment in the concentration camp he was sent to the Russian front. Six months later the news reached Auschwitz that Palitsch had died fighting for the Fatherland.

The multiple deaths of the SS guards strengthened the determination of the Auschwitz authorities to stamp out typhus. One day SS doctors walked into the prisoners' hospital and segregated all people sick with typhus for "delousing." Over 1,000 men were undressed and loaded into trucks. Another truck collected all their clothes, bedding and mattresses for disinfecting, leaving just the bare walls. The men were all gassed in the crematorium. From then on typhus-stricken prisoners were afraid to go to the hospital and simply died wherever they happened to be. Some who had connections were able to stay in hospital by simulating other illnesses.

But even that was not a safe alternative. The hospital was overcrowded and the Germans disliked keeping people off work for too long. As a consequence, a German doctor was sent around every few days to select the weakest patients for the gas chamber.

It was at this time that Thomas came down with typhus. Fortunately, he was safe in hospital; enough people there knew of his work in the camp and were prepared to protect him from the gas chamber selections. We were all deeply concerned about his illness and one of us checked his condition daily. Typhus lasts normally about two weeks, during which time the patient's temperature rises to around 42°C, or higher. At the end of the two weeks the patient is extremely weak, constituting the moment of crisis. The temperature then falls within a very short time to about 35°C or lower, usually resulting in death. Thomas, however, survived. Even before he was released from hospital it was arranged for him to work in the tannery with Stan Kazuba.

In the meantime, the Russian prisoners had built enough barracks in Birkenau to house themselves and the rest — those who were still alive — transferred out of the main camp. The penal block too was sent to Birkenau, but Block 11 remained a place of executions or of imprisonment in the bunkers, still under the control of the local Gestapo.

Shortly after the departure of the Russians the fence dividing the main camp was erected again, separating Blocks 1 to 10 from the rest of the camp.

Exciting rumours started to circulate that a transport of women would soon be arriving. We had been in the camp over two years without so much as seeing a woman, and sometime in March 1942, the rumour proved true. The first 100 women arrived and a series of pathetic love affairs began across the barbed wire. The desire to be with and talk to the opposite sex was very strong on both sides. Men and women sat face to face and just looked at each other through the fence. Talking was forbidden; besides, the distance was too great for intimate conversation and one had to shout at the top of one's lungs to be heard. Communications were with sign language. Having been away from women for so long, we had nurtured an idealized picture of them as kind, sensitive and caring beings, quite incapable of cruelty. That women could beat each other as cruelly as men seemed unimaginable. Yet the female kapos we saw were remarkably rough, shouting and brandishing their clubs, most frequently upon the weakest. Afterwards, I heard that life in the women's camp was much more complicated than in the men's, full of internal intrigues and entanglements which made the art of survival far more difficult.

The expansion of Birkenau progressed very rapidly when the working force of Russians was augmented by selected Jews and some of the new transports from Poland. With such large numbers, new crematoriums were required. The existing crematorium could not handle the job even operating 24 hours a day, burning two corpses at a time in one oven. It had become necessary to burn the dead just outside the building in a large ditch. The smoke from

Close-up of human corpses dumped into the open pit

charred bodies was exhausted not through a chimney but in the marshlands of Auschwitz. It had a sickening, sweetish smell and spread over the ground for kilometres. Over forty years have passed and I still recall vividly that sinister odour.

Priority was given in Birkenau for the building of four new crematoriums and new gas chambers. The chambers were built in the form of large shower rooms and were used almost exclusively for the mass extermination of Jewish families who arrived from all parts of Europe. Thousands of Gypsies were also gassed. The first Jewish transport sent directly to Birkenau arrived in May 1942 and consisted of about 1,500 men, women and children. The new arrivals were ordered to undress, then herded into the alleged shower rooms where the gas, in the form of pellets, was dropped in through the ventilators. The procedure was perfected to such a degree of efficiency that after about ten minutes everybody was dead. The rear doors would then open, the gas would be exhausted, and the dead bodies would be wheeled into the crematoriums. The remaining people in the transport would await their turn, completely unaware of what was going on inside. In the meantime, the shower rooms would be hosed down with water to look as though

Burning bodies in open pit

the previous group had really had a shower.

The whole charade had no humanitarian aspect whatsoever. It was simply an efficient and convenient way to control large crowds with only a few SS men on duty. In subsequent transports a selection was made before the victims reached the "showers." Young, healthy men and women were sent to work in Birkenau and the old, infirm and children went to the gas chambers.

A new working group of prisoners was created to assist the Germans in this macabre operation. Called a "Sonderkomando," it consisted exclusively of Jewish volunteers. They were given special privileges and lived in conditions superior to those of the SS: bedrooms with comfortable beds and clean sheets, changed every

Selection of Jews for work in camp or for death in gas chambers

day; a spacious dining room with good china and cutlery and a living room with a library, checkers and chess; and the best food Europe could provide at that time.* All these luxuries were taken from the Jewish transports who had just been put through the gas chambers. The Sonderkomandos received clean clothes and good quality underwear; they even were allowed to wear watches and did not have to have their heads shaved like the rest of us.

Their duties were to lure the new arrivals into the gas chambers, take their bodies to the crematorium and transport their belongings to a special barracks where a thorough search was made for valuables. The barracks were called "Canada" — meaning the place of affluence. Indeed, people displaced from their homes all over Europe took as many of their valuables as they could with them. The prisoners who worked in "Canada" had to search through these belongings, especially for food, money and jewellery. Some of the warm clothing was sent to Germany if it was in nearly new condition; useful things like leather belts, shoes, briefcases or leather suitcases were recycled for use by the German army. Many valuables found their way into the camp and were used as purchasing power for food or better clothing; the rest was piled up in separate barracks for possible future use. After the war,

---

*See Dr. Miklos Nyszli. *Auschwitz* (Greenwich, Conn.: Fawcet, 1960).

millions of useless eyeglasses, toothbrushes and prostheses were found, all of them neatly segregated into enormous heaps.

At one time, when a large supply of American dollars was circulating, the price of a loaf of bread on the camp's black market was $100. The Sonderkomandos had first choice in food or clothing. Valuables such as gold and jewellery did not interest them; they knew they were soon to be gassed and willingly traded those several weeks of relative luxury for certain death later.

Probably their work represented an immediate escape from the horrible conditions in the camp. But the price — helping Germans in the gassing of their own people — was high indeed. Perhaps each had a spark of hope that before his turn came, something would happen to save his life. Two Sonderkomandos attempted to flee the camp just before they were due for extermination. Once they even received guns from the outside underground army, killing a couple of SS men in the process. None made a successful escape, however, until just before the end of the war.

American dollars, gold and diamonds became very valuable for our organization. We had discovered several SS men could be corrupted by amounts of money they could never dream of seeing in their regular pay. Food was always the most desirable commodity among prisoners, kapos and even among the SS whose menu was good but terribly unimaginative.

When, in 1942 and 1943, the Germans no longer punished other prisoners for one man's disappearance — a change of regulations believed to have come from Berlin — the underground began to assume an active role in arranging escapes from Auschwitz. The families of escapees, however, were still threatened with either public execution in the camp or "life" in the penal company. A major responsibility of our organization, when preparing escapes, was to notify the families ahead of time, allowing them to move to an address unknown to the local Gestapo.

Thomas was very anxious to send an envoy who could personally describe the situation in the camp in detail to the underground headquarters in Warsaw. The first candidates were Bielecki and Gawron. Both men had been arrested for belonging to the underground army and for possession of arms; their chance of survival was nil. Sooner or later they would be executed by Palitsch in Block 11.

We decided to use our influence with the kapos to have them

transferred to the group working with livestock outside the camp. A single barbed wire fence, not electrified, surrounded the area. Prisoners working there were few and the guards known to be inattentive.

Through our contacts, partisan units outside were notified to help them cross the border to the unannexed part of Poland and finally to Warsaw. Indeed, a week later the two men cut the wire fence and disappeared into the foggy night. They reached Warsaw soon after, delivering the first oral report from Auschwitz.

Out of sheer desperation, many others attempted to escape unassisted. A very small percentage were successful. For the most part, the escaping prisoners were Musselmen, indifferent as to whether they lived or died. Those caught would be brought back into the camp in great triumph. The SS would hang a big sign around their necks reading: "Hurrah, Hurrah, Ich bin wieder da!" (I am back again!). The man would be given a drum to beat, paraded before the entire camp at roll call, then thrown into the bunker.

Genuine escapees tried to hide from the large outer ring of guards, hoping that when working groups returned to the camp no one would notice they were missing. Then, when the sentries were

Reception of the recaptured prisoner

taken off for the night, the country would be open for a free walk home. However, it was not that simple. The Germans were very thorough when counting prisoners; in all my five years in the concentration camp, I cannot recall a single miscount. Even if a prisoner did walk away unnoticed, the surrounding countryside was either deserted or had been resettled and occupied by the German army, the SS and civilians. Without knowing where to go, an escapee was bound to stumble across some German patrol or, simply exhausted, would die in the fields. If caught, he too was paraded in front of the prisoners, then publicly hanged. Nothing, however, could discourage men from attempting escape.

One of the most spectacular escapes occurred when an officer, acting as a courier for our organization, fled with three colleagues. Each had worked in the industrial park where they were able to steal machine guns and SS uniforms. In broad daylight, fully disguised and guarded by the SS, they drove down the main road and out of the camp in a convertible car belonging to the commandant of the industrial park.

Needless to say, the boldness of this escape left the Auschwitz authorities furious. Aumeier, the deputy commandant of the camp, warned that all escaping prisoners would sooner or later be tracked down by the Gestapo since the whole of Europe was under German control. Executions would be swift and families hanged. This proved to be no idle threat. One day we found bodies, supposedly of a family, swinging from the gallows in front of the camp kitchen.

The most desperate attempts were made by the Russians in Birkenau, who were treated even more cruelly than their counterparts. They did not trust our underground; after all, only a year before, Russia had sided with Germany in its war against Poland. In time, our organization made contact with representatives of the Russian prisoners. Nevertheless, they continued to act independently.

Preparations began for a mass escape. First, the Russians snatched the corpse of a prisoner who had died during working hours and hid it within the outer ring of sentries. At evening roll call the alarm was sounded and the SS men, kapos and blockelders went out for the search. The rest of the camp in Birkenau, closely guarded, remained standing at attention in the roll call square. The body had been hidden well; after several hours the kapos and SS men came back empty-handed. Then, just loud enough for one of the kapos to hear, a Russian remarked: "If they let us look for him, we'll find him for sure! We know all the places where a prisoner might hide."

With nothing to lose, the SS men decided to let a group of Russians continue the search. Of course, they found the dead body and everybody was happy. They thus became the "experts" in finding escapees. They repeated this charade a couple of times over several weeks until the moment finally arrived for real action.

Once more the Russians hid a corpse, but when asked to search for the escapee, simply walked around aimlessly and made little attempt to locate the body. The Germans were furious. During the search, the whole camp of Birkenau had been standing at roll call for four hours while the sentries kept watch from the towers. In a last-ditch attempt to solve the problem, the commanding officer announced that all Russian prisoners would participate in the search. If unsuccessful, each one would be punished with 50 strokes to the bare buttocks. They went, but as they walked through the fields and between the buildings they collected stones, bricks and anything else which might serve as a weapon.

All at once the Russians attacked the guards and even succeeded in disarming one of the tower sentries. Then they ran towards the river where they believed freedom lay. The other towers opened fire and the alarm brought more reinforcements. SS men jumped into cars and drove to the other side of the river where frequent shots indicated they had found their targets. Most of the Russians were killed but several individuals escaped. The rest were brought back to the camp and hanged.

The building of new gas chambers at Auschwitz for the mass extermination of European Jews made it necessary to smuggle Jewish eye-witnesses out of the camp.* Late in 1943, two Slovenians named Wetzler and Rosenberg planned an escape. They decided to build an underground hideout in the industrial park and wait there for three days, until the posts were taken off the towers. When a prisoner went missing during working hours within the outer ring of sentries and no way was found by which he could have escaped, the guards remained at their posts for the next three days

---

* *Escapes from Auschwitz* (in Polish) by T. Sobarski (Warsaw: Polish Ministry of Defence, 1974).

and nights.

It took Wetzler and Rosenberg about two months to prepare; in a place where an old building had been demolished and where old lumber and broken boards were still lying around, they had dug a hole big enough in which to lie down. On the appointed day, their friends covered them with boards camouflaged with loose soil. They then sprinkled pepper generously around to prevent tracking dogs from sniffing them out.

When the evening roll call revealed two prisoners missing, the usual search was initiated. But the escapees were not found. Three days later, under the cover of night and when the posts were off the towers, Wetzler and Rosenberg walked away to freedom.

Through the intervention of the Polish and Slovenian undergrounds, they were eventually granted audience with the Vatican envoy to whom they made full eyewitness reports and asked for the intervention of the Pope on humanitarian grounds.

Though great danger was involved in escaping from Auschwitz, it was a way to fight back. Nonetheless, the great majority had no desire to escape, unwilling as they were to put themselves voluntarily in a position of immediate danger. The instinct for self-preservation told them to postpone action in favour of prolonging their lives at least a little. This may also explain why the Germans could lead thousands of people into the gas chambers, in most cases without any resistance.

In May 1942, the local Gestapo gave an order to shoot about 170 prisoners — officers or proven members of the Polish underground, some of whom had been in the camp for a year or more. All of them marched to their deaths singing the Polish national anthem, their only sign of defiance. At the time, we thought them very brave. In actual fact, they knew that if they tried to attack the SS guards, they would be shot on the spot. By marching and singing they postponed their deaths for perhaps an hour or two.

Shortly after this execution, 400 more Polish prisoners were summoned and transferred to the penal company in Birkenau. In addition to their red triangle, men in the penal company had to wear a black dot on their uniforms with a red circle just above it. This distinguished them from ordinary prisoners and signified that they were extremely dangerous.

A week after their transfer the first ten red circles were called up and shot. A week later another ten men were executed. When, the week following, ten more red circles were shot, they began to suspect the reason for their transfer. They had been condemned to die, but the Germans, afraid of a rebellion, had decided to execute them in small groups.

This was confirmed by Thomas through his contacts, prisoners working in the Gestapo offices. He immediately gave thought as to how he might save his colleagues who were sentenced to death.

The red circles decided to make a break for freedom, en masse, while they worked on the construction of the Konigsgraben Canal near the River Vistula. In addition to the 370 red circles, the regular penal company prisoners were also prepared to flee. The methods used to effect escapes could seldom be repeated because the Germans were invariably alerted as to what suspicious signs to watch for. Thus, almost every escape from Auschwitz had to employ a different technique.

Their plan was to disarm the immediate guards, run in groups towards the river, swim across and scale the embankment. "Much would depend on individual courage, enterprise and luck. Naturally heavy losses were to be expected — perhaps over 200 prisoners would fall to bullets or be caught and murdered, perhaps more would die and only 50 be saved — but how much better that would be than to wait passively for certain death."[*]

In order that the mass slaughter which had happened to the Russians not be repeated, partisan units had damaged the bridge over the river and were waiting on the other side. Dispatched troops of SS men would have to take the long drive around, giving the prisoners more time to escape.

It was decided that the attempt to escape would take place on June 10th, when the whistle to cease work sounded. It was a beautiful, sunny day, with no suggestion of a change of weather. Suddenly, at about four o'clock, clouds appeared in the sky and rain began to fall; some minutes later this turned into a downpour. In the torrents of rain it was almost impossible to see. Those in the know were not upset by this as it could only facilitate their plans, for work would go on to the end of the day; it never stopped for bad

---

[*] The events are described by an eyewitness, Zenon Rozanski, in *Fighting Auschwitz* by Joseph Garlinski (London: Julian Friedmann Publishers Ltd., 1975), pp. 104-105.

weather. But this time they were mistaken. Unexpectedly, the SS sergeant came out of his hut, looked around and with one long, shrill whistle gave the signal to knock off work. It was only half-past four.

Complete confusion resulted. Prisoners ran wildly from all sides, some towards the embankment and some not at all. When the crisis was over only fifty prisoners with red circles had disarmed the nearest SS men and tried to get away. Thirteen fell to the hail of bullets, a number turned back and only nine reached the Vistula and freedom.

Despite the general order from Berlin, the camp authorities took bloody retaliation for the attempt at a mass escape. The following day, Aumeier arrived and demanded of the 320 prisoners that they bring forth the leaders of the revolt. They silently refused, and immediately the deputy commandant shot 17 men, leaving three for his colleague Hossler. The remaining column of prisoners was led to the bunkers and gassed. On July 8, two members of the penal company who had been recaptured after the escape were publicly hanged.

As the war progressed, conditions in the camp tended to be in inverse proportion to the successes of the German troops in Russia: the less successful the German campaign, the more cruelly prisoners were treated. Jewish families arrived at Auschwitz in larger and larger numbers and the gas chambers were now used to exterminate all Musselmen, all hospital patients, Russians, Gypsies and Poles considered dangerous by the Gestapo. These extreme circumstances demanded that word be sent to the Warsaw headquarters. The bearer of the message had to be a long-time member of our organization, one who could persuade the Polish underground army that an uprising in Auschwitz was absolutely necessary.

I volunteered and my offer was accepted.

The SS kitchen where I was still serving very often worked overtime, after the outer ring was released from duty. Only one SS man guarded us in the kitchen and he could easily be distracted by good food. Before I could actually escape, however, there were several problems to be solved. I knew that if I escaped alone my colleagues would be held responsible and, as a reprisal, possibly hanged. I had to find out whether they were also willing to go. As it turned out, they had been talking about it for some time. When it was decided all six of us would escape, our next step was to notify our families to move to a new address. To assist them, we sent through outside contacts an American $1,000 bill for each family. During the war, U.S. currency was very valuable and a family could easily live on that amount for more than a year.

It was a tremendously exciting time. Replies from families started to come back, one by one, saying they had received the money and had moved into a new place. We were now just waiting for confirmation from my wife. When no word came, two weeks after everyone else's letters had arrived, I began to worry; perhaps something had happened to her. I asked Thomas to make contact once again through our men in the underground army. Several days later he informed me that she had been spoken to personally in Warsaw but refused to move out of her apartment. It was greatly unexpected and a terrible blow. The escape was all set up; we had smuggled civilian clothes to the kitchen and arrangements had been completed with a partisan unit outside to meet us and help us reach Warsaw.

I was frustrated, angry and very unsure what to do. Stan said I should go; my wife had not actually said I should not escape, she had only refused to move out. Perhaps she knew something. Perhaps she had established good relations with the Warsaw Gestapo and they would not arrest her, even if I did escape.

But I had seen the families of other fugitives hanged in front of the kitchen and could not bear to think of my wife being brought to Auschwitz. Two years in the camp had made me believe I could survive almost anything short of execution. But I had always thought of my wife as so helpless that even if she were not executed, she would not survive long in the conditions of Auschwitz.

I told Thomas that I could not go this time, not until I was sure that my wife would be out of danger. Thomas understood, but knew we could not hold back the rest of the men. When I returned to work in the kitchen next day, I told my colleagues of my decision and wished them good luck. My civilian clothes, hidden in the kitchen, had to be brought back into camp; if they were found after the escape I would be suspect. After work I dressed up in the civilian jacket and pants and put my striped uniform on top. For good measure I also took two ham sausages. What would the food matter if I were caught wearing civilian clothes? I got into the camp with no misadventures.

In the meantime, our organization faced the challenge of arranging my transfer from the SS kitchen to some other working group without my being implicated in the impending escape. To achieve this, they devised a fictitious punishment by the camp authorities. The following day I joined the kitchen group as usual but before Mamma had a chance to lead us out, my number was called by the SS man in charge of the working squads. Mamma was disturbed and insisted on going with me to help out if I was in some sort of trouble. According to the guard an order had come, probably from the Gestapo, that kitchen work was much too good for me and I was being transferred back to the general workforce. I fell in with new arrivals who had not yet been assigned to a squad.

Mamma, helpless to do anything, just turned to me and said: "I don't know what you were arrested for out there, but it must have been pretty bad if the Gestapo's still watching you here in Auschwitz. Anyway, if you ever feel hungry you can always come to me."

I was very grateful and thought perhaps we had made a mistake by not including him in our plans. But then I remembered the behaviour of the kapos in the penal company and reminded myself Mamma was also a criminal prisoner whose loyalty was more to Germany than Poland. I also knew that on the day of our escape Mamma and the SS guard would get a sleeping powder with their coffee and so would not be blamed.

My thoughts were interrupted by the kapo in charge of the workforce: "Number 4618! How many times do I have to call you! Join this group!"

I ran to the end of the column which was ready to march out to work, noticing with great joy the familiar faces of Thomas Serafiński, Stan Kazuba and Henry Bartosiewicz.

I had been assigned to the tannery group.

The escape from the SS kitchen had been scheduled for 8 o'clock in the evening on Wednesday of the following week. By then I had been safely transferred to another block where my tannery friends lived. On Wednesday night, as I lay on top of the triple bunk bed, my thoughts were with my colleagues in the SS kitchen. I knew that by now the night shift would be finished and the SS cooks would return to their barracks. Only Mamma and the SS guard would be there having dinner and the rest of the fellows would be cleaning the kitchen. Now was the time they would spike the coffee with sleeping powder. So many things could go wrong!

Sometimes more SS men would come for a second dinner prepared by Mamma as part of a general bribe. Sometimes the SS guard would ask for tea, not coffee. Did they have extra powder for that possibility? If everything went according to plan, Mamma and the guard should now be sleeping and everybody running for the storeroom. Now they would change quickly into civilian clothes, open the window at the back of the kitchen and climb out. The window faced fields; there was not a single building or road where they could accidently run into SS men. If they did everything as planned, they should now be running like crazy, full of the joy of being free!

Being free was more than just escaping from Auschwitz. It was like stepping back through the looking glass to find oneself in a different world. Auschwitz functioned according to its own set of rules. Old prisoners knew these rules and lived according to them. We stole food from the Germans and engaged in the power struggle with the kapos by mutual intimidation and bribery. We considered newcomers abnormal — they could not understand, even when told, how to behave in the camp. They knew what it was to be free, something we only faintly remembered.

At the far end of the fields was a small wooded area where they would be met by the underground men. I wondered what they would do if there were no one to meet them. Were they lost now? I had forgotten to describe the terrain to them, which I had memorised from the map. Did they know which way to go?

This part of Poland had been annexed to Germany and there were already large numbers of Germans working on the railroads, in the post offices and elsewhere, going about their daily business. I hoped my friends knew enough to get as far away from Auschwitz as possible. Sooner or later the escape would be discovered, the SS patrollers would give chase and all military and police units would be notified to keep a look-out for the escapees. If they were caught, the Gestapo would interrogate and torture them to try to find out who had helped arrange the escape. There was no way of knowing how much pain they would be able to take.

Suddenly, all the sirens around the camp started to howl. The escape had been discovered and the chase begun. There was no guessing the outcome; I had to wait until tomorrow. I felt as if I were with them, that life in the camp would no longer be the same.

The morning roll call was no different from any other day.

Everything appeared to be routine, but at the end of the roll call my number was called. Nobody else's, only mine. This is it, I thought. It's about the escape. When I marched out to the front and reported to the roll call commandant, an SS man was already waiting for me.

"Come with me!" he said and marched me to the main gate.

My mind was working overtime. If my colleagues have been caught they must be dead by now or in the bunkers of Block 11. Or the escape was successful and I was about to be interrogated by the Gestapo.

There was nothing cheerful about either possibility. Interrogated prisoners were generally put in the bunkers for softening and as a rule, seldom came out alive.

The SS man led me to the Gestapo offices. I was shown to a room with bare walls and no furniture. I was told to wait and the door was locked behind me. I must have waited for more than two hours, becoming more nervous, more tense with every passing minute. I completely forgot what I was supposed to say when the door opened and I saw two SS men and a man in civilian clothes talking to Mamma. He had obviously been interrogated before me. When Mamma was dismissed, all three walked into the room.

"Why did you not escape with your friends?" the man in civilian clothes asked.

"I did not know they were planning to escape. Besides, I was fired from my job."

Now one of the SS men said: "They must have been good friends to get you a job in the SS kitchen."

"They had nothing to do with hiring me. Kapo Fritz hired me. In fact, I think that they're the ones who arranged to get me fired!"

"That is true," said the civilian, "Fritz told us he hired you. He also said you should not be wearing a red triangle but a green one. You two have a lot in common."

I did not know what else Mamma had told them but they seemed more amused than angry. That was the end of the interrogation. Mamma had saved my life. The SS guard led me back to the main gate and let me into the camp.

My colleagues from the SS kitchen reached Warsaw safely.

Work in the tannery among friends seemed like an anti-climax after the adventures of my previous life. The tannery was about three kilometres from the main camp and consisted of three buildings arranged in a horseshoe pattern, with a large yard in the centre. The buildings and yard were fenced with barbed wire, with towers located at four corners of the premises. Two one-storey buildings were occupied by the tannery, one for the wet work where skins were tanned and one, where I was assigned, for finishing the dry leather. The third building was used by shoemakers and tailors working for the SS troops. Most labour in the tannery was on steer skins, producing leather for shoe soles, but we also dressed fine pelts to make chamois. Occasionally some SS officer would bring in the skin of a deer, a wild boar or a whole fox for private tanning.

When a whole animal arrived, the SS men demanded the meat for their dogs; but, of course, the best portions were cut out by Stan Kazuba for our consumption. Cooking food was not permitted here, but Stan designed an ingenious arrangement.

He had removed several bricks from the top of the large, brick stove in the drying room, leaving sufficient space for a big pot. Since, in spite of ventilation, the aroma of cooked meat could easily be detected, cooking was left for night time. In the morning when we arrived for work, the oven was still quite warm and the drying room smelled more like a kitchen than a tannery. Our first job was to open the windows and spill some of the foul smelling tanning solution on the stove to kill the aroma of cooked meat. Our pot was then removed to a safe place and we would all go about our work. On lean days, Stan used to cook up the cows' ears and udder parts — not a gourmet's delight, but for us a valuable supplement to the regular camp diet. On better days he would cook muskrats, cats, dogs, and when especially lucky, a whole horse. The inconsistent food supply was balanced out by salting meat and storing it under the floor boards in tanning barrels. Though my diet there was not as good as it had been in the SS kitchen, I was never so hungry as in the early days of Auschwitz.

I quickly learned how to use the machines for slicing and polishing skins and even became skilful at dressing skins by hand for chamois. The work in general was not particularly difficult and we could easily produce the required quotas. There was also very

Stan Kazuba

little SS supervision; they considered us craftsmen and did not interfere as long as the work was done.

Once or twice a day an SS man would walk through the tannery and then everybody worked busily. Otherwise, direction came from our foreman, Karl, who was half-German and half-Polish but could speak neither language well. Though Stan had been in the tannery the longest and had become very knowledgeable about all processes, Karl was the only real tanner among us. He did not know, or perhaps preferred not to know, that he was in the middle of a clandestine organization. Whenever the conversation turned to underground army escapes, Karl would immediately find some urgent job at the other end of the tannery.

One day, to help four of our men escape, we had to transport a complete SS uniform and holster with a wooden gun into camp. I had just put it on and was ready to disguise it with my own uniform when Karl walked into the drying room.

He snapped to attention and reported: "Twelve men working group at the tannery — Sir!" Without answering I began to walk slowly around him, pretending to inspect him. He continued to stand stiffly and would not have recognized me had it not been for the others suddenly bursting into great roars of laughter. Karl looked around in complete and utter confusion. Wide-eyed, he looked back at me and I started to laugh as well. Only then did he realize what was going on.

"You . . . you . . . you ain't an SS man!"

Slowly I reached for my wooden gun.

"You . . . you gotta gun! So you think I don't know you . . . I don't wanna know you! This is too much! You can't do this to me, I could be shot with all of you!"

Karl regained his composure slightly. "Now you listen here, I never seen you in that get-up, you understand? I wasn't here!" And, almost running out of the room, he repeated continually: "It ain't fair! I don't know nothin' about nothin'!"

After the fun was over, Henry started to worry. "Do you think this nitwit will report us? He was so scared he might just do it!"

Stan, who had refused to participate in the joke, said seriously: "I didn't want Karl to know anything because I wasn't sure about his loyalty. But what happened is maybe better for everybody. Karl is very cowardly but he's eating meat stolen from the SS. I also know he found some American dollars and a diamond ring in old shoes sent here for burning. He hid them behind the tumbling barrel. Leave him to me, I know how to keep him quiet."

Indeed, from then on Karl was very friendly with all of us. Instead of giving the usual orders he became obsequiously polite and when we had special work to do, did not interfere. As long as the regular chores were done, he was happy.

The only time he was extremely nervous — as were all of us — was the day of our practical joke when he had to lead us back to camp knowing that I wore the SS uniform under my prison garb. At the main gate, where he was supposed to report the number of prisoners returning from work, he almost lost his voice. Fortunately, Henry Bartosiewicz, who was close behind, saved the situation by reporting the number himself, explaining to the guard that the foreman had a bad case of laryngitis.

In the meantime, our organization decided it was in a sufficiently strong position to control the excessive violence in the camp. To a certain extent this was already working. Prisoners who spied for Germans were dying under mysterious circumstances and the kapos, knowing it was not their handiwork, made an effort to be more careful.

When Siegrud and two other infamous kapos were gassed because the SS men had found stashed in their beds gold and U.S. dollars, their colleagues suspected the men had been framed by some secret Polish group in the camp. We simply reinforced their suspicions and compromised them, offering the kapos gold or American cash. It worked, because the behaviour of all kapos in the main camp became almost civilized by the end of 1942.

A different situation, however, prevailed in Birkenau where

the most cruel of the kapos found their way. At that time our influence there was almost nil.

Two men were there whose terror tactics exceeded even German demands. One of them was Bednarek, a Pole from Silesia who spoke fluent German and Polish. He could kill a person with one swing of his heavy club and would do so without provocation — perhaps because he did not like a man's face or simply because he was in the mood for killing. He was illiterate and could not even count properly the number of prisoners under his command. He could neither organize work nor supervise a working party, but at the mere sight of him men leapt frantically into action. In Birkenau, where extermination was still more important than work, he was one of the SS's most popular men.

The other was a Jewish blockelder who supervised Jewish prisoners newly arrived from selection at the gas chamber door. In his block they received their first exposure to the cruel conditions of Birkenau.

No special time was assigned to the once routine sports. Here, the sport drills were incorporated into daily life from morning to night. The blockelder would start his day with breakfast, which he ate outside the barracks standing on the throats of two prisoners pinned to the ground by his helpers. SS men would come specially to see the new "breakfast routine." He also liked to think of the most cruel ways to kill. If someone, while soup was being distributed, looked hungry, he would call the man and ask whether he wanted more. If he said "yes," the blockelder would push his head in the kettle of soup until he drowned.

We decided both these men had to be stopped.

Anonymous messages were sent through other kapos, warning them they would die if they did not alter their behaviour. Of course, this produced no results.

To dispose of a Jewish blockelder was easy because, almost every day, dozens of Jews too weak to work were sent to the gas chambers. One day the badly beaten blockelder himself was among this group.

It was much more difficult to get rid of Bednarek. The authorities considered him a good "German" and consequently he was better protected than other privileged prisoners. More clandestine methods would have to be used.

The lice sharpshooters were called. Several typhus-infected

lice were brought in from the main camp and a trusted Jewish prisoner from Bednarek's block took lessons in shooting technique. Several weeks later Bednarek died of typhus fever. Even in Birkenau, this served as an effective warning to other kapos and blockelders. The message got across, however, that a secret Polish organization was in operation, dangerous to all German kapos and SS men. Though this produced more bearable conditions for the average prisoner, the message also reached the local Gestapo. The Germans were outraged and sent more spies into Birkenau, offering bigger bribes to the informers. Word filtered back that any prisoner who informed on a Polish underground in camp and on its members was to be set free. The secret war had been declared and we realized we could only come out of it as losers.

The first major defeat involved the arrest of Fred Stoessel in October of 1942. He had been one of the first men enrolled by Thomas and knew perhaps more names within our organization than anybody else, with the exception, of course, of Thomas himself.

The Gestapo also realized they had caught a big fish. Fred was guarded round the clock in the bunker of Block 11 by one SS man. He was taken almost daily to the political department (camp Gestapo offices) for interrogations until the end of February.

We knew all about the elaborate torture systems and inventiveness of the Gestapo. Any day the entire organization could end up in the bunker with Fred. A contingency plan went into effect in which new men whom Fred did not know were enrolled and our functions distributed to those who would stay on in the event we could not. Every time Fred was taken for interrogation someone would carefully observe him in an attempt to guess whether or not he had broken down.

One day, I was standing in the doorway of the hospital, opposite Block 11, when Fred was brought back from interrogation. He was always closely guarded by two Gestapo men who watched to see if he would try to communicate with someone. He saw me standing there and probably guessed how anxious all of us were because he smiled at me. Then, when he was handed over to the SS guard from Block 11, he managed with his handcuffed hand to give me the thumbs-up sign.

We also received reassuring messages from Fred through some prisoners who worked in Block 11. He would not betray

147

anyone.

He knew eventually he would be killed and to shorten his tortures asked for a cyanide pill to be smuggled in. Unfortunately he was so well guarded even his food was tasted first by another prisoner. The Germans were determined to keep him alive hoping that sooner or later he would crumble under pressure. We had to get him out of the bunker and into the hospital, and typhus provided our only means. Several infected lice were sent to Fred and in spite of the fact that he had organized for himself an inoculation when he worked in the hospital, he came down with the disease. He was immediately transferred to the hospital, SS guard in tow. The doctors were told to save his life at any price.

No matter how impossible it appeared, we decided to spring Fred from the hospital to arrange his final escape. About that time, the Germans had begun the practice of tattooing the forearms of newly arrived prisoners with their identification number. Old prisoners, however, were difficult to round up and a great many of us still went without one. We planned to put someone else's corpse in Fred's bed with his number tattooed on the forearm.

But the Germans were one step ahead of us; they ordered Fred tattooed for the very next morning. We had to do something before then.

The number was painted on Fred's forearm with tattoo ink simulating precisely the standard print for a real tattoo punched with needles. Next morning, when the Gestapo men went to call the prisoner who usually did the tattooing, they were shown it had already been done and left satisfied.

In the meantime Fred's illness worsened. It was the second week; he was delirious all the time, had lost a lot of weight and was difficult to recognize, even by his closest co-workers. We expected the disease to reach its crisis at any time and, still hoping we could put our plan into action, selected every day one fresh corpse to be substituted for him. Unfortunately, or fortunately, when the crisis came Fred died.

In January and February arrived several transports of Jews arrested in Holland, many of whom were diamond cutters or diamond dealers. They were sent directly to the gas chambers and their belongings searched very thoroughly, of course, in "Canada" by the Germans. Nonetheless, some of this wealth still found its way into the camp.

With such a great number of German marks and American dollars in circulation, food prices on the camp's black market skyrocketed. The cost of a loaf of bread was, at one time, $1,000 U.S.

The tannery also received its share. Odd pieces of leather goods arrived: broken down suitcases, torn belts, unmatched shoes. To salvage some of the leather, we tore out the linings only to find diamond rings, U.S. dollars, or U.K. pounds sterling, usually in large denominations. To remain in the tannery now became more important than ever. With Germany starting to feel the impact of food and clothing shortages, we had fewer skins to tan and had to invent work to keep our jobs.

The steer skins were tanned in large, cemented, rectangular holes in the floor. They were about four metres wide, six metres long, and two and a half metres deep. The skins were nailed to and hung from logs seven metres long which were placed across this tank, submerging the skins completely in tanning solution. Because of the shortage of skins we arranged fake tanks — empty but for the covering logs from which hung short strips of skin, to give the impression the tanks were full. Under the log facade was something akin to a small room, unlikely to be discovered. Out of some unspoken sense of defiance, we started to use this place to play bridge.

Someone in the hall kept watch for the SS guards, but we were once almost caught in the act through our own carelessness. Three of my bridge partners were heavy smokers and our little room was always filled with a gray-blue cloud. One day, in the middle of a game, we received a signal that the guard was approaching. We sat very quietly, listening to the steps of Karl and the SS man coming our way. No sooner had the steps stopped directly above us than we heard the SS man say to Karl: "Look, there's smoke coming out of this tank! Something must be burning! Remove those skins!"

Karl knew we were there. He also knew that, as foreman, he ought not to have tolerated it. Somehow he had to save the situation.

"That ain't smoke from burning, sir . . . that's acid solution, it smokes when the skins are tanned. Make sure you don't breathe it."

Walking some distance away, he continued: "You see this tank here? There's no skins in it, you can even see the solution."

But the SS man was not convinced. He bent over our tank and we could see him from between the logs.

"Funny, but it smells just like cigarette smoke. If I didn't know this hole is full of liquid, I'd think someone were sitting down there smoking."

Bending lower and taking another whiff, he remarked: "And very good tobacco, too. Much better than we can get in the SS canteen."

"Actually, I do have cigarettes," said Karl, finally catching the hint, "from an old suitcase . . . we were gonna burn them. You would like one?"

The SS man accepted the cigarette. We heard the steps getting farther away and this time a more friendly tone of conversation drifted back.

One day, while finishing skins, I felt as if I were catching a cold. The routine work tired me and I sensed I had a small fever. It seemed a mere trifle, so I kept it to myself. We all knew very well we simply could not allow ourselves to be sick. I believe this frame of mind kept me healthy even when I was shivering in sub-zero temperatures, covered with wet snow and dressed only in my striped pyjamas, or fighting off hunger, skin disease and intestinal problems brought on by eating foul food.

But now, something was different. By the time we got back to camp I was burning with fever. It looked like typhus and Stan decided to take me to the hospital for help.

We saw Dr. Dering almost immediately. He took one look at me and said: "It's typhus all right. I must warn you, however, that if I admit you, you may end up in the gas chamber. The Germans are determined to stamp out typhus and are collecting patients every day."

"Surely," replied Stan, "you could admit him with some other disease, as you did with Thomas. After all, as the head doctor it's your diagnosis that counts. I understand the German doctors believe you explicitly."

Dering was not convinced. "I would like to do it for our organization, but Thomas was almost discovered and sent to the gas chambers. I had to stick my neck out to save him."

Then turning to me, he said: "If the Germans should discover that I'm covering for you, we'll both be gassed. I can admit you to the hospital with typhus, but I cannot take responsibility for your safety here."

I had never seen Stan excited about anything, but this time he completely lost his temper.

"You should not call yourself an officer! We are at war! You're in action and you behave like a coward! I know very well you can hide him and save a fellow officer's life! Whose side are you really on?"

At that moment German blockelder Bock walked in and demanded to know what the shouting was about. He was a kind man and probably would have done more for me than Dering. But somehow I felt that if I were admitted to the hospital, I would never come out alive.

"Just a friendly disagreement," I answered quickly. "In fact, we were just about to go. Good night to you both!"

I pulled Stan by the sleeve and we left the hospital.

"You don't know what you're doing," Stan said protectively after we had walked a short distance. "Bock would have helped and our members working there could have made sure you weren't shipped to the gas chamber."

He was now very concerned and kept explaining the situation to me: "You cannot stay in the block because it'll soon be discovered you have typhus. You cannot go to work, it's almost four kilometres one way. You need a place where you can lie down until you get over the crisis. Hospital is the only answer."

It was all perfectly logical, but somehow I had read more into Dering's words than was openly said. I felt strongly that going to the hospital meant certain death.

To convince Stan, I said: "Perhaps you are right, but I would like to reduce my time in hospital as much as possible. The shorter my stay, the less likely I am to visit the gas chamber. Let me see how long I can go to work before my strength gives way. Only the walk to work is going to be difficult. In the tannery I can either stay in the bridge room or climb on top of some sheepskins. You guys can cover for me."

Finally Stan agreed.

We had returned to our block and I climbed straight away into the top bunk. I tried to think how I might survive the typhus without medical aid or even a place to stay until the sickness passed. I could count on Stan's help, marching to and from work, and in the tannery I could find a place to rest. But simply overcoming the disease was a challenge I would have to face alone.

It helped to know exactly what to expect. I knew that men had died from sheer loss of strength, that first they ran a high temperature and then, at the crisis point, it would plummet to far below normal. If I could just keep my strength up, I might stand a chance.

From this day on I applied everything I knew. I drank as many liquids as I could. Stan looked after me like a mother. He always set aside an extra bowl of coffee for me, both at work and in the block. When we had no coffee at work, Stan boiled up some water. Though I had no appetite, I ate what I could in very small mouthfuls, chewing for so long the food almost dissolved in my mouth. I consciously tried to derive as much energy from every grain of food as was there. Finally, I applied the deep breathing techniques I had learned in yoga and sucked into my lungs as much oxygen as I could manage.

In spite of my high temperature I did not want to rest too much, feeling the urgency to move around. I even did my regular chore of finishing skins in the tannery. The distance to work posed perhaps the greatest problem. Every day of high fever weakened me further and I had to make a much greater effort to stay on my feet.

Near the end of the second week I somehow became accustomed to fever and it did not bother me as much, even while marching between the camp and the tannery. I also knew the end of my fever was very near. I discussed it with Stan and decided that if the crisis happened at work, I would fake a physical injury. In the meantime I took my illness so well I started to wonder if it might not be typhus after all. Stan borrowed a thermometer from the hospital and measured my temperature one evening. It was an unbelievable 42°C.

After work I was standing at the evening roll call when suddenly I felt very weak. I was covered in cold sweat, my head swam and my knees were so weak they began to buckle. I whispered to Stan, who was standing beside me: "I think this is it, the crisis. I can still stand but in case I faint, please look after me."

Stan whispered back: "You'd better lay down on the ground instead of struggling. You will feel better and when the blockelder and SS man come by, I'll say you fainted."

What a welcome suggestion! I let myself collapse to the ground, not caring much what anybody might think. After a while, I felt much better.

I saw the blockelder and the SS man walking down the line.

They counted me on the ground. As long as the number was correct, it was immaterial to them whether I were dead or alive. When the roll call was over everybody ran to the barracks for the evening meal, stepping over my body and not paying the slightest attention to my prostrate figure. Some prisoners following work were regularly in a horizontal position when the roll was taken. This was a new situation for me. Suddenly I felt frightfully cold and started to shiver uncontrollably. Fortunately Stan was still at my side; he helped me to my feet and we went into the barracks. I was still alive.

I recovered incredibly fast. Arrangements had been made with the blockelder for me to stay in the barracks for one day so I could sleep. I did, for hours. Next day I felt ready to walk to the tannery with my friends, though that first walk tired me much more than all other marches made while I was sick. I was extremely weak but Stan's kitchen of boiled cows' ears and stewed muskrats helped me regain strength rapidly.

The early months of 1943 brought on our clandestine radio the first good news of the war. The contradictory reports of the BBC and the German radio — both sides claimed victories in the war in Northern Africa — seemed finally to be clarifying themselves. All German news from Africa suddenly ceased and the British broadcasts claimed the enemy had been defeated. It was far away, but it still raised our spirits.

More directly affecting our future was news of the battle of Stalingrad. The German advance into the Soviet Union was finally stopped. The Russians had rallied and with great success. The victorious German army was defeated, at least in two places. We all sensed this was the turning point in the war. To the Germans, it was the point of no return. They had committed so many atrocities on the eastern front it was too late to change their policy. They had forced the Russians to fight and now the Russians fought back with a vengeance.

On our little front in Auschwitz, the local Gestapo was making every effort to wipe out our organization. In February 1943, twenty men, all belonging to the underground army, were arrested and kept in the bunkers of Block 11 for questioning. Fortunately, the arrested men were far removed from our command and thanks to Thomas's method, none of those interrogated knew more than five other men in the organization.

After a couple of weeks in the bunkers, two men were released and the rest executed. Naturally, we wanted to find out what questions had been asked and why these two released men had cooperated with the Gestapo. But in my view insufficient caution had been exercised in the handling of our affairs. I believed that very soon all of us would end up in a bunker.

Thomas was also displeased with the way his underground unit was functioning: it had grown too large to be manageable. Too many people had false ambitions to lead cloak-and-dagger conspiracies and, in the midst of this, political parties began to meddle, not for the good of the prisoners but for the dominance of one party over another.

After the battle of Stalingrad, the Socialist Party, with J. Cyrankiewicz emerging as leader, became more domineering, proclaiming itself to be friends of the Soviet Union and hostile to the capitalistic systems of Great Britain and the United States.

I also heard explanations as to why the Russians and Germans had invaded Poland at the same time. The reason, according to the Russians, was that Poland had been a fascist state and therefore presented the same threat as Germany.

"Why then," I used to ask, "would one fascist state fight another? Shouldn't we have been friends like Italy and not bitter enemies as we are now?"

No such logic would appeal to them. Voices branded all Polish officers as the worst kind of fascists, and since our organization was founded by officers, mutual distrust started to grow and cooperation between the military and political factions became increasingly difficult. We all felt in our bones the time was coming when we would each be found out, bringing to an end what until now had been very useful work.

Thomas decided to escape.

By this time the Gestapo realized we were not just a small group but many people, in all the camps, working together under the leadership of, for the most part, veteran prisoners. They decided to solve the problem in a new and different way.

We received news through our men working in the SS offices that several large transports to other camps were being prepared. These would consist mostly of "the low numbers." After the first list was prepared, the Germans realized the whole system of working squads would collapse since they had come to rely on the expertise of the long-time prisoners in groups such as surveyors, building trades, mechanics, carpenters, doctors and administrative staff. If these men were suddenly removed, total chaos would result. Thus, word got around that key people would be allowed to stay in Auschwitz to train new prisoners; all others would go.

On March 7, 1943, about 1,000 men were summoned at the morning roll call. I found myself again standing next to Thomas, both of us part of a group to be shipped to Buchenwald. We wondered how we could get out of this predicament. After further thought, however, I realized the transport presented no problem. I could not escape from Auschwitz as long as my wife would not leave our apartment; besides, life in Buchenwald might be easier and the journey there might offer an opportunity to escape.

Thomas, however, had already planned his escape from Auschwitz and thus sought to be rejected from the transport. All were to undergo a medical examination, so Thomas arranged for a hernia belt from outside. As soon as the examining doctor saw him he was immediately sent back to the camp. I was passed as fit.

The transport was to leave the next morning. In the meantime, we were locked in a separate barracks guarded by a couple of kapos. I felt utterly alone. All my friends were still in the camp and I was heading into the unknown. Although the transport, according to our information, was destined for Buchenwald, we could just as easily arrive at the Buchenwald gas chambers. The fact that the unfit were left behind made this probability unlikely. But then, the Germans were masters of deceit and many people before us had been lured to their deaths without suspecting a thing.

The evening roll call was over and the prisoners started back to their barracks. I sat at the window hoping that perhaps someone would come to say goodbye. I was almost resigned to the possibility of no visitors when I saw Stan trotting towards the barracks.

"Here, Stan!" I shouted. "In the window!"

He spotted me, came closer to the window and said: "I know a kapo who is at the door. I'll try to get in and talk to you. I also have something for your journey."

I was overjoyed to see him and wondered if he would manage to get through the door. But there he was, all smiles. He opened his jacket to reveal a large package.

"This is the last piece of a horse we've been eating for two months now. I guess you'll need it more than we will in the tannery.

Part II

BUCHENWALD &
SATELLITE CAMP ROSE

Previous page: Aerial view of Buchenwald Concentration Camp

CHAPTER 8

THE SHOOTING GALLERY

Escaping from the train proved impossible. Besides the usual SS guards "riding shotgun" on top of each freight car, all prisoners were still dressed in their striped suits. Even if I could escape, I had no hope of finding help or shelter among the German civilian population.

The train steamed through the night and at daybreak pulled over to a side line and stopped. Each of us listened to the sounds from outside, trying to guess where we were and what our fate might be. Voices shouted in German but did not sound as if they were coming from a concentration camp. After a while the train moved, then came to stop again. This went on all day while we sat in darkness, wanting desperately to know the reasons for these manoeuvres. Finally someone succeeded in pulling a large nail from the wall and with the help of others, made a hole big enough to look through. The reason for the constant delays now became obvious.

Long trains full of military equipment and troops laboured past on neighbouring lines, all heading east. As we waited, we tried to guess, without much success, whether this was a good sign or a bad one. Was a new offensive being prepared in Russia or were these reinforcements to bolster a dwindling German army? Whatever it was, those trains had priority and the prison train was required to give way.

Stan's coffee and meat were real treasures. I divided my provisions with the others, also veteran prisoners prepared for the unexpected, and they in turn contributed generously to the common pool.

In the morning the train, after standing on some siderails all night, started up again. It pushed and jerked forwards and backwards, moved slowly for a while, then came to a full stop.

We had achieved the final destination. Apparently the train was on a side line in Weimar, just outside Buchenwald, letting more military transports through. But this time the doors opened to reveal a row of armed SS guards with dogs and a clutch of kapos running around and bellowing, making lots of noise and commotion. The shouts were very familiar.

"Everybody out! Fast! Fast! Everybody out!"

The kapos were carrying clubs as usual, but with one big difference: they all wore the red triangles of political prisoners and I noticed they seldom used their clubs. The SS men, however, were doing their best to make up for it, generously applying the butts of their rifles, kicking the prisoners at every opportunity and letting the dogs bite those who did not move fast enough. But opportunities for the SS men to abuse us were few because we were all old hands, experienced prisoners. Quickly we fell into columns five abreast and advanced towards the camp along an uphill, winding road for about five kilometres.

It was an exhausting march. Kapos leading the column of about 400 prisoners had set the speed, forcing older and weaker men to fall back where the SS men and their dogs provided proper encouragement. We immediately recognized that a somewhat different system was in place for prisoners of Buchenwald. Here, kapos simply supplied the appropriate standard and the SS guards carried out the actual punishment.

Finally we reached the gate to the camp. The SS men stayed outside and the kapos, still shouting but hardly touching anyone, led us into the showers.

After showering I received a new uniform and a new number, 10688, but retained my shoes and belt. We were assigned to an empty barracks where the blockelder was German, yet bore a red triangle. He was very strict and obviously hostile to all prisoners, but still, he did not rush to beat us.

It was Sunday, our day of rest from work. After the swamps of Auschwitz, the high location made Buchenwald seem more like a health spa. We were on top of a high hill above Weimar, embraced by the beautiful Thuringian woods. On a clear day one could see a stunning panorama of pleasantly undulating countryside. Goethe had found inspiration here in peaceful, tranquil surroundings.

I walked around the camp with Kazik, whom I had known for

Roof-top view of Buchenwald

two years in Auschwitz, and we tried to assess our new situation.

"Did you notice the kapos and blockelder didn't beat anybody?"

"Yes indeed, it makes a nice change from Auschwitz. If we can find some Polish prisoners, perhaps they can tell us more about the place. Let's go along the main road, Kazik. There must be Poles around here."

We continued wandering around the camp until we came to two barracks which were separated from the rest of the camp by a barbed wire fence. The gate was open and nobody seemed to be about. Stopping in front of the gate, we hesitated and considered our options. Previous camp experience had taught us not to enter a place that stood separately, particularly one surrounded by barbed wire.

We were just about to turn around and leave when a kapo ran out of one of the barracks, shouting at the top of his voice: "Get out of here! Don't you know that prisoners are not allowed here? Get out of here fast, you bloody idiots!"

No further encouragement was needed. We ran as fast as we could in the opposite direction, soon finding ourselves amongst a small group of prisoners who had been watching the whole incident with interest.

"You must be part of a new transport from Auschwitz," said one of them. "Lucky you weren't spotted by an SS man. You'd go into those barracks and never come out."

The man was talking in Polish, obviously one of the older prisoners in Buchenwald.

"How did you know we're from Auschwitz?" I inquired.

"I heard a transport had arrived from there and that they'd all received low numbers belonging to prisoners who had died here. Your number, 10688, for example, is obviously not a consecutive one. Hundreds of thousands of people have passed through this place. A transport of Russians that arrived yesterday got numbers from 200,000 on up. I also heard you guys were working in 'Canada' and brought a lot of gold and American dollars with you."

"Yes," said Kazik, "I brought a gold watch in my asshole and it's still ticking. Do you want to hear it?"

"Very funny. I don't care what you have or where you keep it, but I do know that for some of those treasures you could buy yourself a good job. I'm not trying to pry, I'm just an honest businessman. For example, I can offer you 100 marks for your shoes and a decent pair in return."

I took an immediate dislike to the man and tried to get rid of him.

"Thanks for your generous offer, but for your information we have survived three years in Auschwitz and know what is what in a concentration camp. We're quite capable of taking care of ourselves."

The man appeared to be apologetic. "Hey, I'm sorry. Listen, my name is Joe, from Barrack 11. So I mistook you for a pair of suckers. No harm in trying, is there? Just keep me in mind when you need to make a deal or two."

Kazik seemed more tolerant of the fellow and his proposition. "It's okay, we're not offended. Only tell us what kind of precious shit the Germans keep in those barracks and how come the kapos here are so polite."

Joe's eyes darted around momentarily. "Well, maybe I could give you some pointers. But first let's get away from here."

We followed Joe down the road between another stretch of barracks where there was almost no traffic.

"You don't look like communists to me," he said, pointing to the surrounding barracks, "so for guys like you this place is off limits. These are hospital and convalescent barracks, for communists only. Others die there.

"This camp was at first ruled by criminals like in Auschwitz.

About a year ago the German political prisoners, all communists, managed to convince the camp authorities that the kapos were stealing from SS magazines and corrupting the guards. The commandant believed them and replaced them all with political prisoners. When the communists took over they killed almost all the green triangles in the hospital, in the convalescent wards, or simply poisoned them in their own barracks. The remaining few were framed for trying to escape or for conspiring with the SS guards. They and the framed guards were finished off in the gas chambers. I also heard your transport consists of Polish fascists and you may all end up like the green triangles."

"Shit!" exclaimed Kazik. "How do we deal with these animals?"

"Oh, it's quite simple. First, you don't call them animals. There will be many spies in your barracks who already have some information about your activities in Auschwitz. Now they'll want to fish out the fascist leaders among you. Just tell anyone who has ears that you're communists. Then you might be okay."

Such political intrigue seemed almost too bizarre and I silently questioned its validity.

"By the way," I remarked aloud, "you still didn't say what is in those barracks we were chased away from."

"That's a different story," he continued. "They say American and English pilots shot down over Germany on spying missions are kept there. There is even supposed to be a Polish spy who was parachuted to the Polish border. Prisoners who saw him say he was dropped by an English plane. If you get too close to those barracks, the Gestapo may accuse you of trying to communicate with spies."

Kazik was visibly upset by this rash of troubling news and wanted to put an end to the unpleasant conversation. "You're a real fairy godmother, you know that? Nothing but cheerfulness itself. May Allah dig crooked holes in the path of your life."

With these words Kazik bowed low, hands pressed together in the style of an eastern salute. We returned to our barracks in silence, contemplating the new situation and the best way to deal with it.

After roll call the next morning our entire transport was assigned to the heaviest work in Buchenwald, at the stone quarry. The brilliant sunshine and fresh air of Sunday had been replaced with a cold morning fog. On grey days the Buchenwald hill was all

The stone quarry

in cloud and on clear days the wind was often so strong and bitter that, with our thin clothing, it seemed to blow right through our bodies. Evidently, unpleasant weather was not exclusive to Auschwitz.

We were divided into smaller working groups, each with a kapo and SS man in charge. My group worked at widening a road leading into the quarry. We were given shovels, picks and wheelbarrows, and again, as in the first days at Auschwitz, experienced the rigours of hard labour. By keeping a sharp look-out, we soon learned where danger might come from.

On one occasion a shot reverberated through the quarry and a prisoner fell to the ground, dead. In Auschwitz, this was an uncommon occurrence — killing was generally done by the kapos, while the SS guards would shoot only escaping, or seemingly escaping, prisoners. Here, however, a man was shot for no obvious reason. At least, it appeared so to us at the time.

Later we learned that role-playing, or story-making, preceded such an execution. The story was made up by the kapo; he might send a prisoner to the other side of the quarry to bring back a pick, ordering him to do it on the run. A running prisoner could very easily be considered an escaping prisoner by an SS man in the mood for target practice. As a consequence, neither our group nor others fared well. At the end of the day we brought back to camp three dead colleagues.

The blockelder greeted us with a satisfied smile. "You didn't think fascists could be shot in a fascist camp, did you?" he commented snidely.

To most of the men this remark made no sense, but Kazik and I were reminded of Joe's words and alerted to their significance.

Some men who had received minor injuries while working in the quarry — superficial cuts from flying pieces of cut rock or a toe squashed under a stone — were attended to immediately by the blockelder. After the roll call he collected all the injured and took them personally to the hospital. We remembered Joe's warning about the hospital and anxiously awaited the return of our colleagues. Two were admitted for some kind of surgery, and two came back.

I asked them how the hospital was.

"There's no comparison to Auschwitz!" exclaimed one of the men. "They're all very kind here and no criminals among the personnel — all red triangles! They're concerned about how we're doing and asked a lot of questions about Auschwitz and about all of us."

"What did they want to know exactly?" inquired Kazik.

"Oh, nothing special. About my home, for example, my wife and children, and what I did before I was arrested. I just told them I was a family man, that I had been working as a bricklayer and was arrested for nothing, that the Gestapo just picked up hundreds of us off the street."

The other man, who had returned with his wrist neatly bandaged, had more to say: "They asked me similar questions but also wanted to know if there was a large number of Polish officers among our group. I said I was too young to know and nobody would tell me whether they're officers or not. I'd swear they know more about Auschwitz than I do. They also said we had a lot of courage to have a military organization in the camp. Is it true there was such an organization?"

Nobody answered his question, but it was now obvious to us that Joe's knowledge of Buchenwald was better than we had first believed.

Our transport had been separated from the other prisoners and the German communists knew somehow that our transfer from Auschwitz was an attempt to break down the Polish underground. This merely aroused their suspicions towards our group, leaving some of us with little hope of getting a better job or even of finding work at which we could be sheltered from the rain and cold.

Kazik decided he would volunteer to join the stonemasons in

the quarry, shaping rocks with a hammer and chisel into rectangular blocks for building material. Although a muscular fellow, Kazik was not used to physical exertion. He had been an "eternal student" at Krakow University, forever studying law. According to his own account, he paid his way through college by playing poker and bridge. Now he was mad at the rocks, at Buchenwald and at the whole world.

"This bloody hammer I got for my new job must have a mind of its own. Every time I want to hit the chisel, the damn thing comes down on my thumb!"

I looked at his hands. The blue of his thumb contrasted starkly with his raw and bloody knuckles.

"Why don't you come back to our general group?" I suggested. "We're not working that hard and as long as you apply the Auschwitz-type lookout, you can snatch a lot of rest during the day."

"No, Kon, I'm not about to let some kapo send me across the quarry to pick bullets out of the air. I've never played ball, I'm no good at catching!"

His persistence actually paid off. Sometime later he was transferred to the "advanced stonemasons" who had a separate barracks in the quarry where he could work under a roof while sitting on a stool. He became in time a genuinely skilled tradesman, one of a privileged group within the camp, and was the first among us to break away from the hard labour to which we had all been condemned.

Every day after work I hunted desperately for an opportunity to be assigned to an easier job. One evening I ran into Joe again. He listened patiently to my complaints, then took me aside.

"I know some of you guys have money. Perhaps not you yourself, but maybe one of your friends. I need some American dollars or other valuables with which I can bribe some Germans to get a better job for you. Bring it over to me tomorrow and I'll see what I can do."

As an afterthought, he added: "Tell me the number you had in Auschwitz, it may also help."

I replied cautiously to his claim I could track down money or valuables and was even more reluctant to surrender my number, but did so in the hope it might be of use.

"Good," said Joe. "You had a low number — you know how

to behave in a camp. Come and see me tomorrow. I'm sure I can find a kapo who can do something for you."

I still had the money Stan had given me in Auschwitz for exactly this kind of emergency and decided to put it, or a portion of it, to use. The next day I went to see Joe as planned.

"I found a friend more clever than I who managed to smuggle in some American cash. He said if I could also get him out of the quarry in the near future, he'd give me 50 dollars."

"Good work," said Joe, obviously pleased. "Let's go to the German barracks. I know a kapo who'd like to meet you."

I walked with Joe across almost the entire camp. Finally, outside the barracks, I was introduced to a friendly young German named Horst.

"Joe has told me all about you," he said smiling. "Come for a walk with me. I'm sure Joe will excuse us."

Joe immediately turned and departed. Horst and I walked on in silence. I did not know what to expect nor what to say.

Horst opened the conversation: "A few days ago I met one of your colleagues from Auschwitz. He told me that you were active in the underground army there."

I was startled by his directness, but having been briefed on the attitude of German communists to our organization, replied without hesitation.

"I don't know who told you that but I can say it's not true. I was never connected in any way with the Polish military."

"But you are quite healthy," Horst persisted. "How could you escape being called for military service? It was compulsory in Poland, wasn't it?"

"I did not serve because I was at the university studying engineering. We were exempt from service until graduation and the war interrupted my studies."

"That may be so," he assented, "but your colleague told me you had frequent conferences with Dubois in Auschwitz."

The extent of Horst's knowledge of Auschwitz surprised me — even such details as who was talking to whom. But I also knew this particular contact would not be incriminating in the eyes of a communist.

"Yes, that's true," I replied confidently. "I wonder who the man was who told you that? I did know Dubois in Auschwitz. He is much older than I, but I have great respect for him. He is a very wise man."

Horst merely smiled. Instead of answering my question, he kept asking more of his own. "What did you talk about with Dubois? I know that he belonged to the underground organization."

"I didn't know about his activities in any organization in Auschwitz," I answered quite truthfully. "He was my mentor on socialism. I think he must have been an important person before the war in the Polish Socialist Party. You see, as a student, I did not know much about political matters or ideas."

"In that case, I'm glad you're one of us. I was arrested by the Gestapo because I belonged to the German Communist Party. After the war all socialists and communists will build a new world."

This was not exactly what I had meant but I did not try to correct Horst. Inasmuch as I had admired the socialist ideas of Dubois, communism to me represented the Russian system, which I knew quite well. I had been under Russian occupation for several months in late 1939 and had seen with my own eyes how the Polish population had been terrorized. My parents had been arrested by the Russians and sent to Siberia solely because they belonged to the Polish intelligentsia.

While in Auschwitz I heard that the Russians had executed about 4,000 Polish army officers in the woods of Katyn, just because they were officers. During the last stages of the Polish campaign, when we were retreating east from the German assault, I was taken prisoner of war by the Russians and could have ended up in Katyn with the rest of my colleagues.

Thus I was very sceptical about Horst's equation of socialism and communism and could not restrain myself from expressing it to him.

"Do you know anything about Russian communism? It does not seem that it has anything in common with socialist systems or with your ideas of communism."

"That may be so to you, but communism is still in the process of evolution and continues to have many opponents, particularly among the remnants of the Russian intelligentsia who are quite obviously enemies of the proletariat. The party must endure great hardship and fight many battles before a true communist system can really be enjoyed."

Not satisfied, I pressed on: "Have you heard about Katyn? All those Polish officers shipped to Russia as prisoners of war and all of them shot in the back of the head. The Germans exterminate Russian prisoners of war in concentration camps, but the Russians were first to perpetrate the crime. I know some people claim that the Katyn massacre was carried out by German SS troops, but how is that possible? The Germans claim they discovered the mass grave and are now using it as their main anti-Russian propaganda. So who do you think is responsible for this crime?"

"You should not call it a crime before you know all the facts!" exclaimed Horst, visibly angry at my question. "Polish officers are all enemies of the proletariat! They've all been indoctrinated to fight communism and socialism! None of them can be re-educated to work for the good of their country! They're clearly an anti-revolutionary and anti-socialist element that must be destroyed!"

At that moment I was glad Horst did not know I was also one of those "evil elements." I adopted again the role of the naïve student, anxious to hear Horst admit that the Katyn atrocity was the work of the Russians.

"Then, in order to avoid any future problems those officers might cause, the Russians had no choice but to eliminate them as a kind of preventative medicine?"

"That's it, exactly — preventative medicine. I see you finally understand. The Russians are committed to liberating your country from fascists and to establish in their place a true and just proletariat society."

My conversation with Horst brought even more to light the attitude of the German kapos towards our transport and that they intended to apply their own brand of preventative medicine to us. Knowing some Polish officers and intelligentsia were among us, but not knowing who they were, posed a problem to which there could be only one simple solution — eliminate our whole group.

This was my first exposure to the powerful manoeuvrings of political parties. I would never have believed different political views were sufficient to cause people to kill others. Yet, now I found myself belonging to a group which, because we were not communists, was considered by some in the camp to be as much the enemy as the SS guards.

My feigning may momentarily have won Horst's approval, but it seemed the impression did not last. I never got a better job and Joe never came to claim his 50 dollars.

After my talk with Horst I decided to stay away from him, and from Joe. It was too dangerous. Sooner or later the truth would come out that I was an officer and a member of the underground army in Auschwitz, and hence an enemy of the proletariat. I did not ask whether any better jobs were available in the camp and decided to blend into anonymity with the other prisoners. I knew how to survive in a crowd, which presented considerably less risk than high visibility.

Buchenwald differed from Auschwitz not only in respect to its kapos. It had a bigger canteen with a larger variety of goods available to prisoners. On certain days one could even buy food. The problem was, we had no German currency to purchase anything.

One morning when Kazik was very depressed and the both of us were feeling quite hungry, I decided to do something about our situation.

"We need money," I told him. "Maybe its possible to exchange some of my American dollars for German marks."

"But we don't know anyone we can trust," said Kazik. "I'd forget about Joe, particularly as he introduced you to Horst. How much do you have? Maybe I can ask around to find out if such a transaction is possible here."

"Let's see what we can get for 50 American dollars."

Kazik was a far more outgoing person than I and could talk to just about anybody, about anything, making friends almost instantly.

The next day he reported his findings. "I've been talking to a guy I played bridge with a couple of days ago. He's also a poker player and has loads of money. He said he can give us 75 marks for the 50 dollars."

"So you've found some gamblers here already," I said, pulling a $50 American bill out of my belt and handing it to Kazik. "The amount he's offering isn't much, but we have no choice."

Kazik took the money and left immediately, disappearing for the entire evening. Just before curfew he returned, very excited, and climbed onto the top bunk with me.

"There you are," he said, handing me a wad of bills, "150 German marks."

"How did you do it? Why did he give you more?"

"He didn't. We played poker and, of course, I won. I tell you, this place is full of suckers. I'll double this money again tomorrow."

Though elated by the return on our investment, I was not in the mood to take further risks, especially if none were necessary.

"We need food, Kazik. What if you run out of luck? I'll visit the canteen tomorrow and get us something to eat. If you want to continue playing, why not take just your winnings?"

"Kon, you do not understand. Winning does not depend on luck. When I win, I win big. When I lose, I lose very little. This is ability, not luck. Just you wait — we'll be living like kings!"

Kazik was as good as his word. He would play cards anywhere at any time with anyone. And he was winning. After about a month, I no longer knew how much money we had and we were no longer hungry.

Through his card-playing friend, Kazik managed to get transferred from the stonemasons to the stone sculpturing group. Although he had no artistic ability, he made friends quickly and secured himself a good position.

I was still, unfortunately, with the general working group swinging a pick or pushing a wheelbarrow. The kapo was more tolerant towards me, probably because he had seen me talking to Horst. When my group got larger I was given the responsibility of keeping count of the loads delivered to the stonemasons and the number of prisoners working among us.

Our morale soared when we watched the sky to see squadrons of American or English planes flying overhead. More and more such flights took place near the end of 1943 and barely a day would pass by in which the air raid alarm did not sound. One day the whole quarry stopped to watch the raid on Jena, only 10 or 20 kilometres away. There must have been thousands of airplanes flying, wave after wave, covering the whole city with bombs. After about an hour we could see only flames and dust. The city no longer existed.

My own experience during the Polish campaign of 1939, when the German Luftwaffe had dominated the skies, had convinced me of the decisive power of air supremacy. I realized now that the Germans had lost their superiority in the air and therefore were very soon going to lose the war. In spite of Germany's many successes, we had been living continuously with the hope that sooner or later the Nazis would be defeated. Now it was a certainty, and I could justify my own hopes of coming out of this war alive.

The next raid boosted our morale sky-high. It was on Buchenwald itself.

I was inside the camp that day. I had been assigned, with a small group of other prisoners, to repair the roads in the main portion of the camp. First we saw a small airplane circling above the camp at quite a low altitude. The sirens did not even announce its presence. The plane made a large circle of smoke directly above us, dropped a smoke flare through its centre and left. We were not sure whether it was a German plane or one of ours.

Not long after the alarm was sounded. We still did not think Buchenwald would be bombed, believing the location of the concentration camps to be well known in England. But what came that day surpassed our wildest dreams.

The first wave of planes came in at a very high altitude. Then we heard the whistle of falling bombs and the whole area where the German SS troops were stationed exploded at once. Though the barbed wire fence of the camp was next to the German barracks, not a single bomb fell inside it. Then came the second wave and it blanketed the southern part surrounding the camp where the SS supply barracks were located. Prisoners stood in the middle of the camp not even trying to take cover, so sure were they that the allies would keep them from harm.

The German guards all left their towers and ran to the bomb shelters. Even the kapos took cover, evidently not trusting the American pilots. A third wave came and its bombs crashed down on the eastern side of the camp, into the woods where many SS men had run for cover.

Then it stopped. We looked around, but no guards were in sight. Moments later the unbelievable happened. Through the open main gate came wounded SS men supported by their prisoners. I saw two men, one in uniform and one in stripes, both wounded, stumble into the camp together arm in arm, propping each other up. Exterminators and their victims were now suddenly united in the face of common danger.

The camp management was not pleased. By the next day the commandant had put an end to the fraternization and everything had returned to normal.

Within a few weeks the entire incident seemed to have been forgotten. The political friction between the prisoners did not change; Buchenwald communists still tried to exterminate our transport and the SS guards were back at their regular duties, shooting prisoners at every opportunity.

I was still working in the quarry and for the first time since my arrest I developed a cold. It persisted for two weeks and I could not shake it off. By the third week I had started to cough, lost strength and felt feverish, especially in the evenings. After having been through typhoid fever, a cold seemed nothing to worry about. But when I began to cough blood and felt pains in my chest, I came to the conclusion that somehow my cold had evolved into pneumonia.

There was still a risk in being admitted to the hospital and I found myself in exactly the same position as when I combated typhoid in Auschwitz. I had no choice but to go to work, although the quarry was not the best place to convalesce. The aspirins Kazik bought me from the black market provided some relief, but I knew that winning the battle depended primarily on my own resources. Fortunately a crisis or absolute necessity always generated in me unusual inner strength and fighting pneumonia proved no exception.

I meditated again, trying to direct all my energy against the disease, and at every opportunity exercised deep breathing in order to absorb as much energy from outside as I could. The weather did not cooperate; it either rained or the whole camp was in clouds. But my condition started to improve. Using a 50 dollar bill from my belt, I asked Kazik to get me anything nutritious he could find in the canteen or buy on the black market. Again I chewed my food very thoroughly to derive from it every last bit of nutrition.

In time my inner strength won out, as it had once before.

Meanwhile the second transport of prisoners from Auschwitz arrived at Buchenwald. As soon as they had emerged from the admitting rituals, I went with Kazik to see whether any friends were among them. Several men, all from the penal company, had been separated from the rest of the group for transport to some satellite camp to do extra hard labour. In this group I recognized Jan, who had arranged my first job with the surveyors. He had also been a member of our organization, which made me all the more anxious to talk to him.

We took Jan back to our barracks, treated him to some food from the canteen and a cigarette, and began pumping him for the latest news from Auschwitz. Naturally, my first question concerned

Thomas and the organization.

"Shortly after your transport left for Buchenwald, Thomas escaped," Jan said, savouring the cigarette. "He must have known it was too dangerous to stay any longer. Too many slip-ups, the Gestapo knew too many names. After his escape they arrested 30 people, all belonging to the organization and occupying leading positions."

"Stan Kazuba and Henry Bartosiewicz," I said, anxious about my friends in the tannery, "were they arrested too?"

"Strange you should ask," Jan replied. "For some reason Stan was not arrested and Henry was the only man released from the bunker. All others were eventually shot. Henry said he was released because someone paid off the Gestapo with gold collected from Jewish belongings. There were ugly rumours circulating about these two guys."

Knowing both men well, my immediate reaction was defensive. "Stan would never cooperate with the Gestapo. He's much too honest and kept too low a profile for anyone to associate him with our group. That could be the reason why he was missed. As for Bartosiewicz, I'm not sure. Although he'd talk to almost anyone who would listen about his work in the underground, the story of buying his way out of the bunker isn't very believable."

"But I heard it from many people," said Jan. "I was also told the tannery had tons of gold, even more than 'Canada.' Surely he had lots of opportunity to organize some there."

"You're mistaken. I worked in the tannery and know that every bit and piece of leather had previously been searched by the more experienced fellows in 'Canada.' They could find anything, even stuff hidden in the most unlikely places, whereas we found precious little.

"Also, Henry was too concerned with impressing people to make many friends. I can't imagine anyone risking his life to bargain with the Gestapo for Henry's release, even if that were possible — which I highly doubt. The Gestapo had all the trump cards. They would have taken the money, then killed both Henry and the one who delivered the ransom. Remember Fred Stoessel? If anyone was in a position to raise money or gold, it was him. As you know, he died while in custody."

Although upset about the news of my friends in Auschwitz, I found some compensation in my no longer being there. Unlike

Thomas, I could not have escaped without endangering my wife and may very well have ended up before the firing squad.

Next day, following evening roll call, I went with Kazik to visit again the new arrivals and to renew my talks with Jan. We found him in the company of three other prisoners engaged in a very animated discussion. As we approached, a tall, strongly-built fellow who had seen us with Jan the day before turned to us directly, displaying a mixture of fear and anger.

"Maybe you guys can tell me what's going on here. You see, I was sent here with my friend Adam — both of us served together on a merchant ship for ten years and know each other like brothers. Anyway, when we're going through the showers, we seen this SS officer standing there with a young woman. Here we are, all bare naked, while this broad looks us over without blinking an eye. She's not bad looking either, so naturally Adam winks at her. She smiles and winks back, then says something to this SS officer. So he takes Adam aside, says something to him and out they go through some side door."

The man paused, noticing that the others were listening, and shook his head. "That was three days ago and I ain't seen Adam since. Just what kind of monkey business is this?"

Everybody laughed and one man remarked: "I heard there's a whorehouse here, but I didn't know they were selecting their clients. Maybe the Germans now have special units for SS whores!"

Kazik could not resist adding his own quip to the general speculation. "It seems your friend must possess some special features that led her to select him over you."

The man maintained his grave expression. "I don't give her the wink, that's all. I just hope Adam ain't got himself into trouble on account of this whore."

We left the sailors conjecturing on the details of Adam's encounter and spent the rest of the evening with Jan, engaged in our own debate over recent news from the eastern and western fronts.

The following day, a Sunday, I decided to accompany Kazik on his regular trip to the poker table, curious about how the big game was played and what kind of people were playing it. Among those in attendance were two Dutchmen, a Frenchman and several Germans, one of whom held the floor by telling amusing stories with the flair of a professional comedian. It turned out he was a professional actor arrested for impersonating a famous Austrian

Karl Koch—Deputy
Commandant of Buchenwald

fighter pilot, the most decorated man in the whole of Germany.

"I procured for myself an air force colonel's uniform with all the proper accoutrements," he informed us, "then sent a telegram to the mayor of Vienna, notifying him that I would be arriving there on holiday. The mayor had arranged a glorious reception at the railway station. A band was playing, children presented me with flowers, several officials made speeches praising my bravery, and the most beautiful girls of Vienna competed for my kisses.

"The mayor offered me a suite in the best hotel in Vienna for the duration of my stay, which I accepted on only one condition — that I receive the same rooms Hitler had occupied when he visited the city. All my wishes were granted, which left me with a very busy week. I attended several banquets in my honour, accompanied the mayor and other city officials to an opera, and also visited a hospital where wounded soldiers from the eastern front were treated.

"One day, however, I myself was visited by the Gestapo and that brought down the curtain on my performance. They evidently failed to appreciate my thespian abilities and sent me to a concentration camp. No sense of humour whatsoever!"

Inspired by his story, other men in the group began, in turn, to tell their own amusing incidents. Among them was Kazik, who found this an ideal opportunity to relate the episode of Adam and the woman who winked at him in the showers. After he finished his story, however, nobody laughed.

"What the hell's the matter with you?" he asked, looking about him at the blank faces. "Do you need a professional comedian to entertain you? Am I not good enough?"

An awkward silence followed, eventually broken by the actor who now spoke in a very serious tone.

"My guess is that you are a newcomer. Otherwise you would know that the woman inspecting the naked prisoners is the wife of the camp's deputy commandant. She thinks of herself as a great artist. As a matter of fact, she possesses in her home quite a collection of lampshades made of human skin. They say she selects men with tattoos that appeal to her taste and calls her work creative art.

Ilse Koch — wife of Deputy Commandant Koch

"I am sorry about your friend," he concluded, "but I expect that by now he is a part of her creations."

The story was so macabre that when we related it to the sailor, neither he nor we could accept it as plausible. It was inconceivable to us that the wife of an officer — or any woman, for that matter — could perform such an atrocity. Unfortunately, the story proved

Lampshade and other items made from human skin

true and Adam's tattoo is still on display today in the museum at Buchenwald.

On Monday I returned to my work in the quarry. There was more bad news. Our kapo had been transferred somewhere else, replaced by a German communist who had no qualms about beating prisoners. I retained my duties as recording clerk for our working group, which gave me more opportunity than the others to talk to the kapo. The new man firmly believed all of us were fascists and thus due for extermination.

One day we found him in an exceptionally bad mood. "You bloody fascists!" he shouted. "You may have been bosses in Auschwitz but here in Buchenwald your time is over! I'll see that you all end up in the crematorium!"

Thinking that he was perhaps genuinely misinformed, I attempted to appeal to his logic.

"Mister Kapo," I said, addressing him as he desired, "we were never bosses in Auschwitz. The green triangles were in power there just as they were some time ago in Buchenwald."

"All political prisoners were united against the fascist SS," he retorted. "I know all about you guys. You're part of the Polish intelligentsia and therefore enemies of the proletariat. This is clearly spelled out in the Gestapo files. I know about you especially — given the chance to become a good socialist but instead attacked the Soviet Union and its policies. I'll deal with you later!"

There was no point in arguing further. To continue would only increase his anger and endanger us all. Instead, I devoted my efforts to keeping a scrupulous count of the men and to recording the work they produced. The others were also careful to avoid giving him an excuse to attack us. However, our attempts to placate him proved futile.

On Saturday, just before work finished, the kapo turned to me and announced that I was to check every working group in the quarry to see how much they had produced.

"I want to know how their efforts compare with our own," he said.

We all knew this was a dangerous assignment. To walk around the quarry was like parading in front of a shooting gallery. But I pretended not to suspect any foul play.

"It's almost the end of the day," I said, "and we should have one more load of rocks ready. Allow me to help them complete this

178

task, then I'll check on the other groups before we leave for camp."

The kapo looked at me with a sly smile. "You're afraid to do what I asked for fear of being shot. Well, this time you're wrong. The SS guards on duty today are not the kind who shoot prisoners. Nevertheless, every day from now on you will inspect these working groups, never knowing when a trigger-happy guard is looking for a day off in Weimar! And you will start Monday."

I returned to camp very depressed. Kazik shared my concern.

"Somehow we have to find you another job. This kapo is no doubt a killer and should be taken seriously. Tomorrow is Sunday and we will spend the entire day, if need be, to get you out of this working group."

Sunday morning brought yet more bad news. Someone had stolen my belt with the $1,000 in it. Prompt investigation traced the theft to four men who were working as carpenters and also engaged in a side business, making wooden sandals with leather straps, which they exchanged with other prisoners for food. We pressed them hard, but no threats and no amount of persuasion would induce them to return the stolen belt.

Then Kazik applied bribery. "Accepting that none of you stole it, I'll offer 50 marks to the man who finds my friend's belt," he told them.

It worked. By evening one of the men collected the reward and handed over the belt. But upon examining it, my worst expectations were confirmed. The lining had been cut open and the money was gone.

Kazik's efforts to find me another job were also unsuccessful. We had done everything possible, but on Monday morning I was faced with marching back to the quarry with my group.

We were working at our usual place when, just before noon, an SS guard and another man visited us. The man, a German prisoner, asked us to stop what were doing and assembled us together.

"I am the foreman of the factory at Weimar," he said. "It is a metal manufacturing plant and we need more skilled men there — toolmakers and machine tool operators who have at least 15 years' experience in the trade. Is there anyone in this group who meets these qualifications?"

Without thinking twice I raised my hand. The foreman looked at the rest of the men, but nobody else volunteered.

"Where did you work previously and what were you doing?" he asked.

I was completely unprepared for this question. The only machine tools I had ever seen were in pictures, and one year of studies in mechanical engineering was no qualification at all. Still, I could at least talk with some degree of sense about engineering problems, perhaps enough to get out of the quarry and away from the threats of my kapo.

"I am too young to have 15 years of experience but I worked as a machine operator in a Warsaw tractor factory for the last eight years and am quite skilled."

The foreman seemed pleased and I suspected he had found few qualified men.

"I am glad you are honest," he said. "If you can do the work, you'll have a very good job. But if you lied to me, you'll wish you had never been born."

CHAPTER 9

SLAVE LABOUR AND RELIGION

I returned to camp with the foreman and three other prisoners.

"I don't care what you are—fascists, communists or common criminals," the foreman told us as we trudged out of the quarry. "All I'm interested in is your ability to stand at the machine tool and produce your norm as set by the engineers.

"From now on, you'll have a roof over your head and will receive extra food from the factory, provided the management decides you deserve it. In short, consider yourselves lucky. Working there is as near freedom as you'll likely get. The camp is only a place to sleep and nobody here has any authority over us. Tomorrow you will spend all day in Weimar."

Once in the camp we were shown to a separate barracks reserved for prisoners employed at the Gustloff Werke factory. For the first time I found myself isolated from my Polish compatriots. My new companions, two of them Dutch and one French, were from the penal company. The Frenchman introduced himself as André and although he spoke no German, he had no difficulty following my limited high school French. My understanding of him proved a different matter, particularly as he broke into a lengthy monologue about himself and his situation within the camp. From what I could discern, his story sounded surprisingly similar to mine.

"I thought I was done for. The SS guards were shooting us for sport and I knew that eventually we would all be killed because we had each belonged to resistance movements. One day we're condemned men and the next day they send us off to a factory to make bombs or whatever for their war effort. But they won't get much work out of me. I had barely finished my apprenticeship as a machine tool operator when I was arrested."

He was so happy to have escaped the penal company and so pleased to have someone to talk to, he did not mind that I understood only every other word. The two Dutchman spoke perfect German but were more private and talked only to each other.

At about noon the foreman called upon me and André to accompany him to the camp kitchen to organize some food. We waited outside while the foreman collected together the supplies — two small kettles, one containing soup and the other coffee, two loaves of bread, half a kilogram of margarine and some beet root marmalade. The food was enough for ten men and we marvelled at his ability to organize it. Back at the barracks, he declined his portion and passing the food to the four of us, watched us devour it in a matter of minutes.

The foreman then declared a rest period and announced that one of us would have to stand or sit outside the barracks to keep a look-out for any SS man who might happen that way. The two Dutchmen volunteered while the foreman, André and I went to our respective bunks. Even for a veteran prisoner like myself, this was a new situation: to be allowed to sleep in the middle of the day without fear of punishment. But I could not sleep, nor could André who lay in the bunk beside me. Not having a common language in which we could express our thoughts and feelings, we lay silently next to each other, contemplating our own affairs.

For me, the bliss was only temporary. Tomorrow I would have to prove myself as a machine tool operator and then the truth would come out. I could see myself taking André's place in the penal company. On the other hand, the situation in the quarry had become very dangerous; I had had no choice but to assume the risk of volunteering for the factory work. The decision was made and worrying about it provided no advantage. Consoling myself with this thought, I was about to fall off to sleep when André, still wide awake, decided to attempt another conversation.

"What are you going to do after the war if we survive it?"

"I don't know. Perhaps finish my studies in mechanical engineering. After that, I suppose I'll get a job somewhere in Poland."

"What if the Russians occupy the whole of Poland? What would you do then?"

I pondered on the question for a moment, attempting to imagine that such a thing were possible. But my mind was geared towards more pleasant thoughts.

"I don't think the Russians can succeed. The Polish government is still intact, as is the Polish army now based in England. The Americans and English would never sell their best allies to the Soviets, particularly as the war started in defence of my country."

"You are very naïve, Kon," André chided. "Politics is a dirty business, everybody looks after their own interests. They call it patriotism. We have seen a lot of it in France. Our Vichy government cooperated with the Nazis even though they occupied France and arrested and killed thousands of Frenchmen. Meanwhile De Gaulle sits comfortably in England thinking he will become the next Napoleon by doing nothing. Only a small fraction of the French people are in the Resistance for the love of France."

"Maybe so," I replied, dejectedly. "But if I can't go back to Poland, I don't know what I will do."

As if struck by a sudden idea, André sat up in bed and said excitedly: "I know what we can do, Kon. Nobody is likely to appreciate the service we have performed for our countries. So when the war ends, we should go to some German port and confiscate a yacht on behalf of the former prisoners of Buchenwald. I've always wanted to sail around the world. We'll take it to France, stock up on good wine and then set out on our travels. What do you say to that?"

Although I had never sailed in my life, the idea sounded pleasant enough. Perhaps too pleasant, considering our circumstances.

"I think we should first concern ourselves with contacting our families. My parents are somewhere in Siberia and my wife — God knows where she is now, or even if she's still alive."

His enthusiasm was undampened. "Well, all right, let's agree then that if we are separated, you will come to see me in France. I live in Creteil, near Paris. It's a small place and you should have no trouble finding me in the telephone directory. After the war all members of the Resistance should be well known throughout France. We will have our own private glory and as for me, I'm sure I will have a yacht."

I appreciated André's musings. They allowed me to renew my ability to daydream about the future, an activity that not only provided an escape from the dread of reality but helped considerably to preserve one's sanity.

Escaping Hell

The working day in Buchenwald spanned 12 hours — from six in the morning to six at night, when the first working groups began arriving back at camp. Prisoners employed at the Gustloff Werke in Weimar, transported by truck to and from the factory, usually returned to camp about an hour after everyone else, delaying the evening meal. I decided to visit Kazik during the interim to share with him the day's developments. He had expected to see me return with the group from the quarry and was naturally worried about what had happened. My story only made him more anxious.

"I'd be surprised if you could pull it off, Kon. I only hope they give you an easy job to start. And as for the penal company, it seems as rough here as it was in Auschwitz. You'll have to rely on your instincts now more than ever."

The next day the entire block to which I was assigned was awakened an hour before the rest of the camp. There was not, however, the usual rush, swearing or pushing by the blockelders or other camp authorities. New to me as well was the attitude of my co-workers who behaved in a very business-like manner. Perhaps because of the mixture of nationalities — most of the men were either Russian or German, but also among us were Italians, French, Dutch, Czechs, Poles and Yugoslavians — practically everyone occupied himself solely with preparing for work. Unlike the regular working crews, who looked upon their jobs in terms of survival, these factory men moved about with some sense of purpose and actually thought about the nature of their work.

As for me, I was dreading my first encounter with the machine tools and found the other men's confidence extremely disturbing. The fear and loneliness I experienced was much greater than any I had felt, even when faced with more imminent danger. Often, on those occasions, I had been one of many exposed to the same threats. Now I was both alone and vulnerable.

The road to Weimar was very picturesque, winding down the hills and through an old forest; however, its beauty that morning completely escaped me. Everyone sat quietly in the truck thinking his own thoughts and this apparently grim mood made a deep impression — I imagined they all knew the disaster that awaited me at the factory in the valley below.

Finally we drove through the barbed wire gate and into a part of the factory separated from the rest of the buildings by a high fence punctuated with the familiar towers for the SS guards. We emerged from the trucks without anybody shouting the usual "Out! Out! Go! Faster!" All but four of us disappeared into different buildings while we waited by the truck for further directions.

Moments later, the foreman who had recruited us appeared and led us into a large hall full of men and machinery. The place was so noisy it seemed inconceivable that its occupants could think, let alone carry on a conversation. The air was thick with smoke from burned oil mixed with steam. My eyes had barely adjusted to the dim and dingy surroundings when the foreman stopped and summoned us towards him.

"The first job is very simple!" he shouted at the top of his voice. "On a lathe! Who wants it?"

Taking his estimation of the work at face value, I quickly raised my hand.

"You come with me! The rest of you wait here!"

We walked between rows of machine tools, each operated by one prisoner who worked alone; no other foremen or kapos were anywhere in sight. Near the end of a row stood an unoccupied lathe. Here the foreman bent down, picked a shiny piece of steel from a box on the floor and held it in front of me.

"This is the part you're to make," he announced over the deafening crash and clatter of machinery. Then pointing to my left, "And these are the steel bars from which you machine it. More will be supplied when you run out."

He then pointed to several gauges lying on a table. "Check every part. If it does not fit, put it aside. Do not mix good parts with bad ones. It is considered sabotage. Too many rejects — that's also sabotage. I will be back to see how you're doing."

I held the part handed to me by the foreman, not even knowing which end of the machine it came out of. I stopped him just as he was about to leave.

"This is a somewhat different machine tool from what I've worked on. Could you maybe make one piece so I'll be able to see how different it is? I don't want to start turning out rejects."

He accepted my request, not only to save his own neck in the event I made mistakes, but as a chance to boast about his skills on each and every machine in the factory.

"That's why I'm a foreman. Unlike the kapos, who know nothing, I'm a skilled tradesman."

He then stepped up to the lathe, pressed the starting button and went through the motions of making the part from a round, two metre-long bar. My eyes were glued to the machine while he continued to advise me on the factory's chain of command.

"The civilian master who runs this place — he's the guy to watch out for. A very important person in the Nazi party. To him, any mistakes are sabotage, clear and simple."

As he talked, a metal piece dropped down on the tray below. He picked it up and showed it to me.

"Now you must check it so that this gauge goes through — like that, and this other gauge should — oops! It's too small!"

The foreman looked about him, then quickly pocketed the spoiled part.

"The bloody man on the night shift didn't have the machine set up properly. Can you set it up? Or maybe I should show you how."

I never in my life paid as much attention to anyone as I did then. Although the foreman's big body often got in the way, I did my best to memorize all the motions of his hands and the settings of the dials. The next part he produced was correct.

After confirming its dimensions, the foreman turned to me and said: "That is how it should be made. Now go ahead and do it."

I stepped up to the lathe, pressed the starting button and attempted to duplicate everything the foreman had done, setting the dials to the same numbers, turning cranks left and right, and pulling levers in their proper sequence. The lathe responded with strange screeching sounds as the cutting tools moved across the revolving steel bar. I watched it with my heart beating louder than all the noise around me, anticipating the inevitable disaster when the whole machine would explode into thousands of pieces. It appeared to me I had done something wrong, because it took at least twice as long for the part to drop with a sharp "clung" onto the tray. The foreman, who had watched me from behind, picked up the part and measured it with the gauges.

"As long as you make them like that, you'll be all right. Don't be so nervous about it — you've done a good job."

Without waiting for an answer, he turned around and walked away. I just stood there, my heart still trying to leap out of my throat. After a few moments I decided to examine carefully what it was I had done to produce this part. I repeated all the motions without actually machining the metal, simply to see what happened when the levers were moved and the dials turned. I was so engrossed in this examination that I did not notice a fellow operator, whose lathe was back-to-back with mine, watching me with great interest.

"I guess you don't have a clue as to what you're doing," he remarked, peeking out from behind his machine. He spoke half in Polish and half Ukrainian, presumably as a result of seeing the letter "P" for Polish on my red triangle.

The man's face startled me, for his large mouth wore a smile from ear to ear that seemed to register more gaiety than malicious glee at my misfortune. The face was Asiatic, with high cheek bones and small brown eyes set wide apart. In the middle was something that might once have been a nose before it was broken.

"Keep going, you're doing just fine. The foreman will likely let you know how productive you are."

His carefree attitude took me completely by surprise. It must also have been infectious, for I suddenly felt less anxious about my hasty apprenticeship. Guessing the fellow to be a Russian prisoner, I introduced myself in the Russian my mother had taught me as a child, informing him that although my father was Polish, I had actually been born in Kiev.

"No joke!" he said, bursting out in loud laughter and clapping his hands on his knees. "I was also born in Kiev. Only I'm supposed to be a good communist while you grew up to be a good capitalist!"

His reference to politics immediately returned me to my predicament: that my life depended on my performance on the lathe. I turned back to the machine, continuing to trace the effect of my memorised operations. When at last I understood how the mechanics worked, I had forgotten the settings on the dials to make the part fit the supplied gauges. Cutting bit by bit off my steel bar to make it the proper shape, I was startled again by the Russian's voice.

"I'm sorry I laughed, but don't you think it's strange that we're from the same city? Don't worry about the lathe, I will show you how to become an expert at it. My name is Ivan. If you'll step to one side —"

He wriggled his small frame between myself and the machine and began making a part, occasionally turning his head from side to side to make sure the foreman was nowhere in sight. As he worked, he marked the settings on the dials with ink pencil. In the meantime I looked over at his own table where sat a variety of complex machine parts, tools and jigs, as well as blueprints that were little more than simple sketches.

His skill on the machine amazed me. In what seemed a matter of seconds he had produced a part that conformed perfectly to the foreman's specifications. He then explained to me, patiently and logically, how to repeat what he had done.

"Now if you'll excuse me, I should get back to my station before someone notices. If you have any questions, just give me a shout."

Ivan went away and I worked steadily on, making part after part with more and more confidence. I did not even notice the foreman and civilian master standing behind me watching my performance.

"At this speed you won't make your norm," said the master, interrupting me from my work. "Foreman! Check how many rejects he has!"

The foreman motioned me to one side and applied the gauges to each part I had set aside on the table.

"All good, sir."

The master appeared satisfied. "All right. But watch that he improves his speed or he'll be out of here."

With these words he walked away, followed by the foreman. I had passed my first test.

The morning went by so quickly I was surprised to hear the siren announcing the mid-day break. No sooner had it sounded than the hall was suddenly silent, as if the whole world had come to a stop. Only then did it occur to me that one could grow accustomed to the pandemonium that usually filled the place.

Ivan appeared from behind his row and called to me: "You are now a skilled machine tool operator. When you learn some more, you will find out how really difficult it is. Come, let's eat. I'd like to introduce you to some of my friends."

A short distance away a large group of Russian prisoners of war were talking to each other. Two men separated from the group and came to meet us.

"Where did you get this Pole from, Ivan?" inquired one of them. "Have you learned to speak Polish as well?"

Ivan's friend obviously resented me, though this was not surprising. The Russians generally did not mix with other nationalities and were even more reserved towards German communists, despite their political affinity. Most striking was their distrust of everyone, including their own colleagues.

Ivan disregarded the remark. "I would like you to meet Konstantin. Imagine, we were both born in Kiev and he is Polish and I'm Ukrainian! He still speaks Russian, not like Soviet Russian, but much better. I must tell you how he started work here — you won't believe it!"

"Later," remarked the other man, who was busily cleaning and trimming his fingernails. "You have not yet introduced us."

"Ah yes — my comrade Volodia, our resident aristocrat," said Ivan, flourishing his hand toward the tall, handsome-looking young man who had just spoken. His appearance was indeed aristocratic, enhanced by his fair skin, blue eyes and long, sensitive fingers. Both Ivan and Volodia were graduates of a technical college with diplomas as technologists.

"And this is Misha," he continued. "He looks like a pretty girl, but I can assure you he isn't or I'd have made love to him a long time ago."

Misha was a little taller than Ivan, had a dark complexion and large, black eyes shaded by enormously long eyelashes. With full-shaped lips and dimpled cheeks, he probably would have been troubled by the camp homosexuals were it not for his excellent athletic abilities, especially in boxing. He had been a circus performer in the Soviet Union but, thanks to Ivan and Volodia who had taught him technical skills, had managed to secure a job in the factory.

"I wouldn't talk, Ivan," answered Misha. "You're so ugly, even an ape would not make love to you."

The banter was obviously made in good humour, for the three of them seemed a closely knit group within the Russian pack. I liked them almost instantly and only hoped they would accept me as a friend.

By this time the food was ready and we all stood in line holding our bowls. The servers filled them with what looked like some multi-coloured stew.

"Snails again!" Volodia remarked, disgustedly. "Anyone want my portion?"

The boiled snails, a French delicacy, had been shipped from occupied France and were therefore easily attainable. Their manner of preparation, however, was very haphazard: the cooks had simply boiled them in water without even bothering to wash the sand from them. Only a few men tried to eat them; in spite of the fact that we were hungry, the majority of us merely nibbled a bit and disposed of the rest down the drain.

I was naturally disappointed and asked Ivan if this was the extra food we had been promised.

Ivan was less choosy than his colleagues. He had just finished his bowl and had already started in on Volodia's portion.

"Just imagine that this is a good Ukrainian kolbasa, stewed by a German cook according to the best recipe of a French chef. We only get specialty dishes like this when the Germans bring their bounty from another country and find they don't like it themselves. The other day we had real Russian kasha. After that meal my belly was twice its size."

He stuck his stomach forward, patting it with loving tenderness.

The break was now almost over, so Ivan and I started back to our machines.

"You know, Kon, if you haven't any friends here, you're welcome to join our group. In fact, there's a vacant bunk in our corner of the barracks."

"I'd like it very much," I replied, touched by his offer. "But there's a French fellow with me who has no one to talk to and he's sort of stuck with me. My French is poor, but I seem to be the only one who speaks a word of it. We came here together from the stone quarry."

"I understand — your French friend wouldn't enjoy our company. Of course, there's the language barrier, but I think our behaviour may also be too confusing for him."

By the time we got back to our stations the siren sounded again to announce the end of the break. I continued to teach myself the techniques of lathing and even began to produce a sufficient number of pieces to meet my norm. It was then that disaster struck — the tip of one of my cutting tools broke off. I immediately turned to Ivan for help.

"This is what I meant when I said a simple job is not that simple," he advised. "But don't panic, there's a wrench on the table beside your lathe. Remove the tool and come with me to the grinding stone. I'll pretend that I also have to grind my tool, then show you how to sharpen yours. If no one's looking, I can also teach you how to set it back in the lathe and get the machine going again."

This was not the last time Ivan rescued me from serious trouble. Throughout the next several months he not only trained me on the lathe but on several other machine tools. His initial warning proved true: the more I learned, the more difficult the job became. Fortunately, his talents as a teacher were matched by my ability to learn. During my stay at the Gustloff Werke, with Ivan's help, I was to hone my skills into those of a genuinely competent machine tool operator.

Noticing that André was busily talking with a fellow worker, I decided to accompany my new Russian friends on our trip back to camp. We met up again in the supper line, but he had no thought of joining me with his meal.

"Imagine, Kon, I have run into a man from my home town! Must go — I still have to get caught up on the latest news."

Without waiting for a reply André rushed away, eating his soup while he walked. I was somewhat relieved for I was also in a hurry to report to Kazik on my latest activities. At that moment he appeared in our barracks, equally anxious to hear how I had fared at my first day on the job. When he saw me eating my dinner, however, he knew all had gone well.

"So, how did you con them this time? Someday they're going to catch up with you and your tricks and that'll be the end of the little magician. I predict you're going to finish your career high above the crowd — hanging from the gallows."

I then told him the whole story of Ivan and his friends.

"I wouldn't trust those Russians if I were you. You can see what the communists are doing to this camp. Remember what the Czeches used to say about them in Auschwitz — the only good communist is a dead communist."

"I neither know nor care what Ivan's political views are," I replied. "He saved me from the penal company and I've learned enough from him to convince the foreman that I'm a lathe operator."

"Please yourself. But keep your eyes open and don't tell them too much about yourself. The main thing is that you're now working indoors and safe from those gun-happy guards."

He then asked me to be his partner at the bridge table, an

invitation I considered both a compliment and a chance to wind down from the day's tensions.

Kazik was quick to enlighten me. "This is no compliment, Kon. Face it, you're a lousy bridge player. But maybe there's some hope for you yet."

That evening there was no more talk about the dangers of the camp, kapos or SS men. We instead enjoyed each other's friendship while Kazik fed me with last minute instructions on the finer points of bridge.

Within a few weeks I had fully adapted myself to life at the factory. My mechanical aptitude helped me in learning to operate most of the machine tools — a task made easier by the fact that we were mass producing standard pieces. I had also moved to the Russian corner of the barracks where I was quickly accepted as a friend.

The Russians considered me a novelty and I was often the subject of their curious inquiries. Under Stalin's rule, the Russian people lived in complete isolation and were led to believe that the Soviet Union was a paradise compared to the rest of the world. They were told that outside of their country was hunger and starvation; only a few people lived well and the masses of workers were treated as slave labour. Though they suspected it could not all have been true, they wanted me to reassure them that much of it was propaganda.

Volodia was more curious than the others. "Is it true that in Polish stores before the war anyone could buy as much bacon as he wanted?"

"Of course," I told him, trying to satisfy his curiosity in the best possible way. "We always had plenty of bacon, not to mention ham, all kinds of sausage, lobsters, butter, sour cream, a large variety of cheese — all you needed was the money to buy it."

"Aha!" exclaimed Ivan. "So not everybody could afford to buy those things, is that right?"

"Some things, like lobsters or Swiss and Danish cheeses. But bacon, eggs and cottage cheese, for example, were affordable by everyone."

We then compared wages and what an average worker could get with them. It was a revelation to me that skilled men like Ivan and Volodia had to spend more than a month's pay for a new suit, provided it was available in stores at the time they wanted to buy it. Misha, on the other hand, found it particularly difficult to believe that Polish stores carried such luxuries as wrist-watches and radios.

It was then my turn to ask questions. "Tell me, Ivan, what rank did you have in the army and how was it you were sent here?"

Ivan disregarded the question and rose from his stool as if he were dismounting a horse. "I just remembered, I'd promised to see my friend Pietrov in Barrack 14 and it's already quite late. Kon, would you like to join me? Pietrov's a nice guy, you'll enjoy meeting him."

I agreed and the two of us set out across the camp. Neither of us spoke a word for some time. Finally Ivan broke the silence.

"I didn't want to answer you in front of the others. There are many things you'll probably never understand about the Soviet system. One is that nobody trusts anybody — for good reason. The only way to better your standing with the Party is to report something bad about your closest friends. That serves as proof that you value the Party above all else. It's sad that, for this reason, I trust you more than I do my Russian friends, with the exception perhaps of Volodia and Misha.

"The story of how we became prisoners is very shameful. If I told this story in the Soviet Union, I'd be writing myself a one-way ticket to Siberia. But we've had a lot of frank conversations with you and somehow I feel you should hear everything, not only about myself but also about life in Russia both before the war and when it started."

There was no urgency to see Pietrov. We sat on some stones in a far corner of the camp where we would not be disturbed.

"My father," Ivan began, rubbing his upper lip to expose the large gaps between his teeth, "was an ordinary, unskilled factory worker. I'm not even sure he could read or write. Anyway, during the Revolution he met Trotsky who, as you likely know, was the leading Bolshevik with Lenin. My father worshipped the man. When the Bolsheviks took over the country my father became a very important official in the Party.

"You must also know that Stalin and Trotsky did not get along with each other. At that time such disagreements were quickly solved by firing squads. Trotsky had to escape from the Soviet Union and when he did, the hunt started for all of his former supporters. No matter how dedicated a Communist you were during the Revolution, if you'd been a friend of Trotsky you were now an enemy of the proletariat. All of them, including my father, were shot. Executions were a daily routine in those years — many friends of our family were killed and even my mother lived in terror for her life.

"During Stalin's rule the terror continued. Every man in our country recognizes Stalin as a ruthless murderer. Did you know that he has declared any Soviet soldier taken prisoner by the Germans a traitor and doomed to execution when the war ends? You now see our position — none of us have much to live for. After the war we'd either have to stay in Germany, living subhuman lives as German slaves, or return to our country to be shot by our own people."

Ivan paused briefly to stretch his legs. The joviality by which I had come to know him had all but disappeared. In its place was a grave determination to present his story as accurately and convincingly as he knew how.

"Not long after our graduation, the war with Germany broke out and both Volodia and I were drafted into the army. There was no time for real military training. The Germans were advancing deep into Russia so fast that after only two weeks of drill, our unit was dispatched to the front lines.

"I must tell you that during those first months of war, there was no panic among the population. Nobody was afraid of the Germans. In fact, people were so sick of Stalin and in terror of the secret police that we actually looked forward to the German occupation. The whole Ukraine met the German army with flowers. The mood in our unit was the same though none of us could say anything about it. For every 50 men there was one Politruk assigned to spy on each of us, including the officers. Those who were not fully loyal to Stalin had to be executed on the spot."

To me, this was direct confirmation of the German news we had received when the invasion started. I found particularly surprising, however, the hostility Ivan spoke of toward Stalin, which somehow did not jibe with the later efforts by the Russians to stop Hitler's progress and push the German army back into Germany.

"How can your people be so solidly against Stalin and the Communist system, and at the same time fight so successfully against the Nazis?"

"Ah, well, the answer isn't as simple as you might expect," Ivan explained. "Let me finish my story and then you'll understand the whole situation much better.

"When our division, consisting of thousands of men, was captured by the Germans near Kiev, we tried to tell them we'd had enough of Stalin, that we didn't want to fight but simply wished to go home. Our interpreters explained to the German officers the situation in the Soviet Union and assured them we were not their enemies. Some of the officers believed us and preferred letting us go to having to guard and care for such a large group of men. But the authority rested with the SS officers, a breed no doubt similar to our Politruks. So we were instructed to wait until the next day when the SS men arrived and we were marched to a nearby canyon to camp overnight. The Germans posted guards all around us, though we told them this was unnecessary — we were full of hope and had no intention of escaping. They gave us no food or blankets, but left us to sleep on the bare ground with empty stomachs.

"The following morning a car arrived full of German officers wearing swastika bands on their arms and escorted by two armoured cars mounted with machine guns. One of the officers climbed on top of an armoured car and addressed us through a megaphone. He said we would soon be set free but before going home, we should surrender to them all Politruks and officers among us.

"The Politruks were immediately turned over to the SS while our officers gave themselves up later of their own accord. Evening came again, the guards stayed at their posts and still we had no food or water. Some of the more desperate among us tried to escape or steal food from the German soldiers. Sounds of machine gun fire echoed throughout the night from all sides of the camp. By morning almost 100 men had been shot dead or wounded. But the Germans still did nothing to feed or free us. That was when our small group, including Volodia and myself, decided to try our luck escaping.

"Needless to say, luck was with us. After getting clear of the canyon we hid in a village the Germans had burned almost to the ground. The decision to escape had been a good one. From our division, only a handful of half-dead men were marched out of the canyon to be shipped to concentration camps. The rest either died of hunger or were gunned down because they were too weak to walk.

"That canyon, Babi Yar, hadn't seen the last of the Germans' atrocities. Once our men had vacated it, the SS units found it a convenient place to execute Jews. We heard later that whole families, including women and children, were brought there and gunned down into ditches they had been forced to dig for themselves."

In the pause that followed I explained that much the same case applied to pre-war Poland: "After the Molotov and Ribbentrop agreement made Poland the common enemy of Russia and Germany, we were attacked from both sides. Polish Communist Party leaders became both feared and despised by many of my countrymen for pointing out the intelligentsia to the Soviet secret police. Thousands of Polish families were sent to Siberia. Among them were my parents."

Ivan listened with a puzzled look on his face. "But we were told that the Polish workers asked us to protect them from the invading German army. My God, Kon, we considered ourselves a liberating army!"

"That's also what the Polish population was told," I replied. "In actual fact, it was a proper war on both east and west borders."

Ivan lifted himself from his rock and stared into the distance, his small, crooked frame quivering with excitement. "That bastard Stalin is guilty of so many crimes," he suddenly blurted out. "I can tell you that if the Germans hadn't been so cruel, we'd have all gone home and stayed there. They could've marched through Russia without firing a shot. But they forced us to fight for our land and our families. That's why Volodia and I re-enlisted. The war did nothing to make us love Stalin, but it sure taught us to hate Hitler."

"These German communists in camp," I said, reflecting on my friend's story. "If they are truly as loyal to Stalin as they claim to be, why wouldn't the Politruks and officers among you reveal themselves to them? Surely they'd have a more comfortable stay here as a result."

Ivan glanced quickly at me and I noticed for a brief moment distrust in his eyes, so typical of all Russian prisoners. He then broke out laughing and plopped himself down beside me.

"German communists! They think their brand of communism will be different. But you wait — not all of them are so naïve. Some have already picked up on the basic principles of our system: surrender with blind and uncritical obedience to the decisions of the Party and by terrorizing others, make sure they do the same. What they haven't yet learned is to understand us, the people who have really lived under this system. They think, for example, that all Russian prisoners of war are communists. They refuse to believe that Stalin considers us traitors because we surrendered to the Germans instead of fighting to the last man. So how likely are they to believe what our officers or Politruks tell them?"

The bitterness of Ivan's words moved me. When the war is over, I told him, he must come and live with me in Poland instead of returning to the Soviet Union and risking his life further.

Ivan smiled sadly and thanked me. "I believe, Kon, the Germans are about to lose this war. But let's hope it's not to Stalin, otherwise there will be no Poland for you to return to."

It was getting late. On the walk back to our barracks, we stopped to visit Ivan's friend, Pietrov, a man in his late 40's. Ivan did not call him by his first name, as was customary in the camp, but introduced him to me as "Mr. Pietrov." The man was well-built with broad shoulders, an intelligent face and a friendly, open smile.

I was impressed by our meeting and on the way out asked Ivan if he was one of the Politruks or a senior officer in Ivan's unit.

Ivan did not look surprised at this and said: "I would not introduce you to a Politruk. I have not met one whom I could respect. Pietrov was my commanding officer and unlike most officers, not a Party member. The others rose in the ranks because of their politics, Pietrov because of his intelligence and integrity. I respect him for those qualities."

The next day at work Pietrov's name was not mentioned. Instead Ivan, Volodia and I entertained ourselves by challenging each other with mathematical and logical puzzles. We would give each other a puzzle in the morning, then see who would be the first to solve it during the day. With the monotony of our work on the machine tools, we found such mental gymnastics highly stimulating.

I was struck by the quality of their puzzles — especially the ones dealing with physical principles, at which I considered myself quite good. Twice Volodia managed to stump me with deceptively simple questions.

"Since clouds are little drops of water and heavier than air," he posed, "why don't they fall down?"

When the day passed and I could not produce a satisfactory answer, he explained that as the droplets evaporate, their weight decreases faster than their resistance to air.

"You see? Cube versus the square of the radius."

I was completely fascinated and begged Volodia to give me another one.

"All right, Kon. Tell me by tomorrow: Why is it cooler in the mountains and warmer in the valleys?"

Again a day passed and when again I failed to come up with an answer, Ivan came to the rescue.

"It seems to me that the warm air rising from the valleys cools and expands when it reaches the mountains. What do you think?"

The tedium of factory life was broken in the fall of 1944 by a major staffing upheaval. The Germans no longer had enough civilian workers on the two night shifts and decided instead to run the place with concentration camp prisoners only. The entire factory was surrounded with barbed wire and living quarters were built right on the grounds. All the prisoners from Buchenwald who had been working at the Gustloff Werke and the same number of additional skilled men from other camps were moved there permanently, a welcome change for all of us. Now we were totally removed from a system whose only purpose was extermination. Outside, barbed wire, towers and SS guards with machine guns still surrounded us, but inside the camp no kapos and no internal organization existed to threaten our lives.

The real danger came from our allies. Air raids occurred almost every night. When the siren sounded, the civilian foremen ran to the bomb shelter, the lights were put out and we were left to sit on the floor beside our machines, waiting for the bombs to drop. On these occasions, Volodia, Misha and I would go to the end of the hall, near the door, to be closer to a possible escape route should the bombs start falling on our heads.

Because we were at the factory at all times, we now had the opportunity to discover what was being manufactured there. One day as Ivan and I walked alongside the barbed wire to the end of the factory buildings, we spotted the final product of our labour. Several neat rows of anti-tank guns stretched across the yard.

"So this is what it's all about," I muttered to my partner. "What can we do so that these guns won't fire?"

Ivan quickly took me up on my suggestion. "Let's look around our hall tomorrow and try to identify the parts we're making. Maybe we can improve on their design."

The part that proved easiest to recognize was made on my own machine. It was a vertical shaft, obviously the one around which the gun rotated. The dimensions of the shaft were precisely controlled with fixed gauges and checked by the civilian inspectors.

Many years later I appreciated the ingenuity and excellence of Ivan's knowledge of engineering when I remembered what he advised.

"We cannot change the dimensions, we can only change what isn't being checked by the inspectors. Do you see the radius you're making where you've decreased the diameter of the shaft? Instead of a radius, make a sharp notch there. The principle is much the same as when you use a scriber on glass to get it to break at a certain point. The moment the gun is fired, the shaft is subjected to a shock. Let's hope that when this gun starts shooting, its shaft will fracture and the barrel will fall off."

From then on, everybody who worked on my lathe received special instructions on how to machine this shaft "properly."

The other sabotage, almost impossible to discover, was my invention. André worked in the next hall where a small steel foundry was located. There he helped to manufacture a large steel casting, designed to support the gun during transportation. Mould design and metal casting were the only practical part of mechanical engineering that I had learned as a student and during my summer work in the foundry.

André was at that time a sort of prisoner-foreman and had access to all foundry operations. I met with him when we had time off and told him the gist of my plan.

André waxed enthusiastic. "Just tell me, Kon, what we have to do and I and all the French guys working with me will gladly help out," he chattered away excitedly.

Unfortunately, my ability to communicate in French was so poor it complicated matters beyond André's power to understand me. He then suggested that I come to work in the foundry for one night to show him what to do.

The following week, when both of us were on the night shift, André made the proper arrangements and in time my foreman came to see me.

"I didn't know you were an expert in castings, but so much the better. I've been told they could use the help. The master has agreed to let you go, but only for one night. We're also short of machine tool operators."

I walked over to the foundry and was given a tour by André of the various castings his group produced. My attention was diverted by one casting in particular that was about to be removed from its sand mould.

"Look there, André," I exclaimed, pointing to the casting. "Notice the big raiser, the lump of steel that's later cut off. It's that big because, as the casting solidifies, it shrinks and could leave holes inside were it not for the hot molten steel that flows into those cavities from the raiser."

"I understand all this, Kon. After all, I am the foreman here. What is it you want me to do with it? Remove it from the mould completely or just plug it up?"

"Neither. That would be too easily discovered. But when the part is being cast, you might drop a few pieces of cold steel into the raiser. That should solidify the raiser before the rest of the casting, leaving a hollow part in the chassis that will fracture more easily than a solid one. Once the casting is made, your pieces of steel will be melted down with the rest of the casting and no one will notice a thing. Anyway, let's try it."

In a couple of hours several moulds were ready for pouring. André and I collected a few pieces of steel in our pockets and began our inspections, dropping the scrap steel into the raisers as we went from mould to mould. By mistake, André dropped a very large piece into one of the moulds. I decided it was too large and immediately tried to retrieve it, but as we were bending over the mould we heard a voice behind us speaking in German.

"What the hell are you poking there for? Move aside and let me see!"

It was a civilian inspector. We had been so absorbed in our work that neither of us had noticed him walking our way.

"Who dropped this piece of steel into the mould?" he barked. "You know that this is sabotage and both of you could hang for it! Pieruny!"

I recognized the Silesian slang immediately. Pieruny means "thunder," a common swear word among both Poles and Germans living in the Polish part of Silesia.

My German was better than André's so I took over our defence. "Sir, we did not drop it in, we were trying to get it out. It seems to be lodged in the sand mould."

"Well somebody did and you as a foreman are responsible for

this sabotage!" the inspector shouted at André.

I decided to test the inspector's reactions in the hope that he would reveal his nationality. "It must have been one of those stupid pieruny working at the conveyor over there."

The inspector saw through my tactics and replied in Polish: "Do you think that because I can speak your mother tongue you can do what you like here? Get that steel out of there and watch it in the future!"

In the meantime the other moulds, also with pieces of steel in the raisers, were being filled with liquid steel. The inspector looked at André and at me, at the moulds once more, then walked away. Before the end of the shift, however, he was back again and ordered us to take the still red-hot castings out of the moulds, a procedure normally done on the next shift when the raisings had cooled. Obviously he suspected us of being up to no good, for which he himself might be held responsible.

He took out a hammer and started knocking on a casting around the raiser, checking it for soundness.

"You, pieruny," he said to me in Polish. "You seem to know a lot about castings. As long as you make them like that, it's okay with me."

He left me feeling completely baffled. Had we really deceived his trained ear?

In the morning, before going to sleep, Ivan asked me: "How did it go in the foundry? Did you manage to better the German war industry?"

I told him the whole story and Ivan nodded. "I know who you're talking about. He's here as a German but I suspect he's really Polish. He understood what my friends were saying in Russian about this factory and the Nazis. Had he wanted to make use of it, all of them would have been severely punished, maybe shot.

"I doubt very much that he missed detecting the hollow area in the casting, but as long as it didn't show, his own neck would be safe. With protection, people like that don't mind if someone else does the dirty work."

A couple of weeks later another event occurred that this time altered my destiny. One of the men returning from the hospital in Buchenwald brought a message from Kazik, who wanted to see me urgently. Kazik suggested I fake an injury to get into the camp for treatment as an out-patient. I knew it must be something important and set about preparing for my return up the mountain.

The next day I complained to my foreman of a nagging toothache. It was affecting my work, I told him, and therefore had to be pulled. This seemed to him a good enough reason to seek approval for my release, and within 24 hours I was riding with three other prisoners and an escort of SS guards in a small truck bound for the main camp.

The truck stopped at the gate where our guards received orders to return us there by 7 p.m. I immediately set out for the barracks to rendezvous with Kazik. Upon entering the building I encountered several men and the regular staff, but there was no sign of my friend. The blockelder, however, had been expecting me.

"Kazik is at work but will be back before your departure," he said. "In the meantime, he wants me to introduce you to a special visitor."

The blockelder then summoned from a corner of the barracks a strongly-built man of about 40 years old. I was impressed by his red hair, worn longer than allowed in the camp, which distracted me momentarily from his heavily lined though handsome face.

"This is Zigi, the campelder of Camp Rose. Perhaps you know him. He is also a Polish prisoner from Auschwitz."

The man greeted me like a long-lost friend, though I had no recollection of ever seeing him before. His behaviour was both self-assured and full of confidence.

"Come outside, Kon. I would like to have a talk with you. Kazik has told me all about you."

I reluctantly followed him through the door and into the sunlight, where he took me by the arm and led me across the grounds.

"So, I meet up again with a fellow Auschwitz veteran," he began. "My number was 2020. I think we were there about the same time, though I went through a deeper level of hell than you did. My last years, you see, were spent in the penal company."

All this sounded very strange to me. A Polish prisoner from Auschwitz and a former member of the penal company — now a campelder in some other camp. Top positions in the camps generally went to German criminals or communists.

He quickly picked up on my suspicions. "Of course, you no doubt wonder how I got to where I am. Ingenuity! That's what it takes to overcome all obstacles. My mind has been trained for it. Did you know I was chief editor of a Warsaw newspaper and have written many books? Most are detective stories, which is why I've such a good imagination for intrigue."

I stopped and for the first time stared him directly in the eye. "I suppose there are no kapos, criminals or communists at this Camp —"

"Rose," he assisted me. "As a matter of fact, a German criminal was the campelder there when I arrived. It did not take me long to frame him for stealing SS food and planning to escape by killing several guards. Naturally, I made sure I received all the credit for uncovering the plot. When I promised the camp commandant there would be no more escapes and no more stealing, he made me the campelder and had the German campelder shot."

Zigi was so visibly pleased with himself and his story that he seemed to forget why he had wanted to see me. I decided to remind him.

"Ah yes," he said, taking in a deep breath. "Well, Kazik informed me you are an officer and that you occupied an important position in the Auschwitz underground. When I became campelder, I decided that I should save prominent Polish writers and artists in my camp."

"I am neither artist nor writer," I replied. "So what do you want from me?"

"You are a veteran prisoner from Auschwitz. Only those of us who survived the worst in that camp understand life and can soberly size up any situation. Speaking of sobriety — can you make moonshine?"

My patience with this fellow was rapidly diminishing. "Surely this meeting was not arranged so you could conscript me to build a distillery!"

"Good moonshine in this miserable world where people have shit and garbage for brains is the only noble escape," he said, smiling. "Quite simply, I want you to come to work for me in my camp."

"And what would I do in your camp?"

"I wouldn't sneer. It is my camp. I do what I want there. The commanding officer is a dangerous lunatic but I know his weaknesses and by pleasing him I bought his full trust. Do you know that I can go to town in civilian clothing to shop, without an SS escort? Anyway, I heard from Kazik that you worked in the SS kitchen in

Auschwitz and are consequently a good organizer. I want you to be in charge of all food supplies to the camp, including special supplies for your campelder."

"In other words," I replied casually, "you want me to steal food for you from the SS. But wasn't the former campelder shot for doing just that?"

I continued before he had a chance to respond. "Listen carefully. I am now working in the factory at Weimar. There are no campelders or kapos. I am really out of the concentration camp system and the work I do is not too hard. One might even say it's interesting."

"So I've wasted my time trying to persuade you?"

"Let me think about it. When do you need an answer?"

"I was thinking of taking you and Kazik with me tomorrow," he said, running a hand through his hair. "But then I met here a great man whom I also want to take along. Do you know of a Frederick Jarossy?"

"The actor. Of course I've heard of him. Who in our country hasn't? He's Hungarian, isn't he?"

"Originally. But this guy's so talented he would stun you. And as charming off stage as he is on. What's more, he speaks Polish, German and French like a native. Do you know that he's studied literature at the Vienna university and philosophy at Heidelberg? Not only is he a brilliant actor, choreographer and stage manager, he's also extremely intelligent. I'm looking forward to having him in the camp to participate in our intellectual discussions."

"Who else participates in these discussions at your camp?" I remarked, making no attempt to hide the sarcasm in my voice. But Zigi seemed unperturbed.

"I think Polish history will remember me for saving the lives of these people. Among them, there's the great modern writer and poet, Jankowski, who is not useful for anything else in camp but expressing his opinions. He would have been dead by now if it weren't for me. Then there's a highly educated Jesuit, Father Martin. I like to tease him, but he's smart so I made him a camp writer. He maintains all records, something he's good at.

"Also Jan Groski, the best of all Polish criminal lawyers as well as a very fine bridge player. When Kazik and Frederick come, we shall have an excellent foursome. Oh yes, and our guest of honour, young Prince Andrew. I've taken care of him from the day we left Auschwitz. A little sprinkle of Polish aristocracy in our otherwise dreadful lives."

"An impressive list of people, but —"

"I, however, am the ultimate power there. None of these guys knows the first thing about life in concentration camps. That's why I need you and Kazik. You will take care of food supplies while Kazik looks after getting us clothing, shoes, building materials and furniture."

"Sounds interesting. But assuming we decide to go, how exactly do you plan to get us transferred?"

"I'll appoint Kazik responsible for the next transport to be sent to our camp, which I expect will be in two weeks. We're working on some sort of secret weapon — that's why we have top priority in the selection of prisoners."

He then turned and headed back toward the barracks where, while waiting for Kazik, I was forced to listen to yet more of his grand adventures and reminiscences of Auschwitz. Among his stories was a retelling of the mass escape of "red dots" from the penal company, only in his version it had been Zigi who had organized it and who had managed to survive because of his clever handling of the Gestapo.

When Kazik returned from work, I managed to find a little time with him alone before meeting the truck back to Weimar. Considering the impression Zigi had made on me, I was particularly curious why Kazik had elected to follow him to Camp Rose.

"I wouldn't trust this megalomaniac any more than I would a German campelder."

"Well, Kon, there are several reasons why we both should go. First, the camp is only 30 kilometres from the French border, meaning we'll be closer to where the invasion of Germany will begin — which can't be far off. Second, I'll be in charge of clothing, so we can have good civilian suits ready for our escape. And finally, I heard that the camp is poorly guarded, by old men in SS uniforms. Zigi needs us both and believe me, when the time comes to escape, he'll be the first to go."

I pondered briefly on Kazik's argument, which seemed to me a good one. "Zigi told me he's planning to send you for the second supply of prisoners. He also said I could come with you at that time.

By then you'll have a better idea of how things are there and either we both go or we don't go at all."

I was glad to see Kazik again. In spite of my good relationship with the Russians, I felt that here was a real friend. The trust between us was never questioned. I wished we could spend more time together, but the truck to take me back to Weimar was already at the gate. I said a hasty farewell and within an hour was crossing the factory grounds to my barracks.

Ivan, Volodia and Misha met me at the door, each anxious to know the real reason for my trip to Buchenwald. I avoided relating the whole story, unsure as I was about whether to leave my job at the factory. My friend Kazik, I told them, was to be shipped to a different camp and wanted to say goodbye — an excuse they seemed content with.

Life became routine again. Routine work and routine air raids. One night, however, we had a close call. My friends and I had been working the day shift and were bedded down for the evening. About midnight the alarm sounded. By then, they were so common we did not even wake up.

What startled us from our bunks was the sound of several deafening explosions. Grabbing anything within reach, we hastily dressed and ran outside. It was as bright as day. The first wave of bombers had just passed over, leaving the factory two blocks away a fiery inferno. The screams of wounded people bombarded our ears. Men escaping from the fire threw enormous shadows and to us looked like giants. Noticing the guard towers were unmanned, some of us ran for the barbed wire to escape the next raid. A burst of machine gun fire stopped us. The SS guards had built special concrete bunkers at each corner of the fence and were shooting through the wire at anyone who approached it. We had no choice but to return to our barracks to await further developments.

Then came a second wave of planes. Anti-aircraft guns opened fire from all sides and parts of exploded shells fell like rain from the sky. We decided to take shelter inside the barracks only to encounter large fragments of shells crashing through the roof, taking the lives of those unlucky souls caught beneath. Then the bombs fell. It seemed as if all reached the ground together, violently shaking the earth upon impact and clouding the air with dust and smoke. It was hard to judge what was being bombed, though we could see the fire from a neighbouring block licking the sky.

Disregarding the danger at the fence, several prisoners rushed towards it, some managing to open large holes through which masses of panicking people tried to squeeze out. Accustomed as we were to dangerous situations, Ivan and I opted to hold back and encouraged the men closest to us to await a better opportunity. No sooner had we done so than the sputter of machine guns reverberated through the night. The guards must have shot off hundreds of rounds, but surprisingly few prisoners took direct hits. It then occurred to me that this was intentional: as skilled labourers, we were a precious commodity to the Germans. Without us the factory would grind to a halt.

I stepped out of the barracks and shouted toward one of the bunkers: "Don't shoot! We're not trying to escape! We want to get out of a place where we could all be killed, including you!"

The guard stopped firing and obviously scared himself, shouted back: "These are my orders! What else can I do?"

I suggested that he allow us to walk in an orderly fashion and under his guard into a nearby field.

After what seemed an interminable silence I heard him order the other guards to cease fire and emerge from their bunkers. The next order he directed to us: "Come out one by one and walk near me to the hole in the fence! No running! Anyone who runs will be shot!"

We did as we were told and upon reaching the fence, climbed through one after another. Soon we were standing together in the field, guards and prisoners alike in dread of the next pass overhead and thinking foremost of survival.

One of the French prisoners knelt on the ground and started to pray aloud.

"What's he doing?" asked Volodia in a tone that suggested he had never before seen this kind of reaction.

"He's thanking God for saving him from the bombs," I answered.

"Why God? He should be thanking you. *You* persuaded the SS guards to let us out, not Him. The next wave of planes will probably wipe out our factory."

"Then he's thanking God for giving me the idea to ask the guards," I replied, "and for inspiring the guards to accept my request."

"Come now, you're an intelligent man, Kon. Do you really

believe this nonsense? If God is up there, it's easier for him to ask the English pilots to stop dropping bombs on us than to go through this complicated round of business. Besides, our own pilots who've flown above the clouds have told me they've seen no sign of him."

His questions not only seemed inappropriate to me, considering our circumstances, but tested my patience beyond its limit.

"Don't be stupid, Volodia. Wait until the next squadron flies over us. If they miss their mark, we may all find out in a hurry whether there's a God or not."

But we were spared that trial. Moments later the sirens sounded the end of the raid and we returned with our guards to the factory grounds. This time, however, we walked together as a group sharing our relief that the danger had passed.

On the south side of the factory we found even more fraternization among prisoners, civilian Germans and SS guards working together to put out a fire that had spread from the neighbouring buildings to one of the Gustloff Werke mills. The events of that night had so disoriented us that when we finally entered our partially damaged barracks and climbed back into our bunks, none of us could sleep.

Volodia was among the first to take advantage of our restlessness.

"Tell me, Kon, why you said I was stupid about questioning God's existence."

"I shall answer in your own words. You're an intelligent man, so how can you think the world outside of the Soviet Union, where people believe in God, could be so stupid as to expect to see him sitting on a cloud? Is that all you know about world religions?"

"I must admit it sounds primitive," he said apologetically. "But where, then, do people believe God is?"

"He's like a ghost," piped in Misha. "They can walk through walls, appear, disappear and do all sorts of things. My grandmother told me a lot about ghosts."

I was amazed by the naïveté of these people. Perhaps it was my recollection of the man fervently praying in the field that made me want to enlighten them. The story of Father Kolbe in Auschwitz seemed to me a good vehicle, but the point of his sacrifice escaped them. I then drew on a popular version of Einstein's theory of relativity, about which my father had lectured at the university, in an attempt to stress the limits of our intelligence in a multi-dimensional world. My lesson, however, merely prompted questions about my own beliefs.

"I am not a good example because I'm not a practicing Catholic. But I do feel that religion helps set standards for how people should behave, and in that respect is important to society. Without religion, what kind of values can you have?"

Ivan responded quickly. "In the Soviet Union, decent behaviour towards one's comrade is taught to children in kindergarten. Of course, the government abuses these standards from time to time — that is the nature of power. But look at the German people. Their brand of Christianity allows them to murder Jewish men, women and children by the millions without any sense of remorse. So much for their religious values."

As I faded off to sleep, I reflected on the recent news I had received of the Warsaw uprising. The Soviets had advanced to the eastern banks of the Vistula River, overlooking German-occupied Warsaw, and waited there. The Poles then used this as an opportunity to retake their capital and succeeded in holding it for a few brief weeks. In retaliation, the Germans redoubled their efforts and methodically destroyed the city, building by building. I wondered how many of my friends were among those captured or killed. Was my wife still alive?

There were several beautiful autumn days in 1944. When working the night shift, my companions and I spent as much time as possible outside enjoying the sunshine and Misha's entertaining acrobatics. Somewhere he had found a steel pipe for high bar gymnastics and his performances were so captivating, even the townspeople watched him from behind the barbed wire. He also taught Ivan, Volodia and me some circus aerobatics in which he performed the most difficult stunts, held high on a pyramid made up of his friends.

The performances were interrupted daily by air raids. English and American planes flew overhead day and night. Although they dropped no bombs nearby, the recent destruction of the neighbouring factory made all of us tense every time the sirens sounded.

In exactly two weeks time I received another message from Kazik to come to Buchenwald. I was still undecided about accompanying my companion to Camp Rose, but when the time came to visit him I knew I might not return to the factory. That evening, following a day of work, I decided to inform my Russian friends of Zigi's proposal.

My initial, brief announcement was followed by silence. They simply stared at me as if awaiting further explanations.

"There's a small satellite camp near the French border where some Polish prisoners have taken control from the German criminals. My friend has already been there for two weeks and most likely will want me to go with him to this camp. Of course, my decision depends a lot on what he has to tell me. We may find it preferable to stay in Buchenwald."

Misha was the first to react. "If there's a chance to escape from there to France, you should also arrange our transfer."

"I know very little about the camp," I replied, sensing again their innate distrust. "But if I do go and find I can get you there, naturally I'll make the arrangements."

After another period of silence, Ivan raised his hand from his lap and placed it on my shoulder. "In the event you do go, we wish you the best of luck. We will miss you."

The night wore on as each of us considered the possible outcome of my decision. Volodia was particularly supportive of abandoning the Gustloff Werke, arguing that eventually the factory would be wiped out with everyone in it. Again I assured them that I would do everything possible to obtain their transfer.

"But if for some reason I can't," I added, "when the war ends I'll come back to Weimar to join you and we will start a new life together — only not in the Soviet Union."

"I regret I won't be included," said Ivan, giving me a gap-toothed grin. "As long as my family and friends remain there, that's where I'll go."

It was now midnight. We exchanged a final round of farewells, then each departed to our bunks. In the morning I was to be on the truck to Buchenwald.

CHAPTER 10

ZIGI'S KINGDOM

I awoke early with everyone else but almost too late to meet my ride. Without washing or having breakfast, I rushed out of the barracks and towards the gate. The truck was already there, occupied by several prisoners. As the SS guards were about to raise the tailgate, one of them noticed me.

"Faster, faster! You lazy swine!"

With these words he came towards me and attempted to kick me in the rear, but I was running too fast. In one leap I was past the other guard and into the truck, supporting myself on the shoulder of a fellow prisoner.

"A good run," the guard sneered, "but not fast enough if you're thinking of escaping. My bullet would go faster!"

Both guards climbed into the back of the truck and ordered us to sit on the floor. They then took the side benches with their rifles pointed in our direction. After six months at the Gustloff Werke, I found their behaviour a rude awakening to the routine life of a prisoner and decided then and there to decline Zigi's offer. Better to take my chances of being killed by falling bombs than to endure again this treatment. I even regretted not sending a message to Kazik informing him of my decision.

Preoccupied by these thoughts, I was startled by the familiar shouts of "Out!" and "Faster!" when we stopped in front of Buchenwald's main gate. Jumping from the truck, we were each counted and had our numbers recorded by a guard before proceeding past the barrier. I had hardly set foot in the camp when I saw Kazik running to meet me. Our mutual joy at this reunion momentarily put out of mind all my resolutions.

"Let's go somewhere, Kon. I have so much to tell you, I don't know where to begin."

"Then why not start at the beginning," I replied, "for I also have some thoughts to share with you."

Kazik led me to a secluded area behind one of the barracks. I had no idea what to expect from him, but his first bit of news caught me completely off guard.

"I've arranged everything for your transfer to Camp Rose. We should leave Buchenwald about noon in order to catch the afternoon train."

"What are you talking about? Didn't Zigi and I agree that I'd have time to think it over? In fact, I've already thought it over and I'd prefer to stay in Weimar."

Although surprised by my reaction, Kazik quickly recovered his composure. "Don't be angry, Kon. Remember that we also agreed to go together or not at all. I promised you that I'd evaluate the situation and you must hear me out."

We had always trusted each other's judgement and knowing he was right about first assessing the possibilities, I managed to bring my temper under control.

"All right then, why should I leave my relatively comfortable life in Weimar to subject myself to campelder Zigi?"

"Buchenwald still has control over your job at the factory, which could very easily be bombed sooner or later. I don't want to praise Zigi — frankly, he should be wearing a green triangle and not a red one. But although he has the mind of a brilliant criminal, he also sees himself as a patron of the arts.

"You and I have lived with criminals for years and can adapt to their whims and desires. But there are other factors I consider much more important that outweigh Zigi's character. First, the guards at Camp Rose are not actually SS men. They're veterans of the First World War put into SS uniforms. Germany is running out of men! These so-called guards know nothing about concentration camps and most of them would never think of killing a prisoner. Also, we have a radio there on which we can listen daily to broadcasts from London. Did you realize that American, English, Canadian and our own Polish troops are now in France and have taken the whole of Italy? The Russian army is also fast advancing through Poland to Germany. The war may be over sooner than we expect. Frankly, under such circumstances I think we'd be much safer in little Camp Rose when the war ends."

I contended these were solid arguments, but still wanted to

know why he had made the arrangements without consulting me.

"Quite simply, there was no time," he responded. "I had to decide for both of us yesterday. Today we're taking with us 40 Italian prisoners of war, chaperoned by two Camp Rose guards. Believe me, you will see the difference!"

Kazik then grabbed my arm and hurried me towards a barracks where the prisoners' clothing was stored. Following him through the door, I noticed that he had already been there to select two good suits for us. I also saw that the greater part of the clothing assigned to those being transferred had had strips of material removed from the sides of pants and backs of jackets, replaced by either red or blue patches.

"Although we wear civilian clothes at Camp Rose, they are altered to discourage the men from escaping," he explained. "The few of us who have important functions in the camp wear only the red triangle and number, in the usual way."

Apart from the suits, Kazik had bribed from the men working there warm underwear and a couple of turtleneck sweaters, items not usually issued to prisoners. After changing and sewing on our triangles and numbers, we hastily departed for the Italian barracks where Kazik checked on a list the name of each prisoner assigned to us, then marched them in two groups towards the main gate. There they were counted again and, watched over by the two Camp Rose guards, boarded trucks to the Weimar railway station.

After our arrival and the departure of the Buchenwald trucks, I overheard the guards taking instructions from my friend, which naturally struck me as bizarre. I approached Kazik during a break in the conversation and whispered excitedly: "What the hell is wrong with those SS men? Don't they know how to travel through their own country?"

"It's all right. They're just two harmless old goofs who need help. Look, I've taken off my number and triangle. Do the same and go find out where the train to Mannheim is. Freight cars for the prisoners are attached to it. And remember, don't act like a prisoner!"

I walked along the platform, still looking over my shoulder to see whether the SS guards were about to stop me with a shout or a bullet. But they were babbling away to Kazik and shuffling some papers around — likely our travel documents.

To be suddenly unescorted and unwatched for the first time

in years was an extraordinary feeling. The obvious occurred to me: if it's this easy, why not buy ourselves tickets to Switzerland? As I contemplated this exhilarating possibility, I came across the Mannheim train but without freight cars. I stared at it, not knowing what to do, when a railway policeman marched towards me.

"Show me your documents at once, foreigner!"

So it is not that easy to travel across Germany after all, I thought. But having become accustomed to facing all kinds of strange and dangerous situations, I answered without hesitation.

"I'm here escorting Italian prisoners of war. Two Gestapo men and a colleague of mine are at the other end of the platform guarding the prisoners. Don't you know there should be freight cars added to this train? Where are they?"

The words "Gestapo" and "prisoners" had a magical effect. The policeman forgot about my documents and instead started to apologize for his ignorance. I immediately capitalized on his change in attitude.

"You'd better find out who's responsible for this because if the Gestapo is stuck here with the 40 prisoners, someone will be in trouble!"

The policeman clicked his heels and rushed into the station to make inquiries. Meanwhile I walked back to Kazik to tell him I had initiated the search for the freight cars. Our two elderly guards got the greatest kick out of being cast as powerful Gestapo men and assumed the proper authority when, shortly after, the policeman arrived with the stationmaster. Within moments the freight cars were attached to the train and we boarded to find a special compartment reserved in the passenger car for the "Gestapo" — our two guards, Kazik and myself.

As the train pulled out, one of the guards asked me how I had known that the Weimar station had a Gestapo office. This information took me somewhat aback.

"I didn't know," I said. "But since everything worked out for the best, let's enjoy our comfortable compartment. Look, the rest of the train is packed solid — people are even standing in the corridors."

Though the distance between Weimar and Mannheim is short, the movement of military equipment took priority once again and our train seemed to move backwards as much as it went forwards. No sooner had we left Weimar than an air raid warning went up and our train was moved to a sideline. We waited as almost endless lines of military transports passed us at full speed.

It was almost midnight before we reached Mannheim. Passengers and prisoners disembarked while Kazik, accompanied by one of the guards, notified the camp of our arrival. We then climbed aboard waiting trucks and were driven through the countryside past sleepy little towns and villages and occasionally through uninhabited forests and fields. After about 35 kilometres of bumpy roads there appeared without warning the outline of a post tower and barbed wire. The tower appeared to be unmanned or perhaps the guard was sleeping so soundly he had not heard the engines of the trucks as they approached the front gate.

Kazik jumped to the ground and called for the camp security men who, to my amazement, turned out to be two bleary-eyed prisoners. They opened the gate, informing Kazik that the barracks for the prisoners were ready, then led the Italians to their new quarters.

Our own barracks were faintly lit by a small electric bulb. Crude partitions had been constructed from old boards and pieces of plywood, while in some places blankets hanging on strings sufficed to provide some sort of privacy.

"The palace of the management!" exclaimed Kazik, gesturing broadly. "Our room is the latest addition, the one with the blanket walls. We'll be sharing it with Frederick Jarossy and Father Martin, but I think Jarossy is getting better quarters later — a privilege reserved for men with definite functions to perform here."

Jarossy, who was already in bed, rolled over several times and grumbled audibly about the noise and the lack of sleep "in this palace." Kazik showed me my bunk and I climbed in feeling utterly drained.

Yet sleep was not easy to come by that night. In spite of being accustomed to the unexpected, I had seen a new side of Germany that day. On the one hand was the familiar image of the Nazi Party — cruel, arrogant young men who firmly believed in their racial superiority, determined to enslave foreigners and exterminate Jews. On the other were ordinary civilians like our old guards in SS get-ups and the stationmaster, all frightened to death of the Gestapo, bereaved of their families through battle on the eastern front or in their home towns by air raid bombings. They were neither hostile nor friendly towards concentration camp prisoners — just insensitive, indifferent and obviously tired of war.

Once Kazik and I too, as new prisoners, had been part of a nameless, faceless mass working and dying for the Third Reich. Now we had become equally insensitive to the grey, sick and hungry crowd of Italian prisoners who had ridden in the freight cars behind us and were now lying in their own bunks, even more exhausted than I was.

Finally my disturbing meditations subsided and I fell into a deep and dreamless sleep.

We awoke in the morning to Zigi's loud bark: "Up and out, you lazy bastards! You think this is Zigi's sanatorium for the mentally deranged?"

He stood in the middle of the room with his feet planted wide apart, striking his pants with a riding whip.

"I let you sleep two hours longer because you were late last night. What kept you, anyway? No doubt dilly-dallying in Buchenwald instead of rushing back as I ordered!"

Sitting up in bed, my attention was attracted less by Zigi than by the man standing behind him. Dressed in a sleeveless sweater out of which poked the arms of a Musselman, he hissed through a set of rotten teeth each time the whip slapped against Zigi's side. His age was difficult to determine; he might have been 16 or 36. Though he had the complexion of a child, his face supported a long thin nose that looked out of place between a pair of big, bulging, blue eyes. It was his eyes I was most drawn to. Void of gaiety or amusement, they darted across the room with curiosity and cunning inquisitiveness.

"You are wondering," said Zigi, drawing close to my bunk, "who this incredible creature is. Well then, let me present to you Prince Andrew. He's only 19, though he has the mind of a 90-year-old sclerotic crook."

Turning to Andrew, he made a gesture as if to kick him and shouted: "Get out of here, you hiccup of humanity! You offspring of a broomstick and a baboon! Out!"

The man backed off with two long strides, far enough to be out of Zigi's reach, from where he continued to survey the room. Ignoring him, Zigi bowed in our direction.

"I am honoured, gentlemen, to invite you to breakfast prepared by my French chef. I trust you'll be ready in half an hour, at which time we will discuss the affaires d'état."

Kazik and I found what was termed the "bathroom" in an open part of the barracks, identifiable by a water-filled barrel and a bench on which sat a couple of washbasins. For other facilities one had to go to the outhouse, situated about 100 metres away over a stretch of dough-like, ankle-deep mud. Though boards had been put down between the barracks and outhouse, within a week they were gone, stolen by other prisoners for firewood. Zigi then ordered that several stones be laid along the route, a scheme which might have proved successful had it not been for the freezing rain that autumn, making the path particularly treacherous.

Zigi's quarters were located in another part of the barracks, separated by partitions about two metres high. We entered through the only inside door to be found in the camp, one scavenged from the entrance to some former barracks and thus higher than the partition itself. Along a wall stood a triple-level bunk from the top of which the white face of Prince Andrew leered down at us. In the middle of the room was a large table covered with a bedsheet. A huge figure dressed in the remnants of a French army uniform occupied a nearby bench preparing the "specialité de la maison," boiled potatoes sliced and fried in margarine.

"I know this camp hasn't much to show," said Zigi, sitting us down to the potato feast that included bread, beet root jam and coffee. "I've not had enough time to organize things. But with my influence, the Fat One — I mean, the commandant — will allow us to requisition some furniture from old army barracks to be moved here shortly. I can't do everything myself, which is why I needed you fellows to help me."

Seeing his complaint merely as a form of self-congratulations, I reminded him of a more pressing concern.

"We've been led to believe that the end of the war is not far off. Have you heard any recent news?"

Zigi rose from his chair and walked to his bed, pulling out from under it a small radio which he placed on the bench. He then connected it to an antenna that also served as a laundry line, grounded it to a piece of wire sticking out of the wall, and instantly we were listening to the Free French station.

Although impressed by this little demonstration, I was immediately reminded of our radio at Auschwitz and the attempts by the camp authorities to track it down.

"Aren't you afraid the SS will find it?"

"Not at all," said Zigi, making no effort to conceal his pleasure at our reaction. "The Fat One let me buy it in town. I simply explained to him that I love classical music, especially Wagner, and he decided not to deprive me of contact with the German culture. I am hiding it only from Adam and Jan, who would listen to the news all day long at the expense of their work."

"So when do you think the war will be over?" asked Kazik.

"In all likelihood, very soon. But I have no time to think about such things. Now we are here and must make the best of it. For example, I've arranged for you, Kazik, to go to town this afternoon to look over the army barracks assigned to us. Pick out the best and also see what kind of furniture you can organize. The day after you're to be at the railway station to receive clothing from Auschwitz — no doubt all taken from 'Canada', which means it's bound to contain at least a few $100 bills or £50 notes. With that money we could buy the whole bloody camp, including our crazy commandant."

"Maybe so," Kazik replied. "I only hope this damn war ends before buying camps and commandants becomes a necessity."

Zigi disregarded the remark, evidently preoccupied more with enhancing his kingdom than anticipating the day when each of us would go free. Though his domain consisted essentially of a muddy square of land enclosed by barbed wire, it still provided him with authority over 200 or so prisoners. Our freedom would result not only in his loss of power but also its accompanying privileges, reflected in the relative luxury in which he lived and which he needed us to improve upon.

"It's time I introduced you to Grandpa Schmidt," he said, turning to me, "our man in charge of the food magazines for both prisoners and SS guards. He's an old fart but knows his responsibilities. As a widower, he also has to provide for the families of his three sons — each in the Wehrmacht on the eastern front, though he hasn't heard from them for some time, so they're likely imprisoned in Siberia.

"Essentially, Schmidt is a coward, terrorized by the commandant, but still greedy enough to steal from his own magazines to feed the women and grandchildren. He's the guy you'll be working with in organizing our supplies. Which reminds me, I'd better pay him a visit. He's making his rounds in Mannheim today and has agreed to take us with him."

Zigi threw on a warm jacket and departed, giving Kazik and me an opportunity to discuss the day's activities. We had already begun criticizing the campelder and his plans when we were reminded that another ear was closely following our exchange. Andrew's face, however, registered neither interest nor disgust. He merely eyed us vacantly from his lair, then, with the movements of a sloth, climbed down from his bunk, slinked to the table where he took a large pinch of tobacco from a box left behind by Zigi, stuffed it in his own tobacco box, and with the same slow motion returned to his bed.

"Don't mind me," he wheezed on his way up. "Zigi's a bastard. Everyone here is a bloody bastard. Makes it difficult for a fellow to live decently."

At that moment Zigi bounced through the door, pulling off his coat and handing it to me.

"Schmidt is ready to go. You'd better wear this to conceal your triangle and number, at least until Kazik can find you something better. Schmidt hates to appear in Mannheim as a prison guard. He prefers that we pretend to be civilian workers."

"Can I also come along?" a voice squeaked from above us.

"You?" Zigi snarled. "You half-assed idiot! All you ever think about is stealing for yourself. We're going for bigger game — to help Schmidt organize more food for all of us from the central SS supply. You'd not even think of doing anything for others."

"Neither would you, Zigi," whined Andrew. "You just want some sugar for your moonshine. To get drunk like a pig, that's all you want!"

"Shut up, imbecile. You should really try listening to and learning from your elders instead of overworking the remnants of your miniature brain. Let's go, Kon!"

Before Zigi could pull me through the door, I reminded him of an important matter we had yet to attend to.

"Ah yes, presents for the SS," he muttered, then glaring at Andrew, "what have you hidden for us under your mattress, you halfwit?"

"Nothing, Zigi, nothing. Maybe a couple of Gaulois, but they're such poor quality —"

"Let me see, you aristocratic thief!"

In no time Zigi had chased Andrew from his bunk, pulled back the mattress and was busily searching through his pile of belongings. Out came a couple of pairs of gloves, some scarves, a half-eaten chocolate bar, a can of coffee beans, someone's gold bridge with several teeth still attached to it, and four packs of English cigarettes.

"This should do for a starter," said Zigi, handing me the cigarettes and can of coffee. "Now we can go."

Leaving the room, we could hear Andrew wailing: "This is outright robbery! Thieves! It was all mine, legitimately traded for my own bread and margarine!"

A guard opened the main gate for us without any questions and we proceeded towards the SS barracks. There, waiting by a truck, stood a tall, thin man with a Hitler-like moustache, greying hair and eyebrows, and small eyes that darted in all directions. His long fingers were nervously shuffling a pile of papers which he immediately passed to Zigi.

"See if you can make some sense out of these," he complained. "The German bureaucracy is getting worse and worse."

"Schmidt, this is Kon. He'll be your helper in supplying us with food. And don't worry — he's very smart and has a university education. You can trust him, perhaps even more than you can me. I'm sure he'll look after both our interests."

Thinking this was the time to make a good impression on my new partner, I let him know Zigi had informed me of his sons and by way of expressing sympathy, told him my parents were also lost to me somewhere in Siberia. Then I pulled the can of coffee from under my coat and presented it to him. This drew a sour look from Zigi, who had intended it for someone in central stores, but Schmidt was ecstatic.

"Real coffee! My God, I don't remember when I last had real coffee! Now there are substitutes for everything, you know — butter, marmalade, soap." Looking over his shoulder, he whispered, "I wish they'd make a substitute for Hitler, then maybe the war would be over."

Moments later the driver and another guard appeared. We jumped into the back of the truck with Schmidt and started for Mannheim.

What we encountered there seemed to me a miracle. Everywhere stores were open for business while crowds of shoppers flocked through the streets. Had it not been for the number of military uniforms among the human traffic, I would have had difficulty spotting any sign of a country at war.

We pulled up between rows of military barracks on the outskirts of town and walked into the central office to proffer our requisition papers for food. The sergeant in charge, obviously wishing to appear important, admitted us only after a long wait. Seated behind his desk smoking a cigar, the man looked as wide as he was tall, his huge stomach protruding through his unbuttoned uniform and an officious, unfriendly expression on his round, red face. Schmidt also held the rank of sergeant, but in presenting our documents showed he was completely intimidated by this man.

"This requisition asks for too much sugar and margarine," said the sergeant. "You must know there is a shortage of these things in Germany. One cannot get even a decent cigar these days."

He peered out at us from behind his fat cheeks with a sort of question mark drawn on his brow, obviously expecting someone to present him with a box of hand-rolled Havanas. Missing this hint altogether, Schmidt took this opportunity to introduce us and thus relieve himself from carrying the conversation.

"My two helpers," he said, attempting to wave his hand in our direction. "They are responsible for the bookkeeping and can tell you exactly how much food is needed for our camp."

Not wishing to wait for further developments, I decided to interject my own thoughts on the matter.

"I understand, sir, what you mean by bad cigars. I myself have quit smoking, but my uncle in France keeps sending me English cigarettes. Would you like to try one?"

The sergeant immediately snuffed out his cigar and taking a cigarette from a pack I had scooped from my pocket, lit it and inhaled deeply.

"Hmm, very nice. I did not think the English could make such good cigarettes. I smoke both cigarettes and cigars, you know, though I think I prefer, for real pleasure, a good cigar."

"If you like the cigarette, why not keep the pack," I said, handing it to him. "In my next letter, I will ask whether my uncle can send me some good English cigars. I understand Churchill likes smoking cigars."

"Yes, yes," the sergeant replied enthusiastically. "It might be very interesting to smoke the same cigars Churchill smokes. But I am holding you up — let me get your truck loaded. Fritz!"

The call was answered instantly by an SS man who marched before the sergeant's desk, clicked his heels and saluted smartly.

"Take these gentlemen to Bruno and instruct him to fill their truck according to this requisition. Also have him include something special for my friends here."

Fritz took us outside and showed us to the barracks where we would receive bread, sugar and marmalade. On the way we collected potatoes and the ubiquitous turnips, every camp's staple food. We found the truck in the loading bay where a plump man, very much like the sergeant I had recently bribed, stood scowling at us. I had learned the meaning of this expression long before in Auschwitz: nothing special for me, nothing special for you.

I extended a fresh pack of cigarettes to Bruno, Fritz and Schmidt, each of whom welcomed my offer. This was enough to put a smile on Bruno's face. He immediately dismissed Fritz in an obvious attempt to corner any future hand-outs for himself. The rest of the pack I gave to Schmidt, signalling to Bruno that I had plenty more I could easily part with.

Bruno took us inside the warehouse and briefly showed us around. "Take whatever is necessary," he said, thrusting the requisition form at me. "Schmidt and I will be in my office. I haven't seen this fellow for quite a while."

Left alone, I grabbed a wooden cart and went off in search of bread. Zigi stood by and watched in fascination as I loaded the centre of the cart with boxes of sugar, then proceeded to surround this mound with loaves of bread.

"Your reputation as an illusionist was not exaggerated, Kon. Looks like we get our moonshine after all!"

We wheeled our cart to the loading dock only to find Bruno talking to Schmidt right in the middle of the the corridor, barring our path to the truck. As we approached them Smidt's face went white as a sheet and Bruno resumed his unfriendly manner.

"Let's see what you got on your first trip," he said.

"Fifty loaves of bread, Mr. Bruno," I answered, pulling out another pack of cigarettes. "I noticed you liked my brand. Would you care to take the whole pack? I quit smoking last week but my uncle is still sending them. I must tell him to stop."

"Oh, don't do that!" he exclaimed, snatching the pack from my hand. "Such wonderful cigarettes! I have to smoke this terrible German brand — it's all we can get in the canteen. Wait a minute, I have something special for you, too."

He crossed the corridor, unlocked a door and disappeared

momentarily, then emerged with three jars of marmalade in hand.

"Apple jam made with real sugar, not like that beet root marmalade you usually get, sweetened with saccharin. Enjoy it."

"Thank you very much, Bruno. I'll have more cigarettes for you next time and perhaps other treats from my uncle."

The moment Bruno and Schmidt departed for the office, we hastily rolled our cart to the truck where Zigi handled the unpacking while I returned to the warehouse with the driver and SS guard.

"The warehouse manager is a friend of mine," I said, pointing to the empty carts. "He promised not to look at what you take, so be sure to grab an extra loaf of bread for yourselves and two for Schmidt — he has a big family to feed. You can do the same with the margarine, but no more than what I've said. We might be checked on the way out. Now hurry!"

With a smart "Thank you very much, sir!" they quickly seized a cart and ran towards the bread. I stood there wondering what an extra loaf of bread could do to people. After more than four years in concentration camps, an SS man was addressing me as "sir." Obviously the food shortage was afflicting all of Germany and not just the camps.

In the meantime Zigi had reappeared and together with the guard and driver we worked like beavers to stack as much food as possible into the carts. On our way out, we noticed that Bruno had "forgotten" to send someone to count the potato sacks and turnips. I watched the sweat trickle down Zigi's face as we hurriedly shifted the goods from cart to truck.

By the time we finished, the back of the truck was heaped so full we had to perch ourselves on boxes and sacks for the bumpy return to Camp Rose.

Before reaching camp, we made a brief stop for coffee at the home of one of Schmidt's daughters-in-law, a kind lady to whom we delivered a loaf of bread, margarine, marmalade and a sack of potatoes. It was dark by the time we unloaded provisions at the SS barracks, so I persuaded Schmidt to allow us to deliver the camp's supplies before retiring, instead of collecting our goods the next morning. He readily agreed, ignorant of the cartons of sugar hidden between the stacked bread.

The consistency of the soup in camp changed immediately from a watery liquid to one rich with potatoes. Although the prisoners received more food, on average, than those in Buchenwald, they were now permitted to receive Red Cross and private food parcels. Such deliveries were enormously important, for they frequently contained currency with which to barter for additional luxuries.

Neither Kazik nor I had ever received food parcels; in the past, we had been lucky enough to manage on our own. But in these new surroundings, where we could organize more and better food than the majority of prisoners, gifts from outside were hardly necessary. Kazik also managed to secure for us reasonably warm clothing, though his hopes of finding valuables in the garments sent from Auschwitz never materialized.

Now that our basic needs had been satisfied, we again began to think about ways to escape. One day, while discussing our plans, we were surprised to find Father Martin awake and following our conversation with great interest.

"In case the two of you didn't know," he cautioned, "the commandant of this camp is Colonel Busch, a former Gestapo officer transferred here as punishment for an excess of tortures and murders that occurred under his command in Berlin. The gossip says he's related to someone close to Hitler — in other words, he's a mad dog. He personally shot the previous campelder and has announced that Zigi and his helpers will be next in line if anyone escapes. The only way out of here without endangering the rest of us is to make a run for it while at work."

This news only served to confirm my suspicions about everything Zigi had told us before our departure from Buchenwald.

"There," I said to Kazik, "are your mild-mannered SS men! Naturally we were not told of the pack's top monster."

But Kazik showed no sign of regret. "You must admit, Kon, that these guards are nothing like the Buchenwald butchers. That's what makes this place safe. Speaking frankly, we don't have to escape until the war ends."

"Unless," I retorted, "someone else escapes before us and this Gestapo fiend descends on his inmates with guns blazing!"

"Zigi has posted guards in the camp for that very reason," said Father Martin. "He could never rely on the SS guards. They spend most of the time sleeping, a fact of which the Fat One is also aware."

Within days we had a demonstration of what he meant.

Zigi had again hosted us to an evening in his quarters at

which we received the standard fare of fried potatoes. After the meal Kazik, Jan Groski, Frederick Jarossy and Zigi indulged themselves in a round of bridge, Father Martin seated himself at a little table in the corner to work on his book, and Andrew took up his usual position on the top bunk. Adam Jankowski and I, having nothing better to do, were embroiled in a heated discussion about my Russian friends in Buchenwald, a topic that regretfully aroused both his cynicism and snobbery.

It was exceptional that Adam condescended to talk to me at all. A published poet and professor of Polish literature at the University of Krakow before the war, Jankowski fancied himself an arbiter of all things cultural and intellectual within the camp. This self-proclaimed status suited his eccentric appearance. Closely cropped gray hair sprouted from the top of his triangular-shaped head which seemed to extend directly into his neck, leaving no indication of a chin. Also, the deep furrow implanted in the centre of his forehead suggested that he was forever absorbed in thought. Though tall, his stooping posture made him look well beyond his fifty or so years.

"You must have an even lower cultural background than I expected," he told me, "to befriend Ukrainian peasants."

"And what makes you think you're so superior?" I asked. "Surely it couldn't be your incomprehensible poetry. Or are you perhaps related to our bunkbed prince?"

"I'll have you know my family dates back to the 15th Century, each succeeding generation blessed with strong intellectual abilities and heirs to a long, noble tradition."

"But Jan, you've not visited long enough in concentration camps to know of the noble minds I've encountered, many from very frugal backgrounds. My friend Ivan was a brilliant man."

Our argument might have digressed beyond the point of tedium had Zigi not suddenly turned from his cards to add his two cents worth.

"Yes indeed, Kon, good point, good point! Our friend Jan here knows nothing of what we've experienced. Why, I recall events that would make each of you — Kon and Kazik excepted, of course — all tremble like little puppies. Imagine that you were condemned to a bunker with 12 other men, packed so tightly no one could budge, suffocating, starving, deprived of water, everyone's pants full of shit — diarrhoea from hunger! Then to endure carrying the bodies of your executed friends, slipping in their blood, tumbling over their corpses staring up at you with a corpse's eyes, blood gushing from their mouths. What do you know of this, eh?"

Then turning to his bridge partners: "My apologies, gentlemen, for the interruption. Sometimes I succumb to sentimentality. I said three no trump — anybody object?"

As if Zigi's contribution were not enough the white-faced young prince also had a word to share. Descending from his bunk, he squeaked: "You know, Uncle Jan, that many old guys like you were rejuvenated in camp hospitals. All done hygienically. First they were marched naked a kilometre in freezing temperatures, then given hot showers and marched back. Their penises grew twice as long — each a solid, shining icicle. The SS men laughed their —"

"Shut up, you!" screamed Zigi. "You miserable little creep, why don't you tell Uncle Jan what kapo Bruno made you do for your extra food and privileges!"

Andrew only grimaced and hissed something, withdrawing back to his lair. At that moment one of Zigi's German security men knocked rapidly and entered, his face flushed and rigid.

"Sir Campelder, three Russians have escaped from camp!" he reported excitedly, the special band on his arm trembling in a salute.

Zigi threw down his cards and bounded through the doorway, the security man and several of us following close behind. It was already dark, but within seconds all outside lights had been switched on and orders given for the prisoners to fall in for roll call.

From a nearby building we could hear Zigi shouting to his guards: "You bloody idiots! Don't just stand there picking your noses! Run through the camp and sniff those bastards out! If you don't find them immediately the Fat One will shoot you all!"

During roll call it was discovered *four* Russians were missing. The security men scoured every inch of the camp and after searching all possible hiding places, returned with one Russian in tow who had been sleeping in the back of the kitchen. Zigi walked quietly toward the man, looked him over, then struck him in the stomach unexpectedly with all his strength. When the man bent over in pain, Zigi grabbed his head and smashed it against his raised knee, breaking his nose.

"This man was not trying to escape," said a security man,

attempting to pull Zigi away from his victim. "He was just tired and fell asleep there because the wall was warm from the kitchen oven."

Zigi's face flamed the colour of his hair. "Don't tell me what he was doing! He was hiding to escape! Bind his hands and hold him there until I come back."

He then marched through the main gate to the house of Commandant Busch. About five minutes later the two of them emerged, the Fat One wearing only pants, shirt and cap with a riding whip in hand and an overcoat thrown over his shoulder. As he ran to keep up with Zigi, his large stomach wobbled over the belt of his trousers. He looked like raging fury made flesh.

The commandant first went up to the small group of security men, lashing at them left and right with his whip. "I'll have you all shot, you lazy swines! What kind of damned security are you! And where is the man who tried to escape!"

"Here he is," said Zigi, pointing to the bleeding Russian who, released by the security men, was attempting to distance himself from the commotion. He was immediately grabbed and pushed in front of Commandant Busch who pounced on him like a mad dog, kicking and beating him with his whip. In the meantime Zigi walked calmly to the side of a barracks and came back with a piece of iron pipe in his hand.

"Give that to me!" puffed Busch. "I'll kill the bastard!"

Zigi obligingly handed the pipe to the commandant and stood back to watch him deliver blow after to blow. When the man finally fell to the ground, the Fat One jumped on him with both feet while he held the bloody pipe above his head, striking the lifeless body yet a few more times. Then he tossed the pipe aside and proceeded to walk towards the gate.

"I will deal with the security men tomorrow," he gasped to Zigi as he passed by.

"But sir, we have caught this escaping prisoner with the help of my security force. It is hard to say how many could have escaped had it not been for their alertness to duty."

"Oh, I see," said the commandant, still puffing heavily. "Then let this be an example to the rest of the men. Leave the escapee on the ground where he is until tomorrow. I want everyone to see what your commandant does to any man who attempts to escape!"

When the Fat One had walked far enough away to be out of earshot, Zigi turned to stare into the small crowd only to see eyes wide with the horror of what they had witnessed.

"What are you standing there for? Don't you realize that if it weren't for me, all of you would be lying there beside this culprit? Well, I too have had enough. If anyone else escapes, don't call on me to defend you. Next time you bastards can take the beatings. Now get lost!"

He then wheeled about and began walking towards our barracks, a signal for the few of us still standing in the doorway to disappear quickly inside. We stood watching him as he entered, anticipating yet another outburst. But he simply took up his seat at the table and inspected his cards.

"All right, the alarm is over," he announced. "Whose deal was it? I can't stand being interrupted at bridge."

Noticing that none of his partners had any interest in resuming the game, Zigi made a grim face and again tossed his cards aside.

"Okay, go back to your burrows, you cowardly bunch of misguided nobility. Kon, send me the Frenchman with some food — I feel hungry."

Before I could make a move, Frederick decided to break the ice. "You know the poor guy wasn't trying to escape. But you went ahead anyway and murdered, with the Fat One, an innocent man."

"Oh my, oh my!" peeped Andrew's voice out of nowhere. "And what would Uncle Frederick have preferred? To take the place of this miserable Russian Musselman and become himself a pile of mincemeat?"

"You unfortunate imitation of humanity," retorted Jankowski. "What do you know, you were asleep in your bed."

"Goodness, Uncle begins to show some life. Dear oh dear! Well let me tell you, my venerable imitation of Hamlet, that although you may not see me, I can see all things at all times."

By now Zigi had risen from his chair and taken the centre of the floor, directing a hard look at each of us in turn. "This time the squeaky hiccup is right. It was a simple question of one life or ten — including your own. You know damn well how the Fat One dealt with our predecessors. This man doesn't joke!"

In the pause following Zigi's speech I slipped from the room, instructed the French chef to prepare a pot of food, and returned moments later with leftovers of Hungarian ragout which I placed on the hotplate. Zigi did not wait for it to warm up, but grabbed the pot and ravenously polished off its contents.

Andrew looked on delighted. "Good work makes for a good appetite, doesn't it Zigi?"

After this incident everyone's relations with Zigi became very strained. Open criticism was far too dangerous; the only alternative was silent disapproval, which from veteran prisoners such as Kazik and I, really meant something. Unable to find consolation in Andrew's unwavering support, Zigi called me aside one day.

"I think it's about time we organized more potatoes. Schmidt is taking most of them for the SS kitchen. We've got to make another trip to Mannheim bearing proper gifts."

With the assistance of Andrew's margarine, which we swapped for English cigarettes, and a few cigars Zigi had organized from somewhere, we came back from Mannheim once again fully loaded. This time we carried not only an excess of potatoes and turnips but also 20 kilograms of margarine. Under Zigi's orders, an extra five kilograms of margarine was added daily to the soup as an alternative to the riskier move of increasing the prisoners' rations. The addition of a little more fat to their miserable diet was well received; Zigi's previous behaviour was almost forgotten and in time we resumed our regular bridge parties.

A few days after our second food run Zigi reminded me of his plans to build a distillery. "It's almost Christmas and I was hoping we could celebrate it with a proper drink. We have no copper tubing, but with your knowledge of engineering maybe you can come up with a substitute."

I assured him I would try to think of something and with the Frenchman's help, set about the task. We first procured some potatoes, flour and sugar, preparing from these ingredients a mash which we allowed to ferment in a metal container. This concoction was then covered with a bigger pot placed upside down over the container to act as a condensation barrier, and slowly heated on Zigi's hotplate. Since the hotplate was much smaller than both pots, we were able to catch the drops of condensed alcohol on a tray beneath the element. To prevent the condensing pot from overheating, we mounted on top of it a third pot full of ice.

Though I was very proud of my design and Zigi equally enthusiastic, the amount of alcohol produced was so small it never exceeded the amount each of us tasted during the distilling process.

While working on the still, I spent a good deal of time in Zigi's room discussing — when he and Andrew were away — his treatment of the Russian prisoner falsely accused of trying to escape. Among those of us who condemned Zigi, Jankowski was the least compromising.

"That man claims to be an officer but where the hell is his honour? I think he's a fraud!"

"It's certainly a tragic situation," said Frederick. "He is clearly a product of his environment. If I'd gone through that hell hole Auschwitz as Zigi did, who knows how warped I might have become?"

"But look at Kazik and Kon," insisted Groski. "They went through the same hell but don't go around killing people."

Jankowski's stare fixed on me. "I'm sorry to have to tell you this, Kon, but I think you're no better than Zigi. You claim to be a professional officer though you behave more like a thief. I may be only a reserve officer, but I'd never stoop to stealing."

"Maybe," I said. "Still, you eat stolen potatoes fried in stolen margarine, cooked in a stolen pan heated on a stolen hotplate. *All the food you eat is stolen for you.* It seems your officer's honour allows you to accept it, even from Zigi.

"In Auschwitz we fought a different kind of war with different ideas of what is honourable. I wonder how honourable you would be if you were cold, dying of hunger and tortured by the most sophisticated methods, not wanting to betray your colleagues. Yes, we stole things — food, medicine, even a shortwave radio, anything we could use to defend ourselves against the enemy. You cannot judge fairly the behaviour of others unless you have lived through such insanity yourself."

Before Jankowski could formulate a reply, our conversation was cut short by Zigi's return. He inspected the still, drained whatever alcohol was in the tray and downed it in one gulp.

"Good stuff, Kon," he pronounced, smacking his lips. "But at this rate we'll be sucking our thumbs for Christmas instead of quaffing good vodka. However, I might have an answer. The Fat One tells me he's out of schnapps, so I made a deal with him. If he gets us alcohol or a still that works, I'll make him the golden drink of the gods. Which reminds me — anyone here know how to make krupnik?"

A broad smile beamed from Frederick's typically sullen face. "Get me the proper ingredients and I'll prepare you a Hungarian style krupnik that makes even the Polish kind seem tame!"

Zigi placed an arm around Frederick's shoulder and together they departed for Busch's house, returning several hours later with news that all had gone well.

"This man's a genius," exclaimed Zigi, ushering Frederick through the door. "With only some vodka, honey and spices, our creation impressed the hell out of the Fat One. In fact, he liked it so much he's promised us the materials for a still, to make sufficient quantities for his Christmas party."

Sure enough, within a couple of days we received a complete set of distiling equipment confiscated by the Gestapo from a nearby village. To ensure that we had an ample supply of ingredients, Busch sent us on another trip to Mannheim, only this time he phoned ahead to the local Gestapo. When we arrived at central stores, the sergeant in charge was so terrified he hardly knew how to please us. He offered us cigars, passed us a bottle of cognac and ordered Bruno to pack our truck with as much potatoes, flour and sugar as it could carry. In the meantime, Frederick joined us from his shopping tour with barrels of honey and a wide variety of spices.

In the end, all of us benefited from this excursion. Busch used his large supply of Frederick's krupnik to improve his standing among higher ranking officers who began paying him regular social visits, while surplus potatoes mixed in a thick soup fed the prisoners for a long time to come. Needless to say, we made enough moonshine to last us through the Christmas season.

On one occasion, while Busch was away, I was delivering four bottles of krupnik to the commandant's house when the door was answered, not by his SS valet, but by his wife. She was a small, very pretty woman with golden hair braided into a long tress and so much younger than Busch she might easily have been mistaken for his daughter. Giving me a friendly smile, she led me into the kitchen where I deposited the bottles on a broad, wooden table.

"So this is what you call krupnik," she said, picking up a bottle and inspecting it closely. "It's a very nice, sweet drink. I had no idea prisoners lived better than we do. You know, of course, that Germans do not have such good things in their houses. My husband tells me you also have Swiss chocolate, real coffee, Danish cheeses and English cigarettes."

Her remark was so unexpected and delivered with such

sincerity it left me speechless. How could this young woman have lived next door to a concentration camp without noticing the true conditions within the fence? She looked so youthful and innocent. Then a thought crossed my mind that this might be a trap. Recalling the young and pretty wife of Buchenwald's deputy commandant who made lampshades from human skin, I decided to be non-committal.

"It's not as good a life as you think, madame. We are concentration camp prisoners and you should know what that means."

"Yes, I know you are enemies of the Third Reich and that you're being punished for that," she replied, her expression changing to one of concern. "But when I meet you individually, you do not look like enemies. Why is that?"

This was one discussion I wished to avoid. Looking about me, I spotted through the doorway to the living room a beautiful baby grand piano with the music of a Beethoven sonata open on it.

"Forgive me for asking," I said, pointing towards the piano, "but is it you or your husband who plays?"

A smile immediately returned to her face. "I play, though my husband knows more about music than I do. Do you also play?"

"Yes — I mean, I did once. I've not touched a keyboard for a long time and have probably forgotten everything."

Even as I said this, I was itching to try the piano.

"I'm sure that you, being a Pole, played Chopin," she said, walking to the piano and lifting some music from a small pile. "His nocturnes are so beautiful, don't you think? Why don't you see how much you remember?"

I could not resist the temptation. Taking the music she held out to me, I seated myself at the piano and started to play. I became so engrossed in the music and the instrument's beautiful sound that I failed to notice Busch standing in a doorway listening.

When I finished he suddenly applauded, saying: "You are out of practice, but your interpretation is very good."

I leapt from the piano bench, my whole body trembling, and began apologizing for the intrusion while in the same breath explaining that I had left some bottles of krupnik for him in the kitchen. Then I backed out the door with the excuse that much work was to be done, and bolted.

In the days following I reflected frequently on our awkward encounter, trying to make sense of how a man who killed with such fury and cruelty might still comprehend Chopin's delicate feelings of love. At moments I thought him a fraud and preferred to forget the whole event. But then it would occur to me: what if this man were actually being sincere? Could it be that we shared an attachment to and appreciation for the beauty of life that music evokes? How was this possible?

As Christmas approached, Father Martin took charge of preparations for the Christmas Eve dinner and service.

Up until the war, the religious significance of a Polish Christmas Eve dinner had become obscured by the length and richness of its tradition. For believers and unbelievers alike, the feast would be meatless. As for the fasting that was supposed to take place until evening, only Father Martin would observe it.

Father Martin had received some altar bread from Poland; cooking without meat was simple because there was none to be had. Zigi did insist that herring be served before dinner with moonshine as the customary appetizer, and shortly before December 24th went to Mannheim with Schmidt. He returned triumphantly with two salted herrings and even a small freshwater fish. Though normally a meal for one, the traditional Polish fare we could anticipate enhanced our festive mood.

Busch gave Zigi permission to chop down a tree in the nearby woods and erect it in the middle of the camp. We had wondered how to decorate it but the moment it was up, French, Italian and Polish prisoners surrounded the tree, each bearing a special ornament made up of Christmas memorabilia sent from home or of prized personal belongings. Electricians among us painted ordinary lightbulbs in different colours and strung the wire from a nearby building. Surprisingly, it worked. No one was electrocuted nor did the tree catch fire.

Finally Christmas Eve arrived.

After dark the Christian prisoners gathered around the illuminated tree and began to sing Christmas carols, each in his own language. One carol could be sung by all: Stille Nacht. Only a year ago, I could not have conceived of such a possibility. But now, joined in song with my colleagues, I could hear even the SS guards singing from the towers.

Eventually the cold and frost drove us from our celebration back to our barracks, but our tree continued to glow until late into the night. The only discordant note was Father Martin's discovery that two polished wooden crosses made for the graves of men who had died that morning had been stolen from their coffins.

Andrew, who had spent the evening draped across his bed, observed the commotion with a wide yawn. "Stop making such a fuss. Anyway, it wasn't fair that poor old Goldman, a faithful Jew, should have a cross erected on his tomb by an atheist like Dmitri while a Jesuit priest prays for his soul. I'm sure he'd turn in his grave."

"How did you know it was Goldman who died?" asked Father Martin.

"It was my business to know. And Ivan, the dentist. Goldman had two beautiful gold bridges in his mouth. We were very kind to him — Ivan could have removed them within seconds but I ordered him to wait until the patient was dead. Or almost dead."

"You, you . . ." sputtered the priest, growing red with anger. "Now I know, God forgive your sins, why his face was smashed and bloody. You and Ivan murdered the poor man before he could die in peace!"

"Now, now, dear Father Martin, you would not have wanted me to commit a graver sin by desecrating a dead body, would you?" Andrew sneered.

"Let us pray on this holy day. I cannot hear any more of this!"

Father Martin began to pray aloud, then stopped suddenly. "So you stole the crosses, too?"

"Not exactly with my own hands, Father. Haven't you noticed the room is especially warm for our holy Christmas Eve dinner?"

This time even Zigi had had enough. "Shut up, you punk! Why spoil Christmas Eve for everyone with your sick behaviour? Let's just start! Martin — do your job!"

Father Martin walked to the table and said a long prayer in Latin over the altar bread. He broke it, gave a piece to everyone and wished us a speedy return home. He also approached Andrew, who silently took his portion.

"Well, now that we've got that over with, let's dig in," said Zigi. "Kon, give us a fill-up of beautiful moonshine. Eat, drink and be merry, but take it easy on the entrée — a mug of vodka and a mouthful of fish should be about right!"

After two full mugs of moonshine, which by my estimate contained at least 70% pure alcohol, Zigi waxed sentimental. "Oh Lithuania, my Fatherland . . ." he recited, only to be interrupted by a squeal of laughter from the prince.

"Forgive him, Lord, for he knows not of what he speaks," squeaked Andrew.

"You uneducated idiot," Zigi slurred. "The poem is Polish — or perhaps they never taught you in the asylum that Poland and Lithuania were once united under one king."

"Of course I knew that. But you've never even seen this place you call your fatherland."

The exchange proved too much for Jankowski who stepped in as the final authority. "Neither of you knows anything about poetry! One requires a soul to understand it and you lost your souls in Auschwitz. You're both on the level of dogs or at best, caged apes!"

By then the moonshine had influenced everyone, including Father Martin, and all tongues began wagging at the same time. Frederick, who lent his support to Jankowski, proceeded to give a performance of King Lear. Zigi plopped his head on the table and cried, sorry for himself and the whole world. Andrew, having dropped from his bed, bickered with Jankowski while attempting to play a feeble fool to Frederick's Lear. Father Martin, sitting with me and Groski, was busily persuading the criminal lawyer to repent his sins or prepare for damnation.

Groski, in spite of his legal background, was not a talkative man; I had rarely heard him volunteer his opinions on any subject unless asked directly. Still, I had heard enough to know that his mind was pragmatic and logical and his religious outlook that of an agnostic.

To provoke him, I asked: "Aren't you afraid little devils will boil your soul in oil down in hell's kitchen?"

"With what's left of me, they would not get much of a meal out of it," he laughed dryly.

"Don't you believe, Jan, that you have a soul?" asked Father Martin.

"What is soul? When I die, my body, my brain and with it my whole personality will just rot away. Nothing will remain of what you and I know as Jan Groski. And if there were a shred of soul left behind, it would have nothing in common with me."

The priest pressed on. "How can you tell there is no spirit which is you? If you believe in God, you must believe what Christ said about life after death."

"Martin, be reasonable! I don't want to upset you, but even assuming that Christ is God, he said it almost 2,000 years ago. People have a tendency to distort what they heard the day before. Why shouldn't all this be simply a grand fabrication of human fantasy?"

At this point Zigi raised his head, lifted his eyes in our direction and cried out: "Martin, I can see the devil hiding behind the bunkbed! I have sinned so much, he wants my soul! Pray for me!"

He then pulled himself from his chair, teetering back and forth on unsteady legs and shouted at the bed: "You will get shit, not my soul! Zigi is going to outsmart you!"

Unable to keep his balance, he collapsed to the floor, curled up in the fetal position and fell fast asleep.

Andrew slithered over to the snoring campelder and walked around him like a dog sniffing his master but unsure of what to do. Then he took a still burning cigarette out of Zigi's hand, stuck it in his mouth, turned slowly around and crawled up the bunkbed into his nest.

That was the end of the Christmas party.

CHAPTER 11

FINAL ESCAPE

January, 1945, was an unusually cold month. Nobody attempted escape simply because to get away on foot or by public transport, without documents, was impossible. Listening to our radio in Zigi's quarters, it seemed the war had stopped. Polish troops had taken Monte Casino, opening the road to Rome and, indeed, all the way to the Alps. The news bolstered our pride, but the effect was shortlived.

Late that month we heard a broadcast from London that Auschwitz had been liberated. If this were true, it also meant Russian troops had successfully pushed back the German army and re-occupied Poland.

"One enemy defeated only so another can take its place," I remarked.

"Just wait for the spring," said Jan. "American and British troops will finish off the Germans and then boot the Russians back into their own country. For all we know, we might actually stand a good chance of returning to Poland in military uniform."

"Anyone who believes that is a dreamer," responded Jarossy. "Politics is a dirty business. When the Brits and Yanks are no longer directly threatened by Germany, they'll give up on Eastern Europe. Even the radio broadcasts admit Stalin is a 'great friend' of the Western powers. They'll leave the housekeeping to dear daddy Stalin and then you'll see — no more Poland or Hungary and all Eastern European nations a part of the Soviet family."

"Maybe so," Jan conceded. "But if that's the case, all of us now serving in the Polish army under British command will be considered enemies in Stalin's Poland. We'll not be able to return to our own country."

"Nor may there be room for us in England," added Jarossy.

Finding his cynicism too much to bear, I immediately lashed out at Jarossy. "You're a Hungarian and don't know the traditions of the Polish army. This is not the first time we've fought for Poland outside our own borders."

"Perhaps. I say this, however, not as a Hungarian, but as an older and more experienced man than you are."

Indeed, Jarossy's predictions proved far more accurate than any of us would have expected. Despite enormous sacrifices, the Russians continued to push towards Berlin. Psychologically and politically, it was a brilliant move. The more territory now taken by Stalin's army, the more would be under Russian control when the Third Reich collapsed in defeat. Furthermore, the Red Army's capture of Berlin would signify that Russia and not the Western powers had won the war.

As the end of the war approached, we began to hear of further atrocities committed at Auschwitz and Buchenwald where the SS embarked on a futile attempt to dispose of all witnesses. In small Camp Rose, however, we felt no imminent danger from our guards, many of whom had grown tired of the war and looked forward to a future of peace and prosperity. It therefore came as a great surprise to us when one day Zigi announced that Busch had ordered the erection of an electric fence around the camp.

"This is crazy!" exclaimed Kazik. "Don't you see that once his fence is built, the Fat One can call upon the Gestapo to machine gun all of us and obliterate any evidence of his own behaviour?"

"He'd never do that," Zigi replied casually. "The guy will be too busy trying to save his own neck. But while this project's under way, I don't want to deal with any more escapes or encounters with Busch."

Work on the fence started a few days later with the assignment of a special group of prisoners, supervised by a civilian technician, to attach insulators to the barbed wire. Almost immediately the Russian prisoners, in particular, voiced strong opposition to the fence. One morning it was discovered the insulators had been smashed. In a fit of anger, Busch ordered his guards to fire sporadically at night between the towers and to shoot any unauthorized prisoner seen within 50 metres of the fence.

On a night shortly following the completion of the fence we were awakened by the sound of gun fire. Zigi dashed from his bunk and commanded his security men to check all barracks for any missing prisoners. He then met with the guards who said they had fired at the sight of sparks flashing in the dark. A thorough search was conducted along the fence but nothing turned up. When the security force reported that all men were accounted for, he called off the search and returned to his bed.

Next morning the guards came upon the German shepherd belonging to Busch, its partially singed carcass lying next to the fence. No one knew why the dog had come in contact with the fence but Busch directed his fury at the SS guards. Later we found out what actually had happened.

Each night before going to bed Busch let his dog out for a run. Some Russian prisoners saw this as an opportunity to take revenge on the commandant and began throwing scraps of meat to the dog over the fence. On that particular night they deliberately deposited the scraps on the camp side of the fence, knowing the animal would electrocute itself trying to get at them.

"They must really hate Busch," I remarked upon hearing the story in Zigi's room. "To kill his dog, they sacrificed the little meat they get."

Andrew's face suddenly peeked down at us from the edge of his bed. "On the contrary. Those Russians have more meat than you think. They set traps on their way in from work and catch all sorts of animals — rabbits, cats, even big juicy rats from around the kitchen."

"Disgusting," scowled Father Martin. "How can they do it?"

Andrew grinned broadly like a Cheshire cat and snickered. "Actually, I tried fried rat myself. It's certainly better than the stuff we get from the kitchen. And you know, of course, what happened to Busch's dog. They offered to bury him, so no doubt he too ended up in the pot!"

Some weeks later Schmidt informed me that we would be making another trip to Mannheim to stock up with as many provisions as possible. "The army is taking our trucks tomorrow. They must be desperate at the front. Have you heard any news over our radio from England or France?"

"Unfortunately, the broadcasts aren't telling us what is happening in the west. But in the east, the Russians are already on German soil."

Schmidt frowned and shook his head. "Oh dear God, dear God. Do you think they will take the whole of Germany? Why doesn't Hitler negotiate with the Americans and the English? From what I've heard about the Russians, they leave nobody alive."

"Don't worry, Schmidt," I said, patting him on the arm. "The war will soon be over and I hope your sons get home safe and sound."

We arrived in Mannheim to find the central stores so packed with trucks we could barely make our way to the warehouse. Inside, the corridors were jammed with SS men pulling hand carts stacked with food. Filing our way through the crowd, we finally located Bruno in his office, greeting us with his customary scowl.

"All the food is gone — to be shipped to the front, or so they say. There's nothing for you here."

I placed a pack of cigarettes on his desk and he agreed to allow us anything we could find. We returned to the truck, seconded the driver and guard, grabbed two empty carts and ran back into the warehouse.

Bruno was right; the place had almost been stripped clean. Picking up whatever was edible, we decided to try where the potatoes were stashed and had more luck there, loading on our carts enough sacks to fill the truck.

"Imagine, nobody in charge!" said Schmidt on our return to camp. "Sheer anarchy! The Russians must not be far off."

We stopped outside the main gate and preparing to enter the camp on foot, spotted more of what seemed like anarchy. A new detachment of SS men were disembarking from trucks while Busch paced about nearby, obviously excited. Upon seeing us, he barked to Schmidt to escort me to the gate — a most unusual order as I always walked there unaccompanied — and directed our truck to the SS stores.

At our barracks I found my colleagues in high spirits, each claiming that the war had ended because no one had gone to work. Jan was busily tuning the radio to all stations, including the German network, but could find no news of anything out of the ordinary.

Finally, Zigi was called to see Busch. When he returned, he looked grim and worried.

"The war is not yet over, gentlemen, but according to Busch it soon will be. He says German scientists have produced a secret weapon that will blow up the whole of England. And Russia, if they refuse to surrender."

"Bullshit!" shouted Andrew.

"So our boy's scared, is he?" said Zigi. "Ready to scram from here to save his own neck?"

"Whatever the Germans decide," replied Andrew, "I know what we have to do. A detachment of young and mean looking SS guards has just arrived from the Belsen-Bergen camp with orders to deliver us there, dead or alive. By tomorrow our trucks will have left for the front and we'll be forced to get to the Mannheim railway station on foot. Schmidt has requisitioned horses and wagons to load whatever food we have and the sick from the hospital."

Zigi, who had obviously volunteered much of this news to Andrew, made no attempt to contradict it. Anyway, there would have been little need for him to do so. We all knew our small camp was located here because prisoners were working on some secret project that involved digging tunnels and chambers for an underground factory. No one knew for certain what the factory was intended for, but it seemed that they had finished their work and our camp was no longer needed.

"This time Andrew could be right," I said. "What I saw in Mannheim today doesn't look like a nation winning a war. There was panic everywhere, stores were actually being looted. Remember that we're very close to France. Perhaps the allied invasion from the west has begun and as a result they're shipping us deeper into Germany. They may even have other, more sinister plans. We must be alert and ready to defend ourselves."

"Nonsense!" exclaimed Zigi. "I want to make clear that there is no danger. I will lead the march in front of the column and ensure that no one is harmed. Who knows, perhaps Belsen-Bergen is waiting for a leader like Zigi. You guys just stick to me and you'll be all right."

In spite of these assurances, none of us could sleep that night. Kazik and I talked almost until dawn and decided to keep clear of Zigi whose interest, if anything, centred on preserving his position of power. That morning, while Zigi organized the columns, five abreast, and counted prisoners, Kazik and I opted for helping Schmidt load the wagons with food.

About mid-morning, flanked by two rows of the new SS guards, the first column of prisoners marched out of camp with Zigi proudly parading at the head.

For some reason we did not take the direct route to Mannheim but followed a sideroad or walked through empty fields where it was easier for the guards to watch us. At 2:00 o'clock we stopped briefly to receive a lunch consisting of bread, margarine and coffee, then continued on our way. Kazik and I kept watch for an opportunity to escape, but on the few occasions when one did arise the guards were also alert.

Only when the sun began to set did it become clear why we had taken this route. The whole column, including horses and wagons, was herded into an empty forced labour camp. Once all prisoners had assembled on the grounds, the guards marched through the gate and assumed their posts in towers outside the barbed wire fence.

Left on our own, Kazik and I set out to explore the camp. We located first a kitchen where our kettles of coffee could be warmed. Upon visiting other buildings, however, we were surprised to find that we were not alone. Occupying several barracks were about 100 men, the remnants of a large work force that had been shipped there from the Ukraine a couple of years previously. Most of this force had since been transferred to other places while those too sick or weak to march had been left behind, without guards.

The presence of other prisoners gave me an idea. "Tomorrow morning we'll get lost among those Ukrainians," I suggested to Kazik, "then let the rest of our group march away under Zigi's leadership."

"It just might work. We can pretend to be working in the kitchen. After all, the SS guards don't know us and I'm quite sure Schmidt wouldn't give us away."

Next morning, after everyone had received a cup of hot coffee, Zigi again assumed the role of campelder, forming columns and keeping order. Meanwhile Kazik and I remained in the kitchen pretending to be civilian labourers. Just as the SS sergeant gave the order to march, we heard Zigi shout for everyone to stay where they were.

"Please, one moment! I haven't completed the count!"

The new SS guards could not have cared less how many prisoners there were. No longer under Busch's command — the commandant and his wife had left Camp Rose by car the night before — they simply wished to deliver their charge to the camp at Belsen-Bergen without incident. Besides, only Zigi knew the number of prisoners being transferred.

But before the sergeant could repeat his order, Zigi shouted: "There are ten men missing!"

"They will come out in a minute when I start shooting down those Ukrainian workers who are hiding them!" announced the sergeant.

He then fired a series of machine gun bullets at the feet of the Ukrainians who were standing watching our departure. The shots were enough to convince Schmidt to come to our rescue.

"Everybody's here!" he shouted to the sergeant. "I have instructed some men to help load the rest of the provisions from the kitchen. You can go, I'll see that they join the end of the column."

Wearied by the delays, the sergeant began marching the prisoners out of the camp as Schmidt entered the kitchen.

"Now you have to come," he told us, "thanks to your stupid Zigi. I know you wanted to stay. Perhaps you'll find another opportunity in Mannheim."

We followed him out through the door and joined the rest of group on their trek towards the city.

As the daylight turned to dusk, I considered the possibility of grabbing Kazik and sneaking from the ranks into the darkness. I turned several scenarios over in my head, but none seemed feasible. The night soon closed in around us and noticing we were nowhere near Mannheim, I began to feel edgy, longing for the chance to make a dash for it. At that moment we were startled by a burst of machine guns and the sudden glare of the guards' flashlights. Two Russian prisoners had had the same idea; they now lay dead on the ground a short distance away.

We were still looking for an opportunity when our column came upon a small railway station outside the city. Because Kazik and I were at the end of the column, we were ordered to load food and kettles of cold coffee for the SS guards onto the last of a line of waiting freight cars, several of which the prisoners were already boarding. We transferred kettles and supplies from wagon to car, then hopped in after them as a guard pulled the door closed behind us.

Not long after, we felt a sudden jerk as the train started to move. The motion was familiar: forwards and backwards, a quick stop, then forwards again. Though we had lots of room to move about, any hope of escape seemed impossible. We thus resigned ourselves to our fate and fell fast asleep on the wooden floor while the train shunted back and forth.

We were abruptly awakened by the sound of the door rolling open.

"Come out, you two," said Schmidt. "We have to get some hot coffee for the guards from the station."

Grabbing a 50-litre kettle between us, we jumped down from the car.

"Where are we, Schmidt?" I asked, squinting as my eyes adjusted to the yellow light of dawn.

"God knows. We didn't get very far, that's all I know. Those two air raids in the night could have finished us off."

Kazik and I looked at each other in puzzlement. Apparently, we had found the anti-climax of our unsuccessful escape attempts so wearying, we had slept right through the night. Schmidt shook his head in disbelief, muttered something, then followed us to the station.

While we were walking, an SS sergeant called out from behind: "Schmidt! Come and join me for a cigarette. I'll send some younger man to guard those two prisoners."

He then appointed a fellow named Franz to accompany us. Franz was one of those eager to please SS men. Taking Schmidt's place, he ran behind us pushing us with the barrel of his rifle and shouting: "Quick! Quick! The SS guards want their coffee!"

We crossed several rows of tracks to the station restaurant where we found a half-asleep attendant standing behind the counter.

"Here!" cried our young guard, pointing his barrel at the kettle. "These prisoners are to fill this with hot coffee for the SS men."

Unintimidated by the shouting and gun-waving, the attendant answered in a lazy voice: "There is no coffee."

"How come there's no coffee? There must be coffee for the SS or someone will get hurt here!"

"Coffee will be ready in about three hours," the attendant replied indifferently. "Either wait here or you can go to the labour camp kitchen behind the station. They usually have coffee early."

Franz paused briefly to think the matter through, then huffed at the attendant and marched Kazik and me through the back door of the station. Several hundred metres away we could see a huge camp spread across the valley below.

"Run! Run! Quick! Quick!" shouted Franz, prodding us repeatedly with his rifle.

We followed a dirt road down the hillside and into the camp. Passing through the gate, we noticed the absence of any guards or prisoners. Either the occupants had already gone to work or the camp had recently been evacuated. In any case, there was no one to ask for directions.

While Franz walked a short distance from our side to survey the grounds, I whispered to Kazik: "This is it — we have to disarm this guy and go."

Franz turned suddenly to face us, his rifle waving in the direction of a nearby building. "There's the kitchen! Over there! Fast! Fast!"

The three of us rushed towards the building, but upon arriving at the door, the young SS man made a mistake. In his hurry to get coffee he entered into the kitchen first, with Kazik and I following right behind. While Franz looked around for a sign of life, we quietly put down the kettle and came up on both sides of him. Kazik jumped from the left and grabbed his head under his arm, skilfully applying a wrestler's hold. I instantly took hold of the rifle and pulled it from him with such force that it dislocated his shoulder, causing him to yelp with pain.

To put a stop to his cries for help, I pushed the barrel of the rifle into his back. "You make one more noise and you're dead."

The guard gasped under Kazik's tightening grip, then whispered: "Please don't kill me. It's already the end of the war and the Americans aren't far from here. I also want to go home."

"Shut up and lie quietly on the floor," said Kazik, throwing him down from his neck hold. He then took out a penknife and quickly removed the red triangle and number from his jacket and my own.

"We're ready to go. Only what are we to do with this SS beauty who likes poking people with his gun?"

Before I could reply, Kazik grabbed Franz by his dislocated shoulder and pushed him down again. "You wanted to shoot us, didn't you? You little bastard, how many prisoners did you shoot? Took a pot shot at those escaping prisoners last night, eh?"

The guard crawled to his knees and favouring his arm,

started to sob uncontrollably. "Please don't kill me, I was only doing my duty. I'm a soldier and have to obey orders."

This was a pathetic picture of a man who only moments before had been so arrogantly sure of himself. Though moved by his pleas, I was in no position to take valuable time consoling him.

"Be quiet and you will live," I told him. "But make any noise and we'll have no choice but to shoot you."

Then turning to Kazik, I said: "I'll watch him here. Would you see if there's some place we can lock him in?"

Kazik walked from one end of the large kitchen to the other, opening any cupboards or doors he passed. He then pulled open the door of a warming oven, stooped down to look inside, and exclaimed: "Here's an excellent place, a perfect fit for our little Nazi swine."

Without threats or prodding, the man crawled obediently into the oven.

Kazik grinned at the terrified face that peeked out at him. "We'll wait here for the train to leave. If you make one peep in there, my friend will start shooting right through this door."

He then swung the door shut and locked it. Kazik took the rifle from me, placed it out of sight on top of one of the shelves and motioned me to follow him quietly out of the kitchen. Taking one last look around, we closed the door behind us. After the war I learned that Franz had returned to Belsen-Bergan and reported that he had executed us.

Outside not a soul was to be seen. We walked at a fast pace to the opposite end of the camp and stood at the edge of a field.

Never before did a field look so beautiful to me as it did then. It was a warm spring day, March 27, 1945 — my 30th birthday. The air smelled of fresh soil and from the green carpet before us rose a thin layer of mist, melting under the gentle rays of the sun.

We did not talk. The feeling of freedom and the beauty of nature were like magic, cloaking us in an ecstasy neither of us could share in words. We walked west, out of the hideous familiarity of an inverted world and back into the strange and distant life we had left behind five years before.

Epilogue

The heroic fight of the Polish Underground Army in Auschwitz received little attention either from Poland's communist government following the war or from the exiled Polish government meeting in England throughout the war and after. Germany's surrender made little difference to Polish soldiers serving under British command who wished to return home; the Soviet Union quickly instituted a communist government in Poland that regarded all such soldiers as enemies of the people. Most officers did not return to Poland, nor were they forced to, though Winston Churchill issued a letter to all Polish ex-servicemen strongly urging them not to forsake their "free" country. Those who did return were subsequently persecuted and imprisoned.

Although Soviet prisoners of war had been labeled by Stalin as traitors, they were repatriated by force along with other Soviet citizens in a joint effort by the allied armies of Russia, England and the United States. Such was the fate of Ivan, Volodia and Misha. Their experiences following the war, as well as those of others who played a part in this story, were no doubt more bitter than what has been recorded here. It is to their courage and spirit that my story is dedicated.

Mietek Lebisz

Mietek was among the last men I knew who believed wholeheartedly in an officer's honour and chivalry — a man who charged like a Don Quixote in defence of a Jewish prisoner being tortured by sadistic kapos. This characteristic was no doubt partly responsible for his death in Auschwitz, where both his common sense and sense of humanity were taken from him, leaving him a creature governed solely by the instinct of self-preservation.

Dr. W. Dering

In 1946, Polish Prime Minister Joseph Cyrankiewicz requested that Dr. Dering, then living in London, England, be extradited to Poland as a war criminal. Dering was imprisoned and while awaiting deportation, appealed to the organization, the Former

Political Prisoners of German Concentration Camps, to collect information about his activities in Auschwitz in the hope of rehabilitation.

As vice-chairman of this organization, I wrote 300 letters to former inmates of Auschwitz; out of 200 replies, almost all were positive and none insinuated war crimes. This information, as well as Dering's successful confrontation with a former Jewish inmate allegedly castrated by Dering, secured his release. Several years later he was knighted for his medical services in the British colonies.

In 1958 Leon Uris published his novel *Exodus*, in which he stated that Dering castrated Jews, made selections to the gas chambers and performed on Jewish men and women experimental surgery in the name of German "research." Dering sued Uris for libel. After several days of deliberations and arguments presented by the best English barristers, the court ruled in favour of Dering but ordered that the damage to his honour be paid in the sum of one farthing.

During the court procedures Uris provided witnesses of men and women whose testicles or ovaries were removed by Dering following irradiation. This practice was carried out at a time when about 3,000 Jewish families were gassed daily. Ironically, the witnesses speaking against Dering were alive to testify because of their selection for experimentation rather than for the gas chambers. Uris later described the case in another best-selling novel, *QBVII*.

Dering died of cancer in London in 1972.

Frederick Jarossy

Jarossy was among the prisoners at Camp Rose transported to Belsen-Bergen, many of whom perished while in transit as a result of air raids and outright murder by the SS. He eventually settled in England where he continued his acting career. He died in 1958.

Maximilian Kolbe

Kolbe's heroic sacrifice in Auschwitz was recognized by the Vatican in 1971 when he was beatified by Paul VI. In 1982 he was elevated to sainthood by John Paul II.

Stan Kazuba

Kazuba became commanding officer of the underground army in Auschwitz a year before the camp was liberated by the

Soviet army. Three months before liberation, the communist political organization headed by Cyrankiewicz released him of his command. He remained in Poland following the war, working at odd jobs and without receiving any recognition for his service in Auschwitz. He retired in 1965 while living in extreme poverty in Warsaw.

Henry Bartosiewicz

Bartosiewicz returned to Poland and as a non-communist worked at odd jobs while keeping in touch with other former prisoners of Auschwitz. He died in 1979.

Witold Pilecki (Thomas Serafiński)

Following his escape from Auschwitz, Pilecki took part in the Warsaw uprising of August and September, 1944, and was again taken prisoner by the Germans.

After the war he found his way to London, England, where he made a full report on the activities of the underground army in Auschwitz to the commandant of Polish Military Intelligence, General Pełczyński. For some unknown reason, the general classified this report as secret and only 30 years later did it reach public scrutiny. Thus no one who took part in this organization, including Pilecki, received any military recognition for the special services performed.

Disillusioned and bitter, without even a promotion to the rank of major which was due to him five years earlier, Pilecki decided to return to Poland. There matters were even worse. Former prisoners who after the war became devoted party members, occupying influential positions in the communist government, crudely falsified the history of the resistance fight in Auschwitz. The most prominent among them was Joseph Cyrankiewicz, who became Prime Minister of Poland during the Stalinist era and stayed in power for many years, outlasting numerous changes in policy over the period of his rule.

Shortly after setting foot on Polish soil in the summer of 1945, Pilecki was arrested as an enemy of the Polish People's Republic. He was executed on May 24, 1948. Ironically, one of Poland's great unsung heroes died in the same Warsaw prison where Mietek and I had faced for the first time Nazi atrocities — his execution a result of native communist justice.

About the Author

After escaping and marching west for two days, he finally met American forces who directed him to the liberated camp of the Polish prisoners of war. They were partisans taken prisoner in 1944 after the Warsaw uprising. There was no officer among them and they were happy to have a Polish commandant. The American army appointed him and his men as an Auxiliary Military Police and they had an opportunity for the last two months of the war to chase remnants of the German 9th SS Division in the Hartz Mountains. After the war he rejoined the Polish Army under British Command in England.

Like several of his colleagues in the Polish Underground Army who received no recognition for their services in Auschwitz, the author decided against returning to live in his homeland. As an officer in the Polish Army under British command, he chose to settle in England, where he completed two Dipl. Ing. degrees in Mechanical Engineering and in Metallurgy at an external college of the University of London. Later he obtained a Ph.D. from the University of Cambridge in Materials Science and Biomedical Engineering. In 1951 he emigrated to Canada and held a professorship in Materials Science at the University of Waterloo until his retirement in 1983.

Appendix

For the last 45 years, I have been thinking about my five years in concentration camps. I wanted to know why prisoners in these camps, including myself, behaved the way they did. From my first day in Auschwitz, I was conditioned to behave — instinctively behave — like a hunted animal. I avoided predators by hiding in the "middle of the herd," thus exposing those around me to immediate danger. I became insensitive to human misery and looked with indifference at the death of my colleagues. I was not in the position of predator myself, but witnessing remorseless killings by SS men and kapos, I no longer made judgements about who was a "good" man and who was a "bad" man.

There have been several books written by former prisoners of concentration camps who attempted to analyze the behaviour of men in the camps: Bruno Bettleheim,[1] Miklos Nyiszy,[2] Primo Levi,[3] V.E. Frankl.[4] All of these books have one important aspect in common: they were written by Jewish authors about the Holocaust — the extermination and suffering of Jews in the Nazi concentration camps. They did not furnish me with satisfactory answers to the reasons for general human behaviour. Thus after 45 years, I am trying to provide my own answers.

A new academic discipline, sociobiology, emerged in the 1970s. One proponent, David Barash,[5] makes a very convincing argument that behaviour relating to sex, love, and violence is governed by the demands of our genes for self-replication. We love our mate because our genes wish to reproduce themselves; we love our children because they contain half of our genes; we love our grandchildren a little less because they possess only a quarter of our genes, and so on. We are violent and declare war on our enemies because their genes are in competition with our genes.

According to the theory of genetic behaviour, we are basically selfish. Modern society deals with this problem by creating laws to protect the members of a society against the selfish behaviour of individuals and by treating certain forms of selfishness as a punishable crime. The sociobiologist would argue that an individual increases the probability of replication of his or her genes by avoiding punishment. Barash's argument that "human genes seem to do best if they give their carrier a great deal of freedom of action" contradicts the very principle of genetic theory: that genes do not give any freedom to their carriers. Assuming, however, that this is true, then human behaviour is governed by two separate activities of the brain — the one independent and rational, and the other, often irrational, but aimed at forwarding the programmed purpose of the genes.

Freud argued that instinctual behaviour is repressed by society — that "our social behaviour is greatly constrained and is actually a complex web of lies and deceptions." More recently the psychologist S. Maddie elaborated on instinctual behaviour, dividing it into core and peripheral elements. Core elements are a result of evolution and peripheral elements are developed as a result of experience.

The division of the human mind into the conscious and unconscious is generally accepted by modern psychology. However, what constitutes the unconscious mind is difficult to conceptualize because one cannot relate to it consciously. Thus it is desirable to sort out the activity of our brains into clearer concepts. Undeniably, we have the ability to think rationally and logically, independent of the needs of our genes, our unconscious mind or our instincts. We can also recognize that the mind often works involuntarily, creating emotions which sometimes lead to irrational instinctual behaviour, which may be prompted by our genes, or our unconscious mind; it functions independent of and often contrary to our rational expectations. Perhaps the most important observation one can make is that the rational side of our brain generally does not recognize our instinctual drives. Simply stated, if the rational side were stronger than the instinctual, we would not have wars.

For the purpose of understanding the drives of the unconscious mind or (perhaps more descriptively) of our genes, I prefer to use the term "instinctual behaviour" because we have observed it long enough in the animal kingdom. We are well aware that our brains are almost never silent. But the thoughts which flow through our brain are often uninvited and not useful. We often perceive them as an insignificant and annoying interference with the rational functioning of our brain. In most cases, this activity is related to our various emotions. Love, hate, compassion, jealousy, anger, worry, fear, joy, sexual desire, or the urge for violence create images in our minds and we often act as a result of such images. It is not surprising, then, that most of our actions are emotionally-based. These are instinctive responses. Emotional whispering (chattering) in our brains is instinctively based.

Who has not seen a well-fed domestic cat stalking a bird or some other prey? We can quite understand; the cat cannot help doing it because it is behaving instinctively. Yet humans share the exact same instinct — even to the extreme of hunting. There is no need to document the existence of instinctual behaviour, particularly in regard to sex and violence. One need merely turn on the television to find ample documentation.

Instinctive behaviour is generally understood as a natural, unacquired mode of response to stimuli or an inborn tendency to behave in a way characteristic to our species. Clearly, fear and anxiety stem from insecurity and are reflections of our instinct for self-preservation. Sexual desires and fantasies (as well as love and jealousy) are the result of our sexual instinct, necessary for the survival of our species. The ugliest of our instincts, also related to survival and developed during the millennia of evolution, is that which triggers a violent response.

In retrospect, I believe that my life in the concentration camps was governed mostly by my instincts. There were, of course, rational decisions to be made, but they were also related to the basic instinct for survival. Sensitivity to injustice and cruelty were strong during my early days in the camps. I still remember vividly today the incidence of a Jew being beaten, but not killed, by kapos in the showers. Later, I witnessed starvation of hundreds of men or deaths from cruel beatings, but I think the details of these later deaths were blotted out of my mind by that one instinct. I was determined to survive and nothing should distract me from it. During my last months in Camp Rose I hardly noticed the misery of other non-privileged prisoners. The instinctive conditioning was equally strong in my colleagues who were in the camps for more than four years.

The most surprising discovery for me was that all of our instinctive responses have nothing to do with what we can rationally justify. It is easy to understand that all cats and other animals have similar instincts. It is, however, extremely difficult to admit to ourselves that we also have similar instincts. The instinctive response is generally not an individual one but common to all humanity.

The next obvious question is what is our real self? Each one of us can recognize the dual activity in our minds. One is reasonable, deployed rationally when it is needed, and the other, often irrational and emotionally-based, occurs in our brain and is called by Krishnamurti "chatter."[6] The former is rational, the latter instinctual. The instinctual activity is acquired during evolution and is often called the effect of the environment; the rational activity is the ability of our brain to think independently. This independent, individual thought must be the real "I."

The human race is very much governed by its instincts. I witnessed extreme violence in the concentration camps and became impervious to it, just as my captors did. Fortunately, instincts do not manifest themselves with the same degree of intensity in all people; not everyone in the camps was violent. In extreme situations, like imprisonment in a concentration camp, the instinctual behaviour dominates the rational behaviour and the instinctual drives become prominent. The rational, the aspect of the human brain which makes man distinctive, recedes. Our only hope in preventing recurrences of experiences similar to mine between 1940 and 1945 is to work towards asserting the role of the rational in man's psychological make-up.

---

[1] *The Informed Heart*. Peregrine Books, 1986.
[2] *Eichmann's Inferno — Auschwitz*. Fawcett, 1960.
[3] *The Drowned and The Saved*. Simon & Schuster, 1988.
[4] *Man's Search for Meaning*. Simon & Schuster, 1984.
[5] D. P. Barash. *The Whispering Within, Evolution and Origin of Human Nature*. Penguin, 1979.
[6] J. Krishnamurti. *The Collected Works of Krishnamurti*. Harper and Row, 1980.